*Values such as integrity, a sense of purpose a[...]
who have lived out their greatness. As muc[...]
caution about toxicity and self-deception th[...]
part of self-leadership. The reflection questio[...]
stimulating discussion and demanding accoun[...]*

Ms. Ang Bee Lian, Director of Social Welfare,
Ministry of Social and Family Development, Singapore

This is a very well-researched and well-written playbook for all managers and leaders who aspire to greatness! I loved the many real-life examples that Dr. John has given.

Mr. George Ang, CEO
Revenue Valley Group, Malaysia

This book will change your life. Readers will learn how to unleash their greatness. Greatness and happiness can come together.

Mr. Husodo Angkosubroto, Chairman
PT Gunung Sewu Kencana, Indonesia

I wish I had read this book when I was starting out in my career. I would have avoided many mistakes. I hope the younger ones who are reading this book will benefit greatly and will be able to unleash the greatness in them without making all the painful mistakes.

Mr. Bey Soo Khiang, Vice Chairman
Royal Golden Eagle, Singapore

This book is an exploration into self-actualization. From his wealth of experience in consulting with leaders, John has given readers insights into rising to one's potential in leading self and others. With his signature concise chapters well-illustrated with personal anecdotes, this book will translate leadership theories into practical achievements. This volume is highly informative, deeply inspiring and effectively practical.

Mr. Peter Chao
Founder, Eagles Communications Singapore

This latest book by John is both inspirational and remarkable. It not only provides profound insights into leadership principles, but also lays out a holistic approach to life. His take on the subjects of value, integrity and character as keys to building a firm foundation for a fruitful life is refreshing and needful in this present time and age. John's sharing about sexual temptations is candid and contains many nuggets of truth that we would do well to pay heed to. The learning points that one can glean from this book, if applied to self, family, organization and community, will be transformational. I highly recommend this book to anyone serious about making a difference with one's life.

Mr. James Chia
Group President, Pico Art International

In cognition to unleashing the Greatness in you, John candidly unfolds the obstacles that may inhibit you. His frank and down-to-earth, thought-provoking expository approach challenges readers to be authentic to their shortcomings, and helps to navigate the journey to attain the Greatness in you! Like in many of his books, John speaks directly to the inner man that needs transformation. With his gifted intuitive understanding of human folly, he helps many to overcome bondages and set free to achieve their full potential. A must read.

Mr. Chris Chiew
The Principal, Corporated International Consultants, Malaysia

This book can give you a great insight into your life and can give a deep and hard look into your self. And if you reflect upon it and come upon a plan to bring your life into the next level, you will find that this book can help steer you and take you to a great and fulfilled life which will give God great glory.

Mr. Kobchai Chirathivat
Director, The Central Group of Companies, Thailand

Whether you have risen to the level of CEO or are someone still finding your footing in the path to success, this book offers practical, time-tested advice that applies to anyone striving to be the absolute best they can be. John and I share in the belief that there is always room to grow, to learn, and to improve, and the practical knowledge in this book provides the keys for discovering and realizing the greatness you have within.

This book is filled with powerful insights that serve as a foundation for developing the character, integrity and determination present in all great leaders. And what is more, he demonstrates clearly that this power is something we can all access, something we can all unleash within ourselves.

Just as John has inspired me over the years, I hope you find inspiration in him as well.

Dr. Chatree Duangnet
Senior Executive Vice President and Group Chief Operating Officer
Bangkok Dusit Medical Services, Plc., Thailand

Dr. John Ng has written a book for everyone. Whether your concern is personal growth or an organization's vitality, here you will find words of wisdom. What makes a person great is not easy to distill. Let alone tackling the task of providing an almost step-by-step manual to achieving greatness in one's life. It is all adroitly done by one who can draw on his vast personal and professional life to inspire and guide us to become better leaders. I am richer for having read it. I wish the same for you.

Dr. David Fung, Advocate
Regional Director for Sabah Full Gospel Business Men's Fellowship, Malaysia

A useful took-kit to a leader or someone aspiring to leadership. There is something in it for everyone. In an encyclopedic way, John Ng invokes many real-life examples and powerful quotes to get the reader to reflect on his/her own leadership style. Being bite-sized, the sharing makes up for lack of depth of discussion with a broad canvas hung on a scaffolding that illuminates what he means by "self-leadership". Indeed, a powerful, positive force is unleashed when these concepts are properly understood and applied!

Associate Professor Ho Peng Kee
Associate Professorial Fellow, Law Faculty, NUS
Chairman, Home Team Vol Networking Steering Committee

You are destined for greatness. You are designed to contribute. Whether you believe this to be true or not, I highly recommend that you read Dr John Ng's latest book. You will enjoy the stories he has painstakingly researched on. With every page turned, you will savour John's brand of straight-talking insights, which are the hallmark of John's books. Discover and decide for yourself. This is a book not to be missed.

Ms. Tina Hung
Deputy CEO, National Council of Social Service, Singapore

Easy to read and practical with real-world examples, this book takes me on a personal discovery that helps me uncover my blind spots and equips me with a shield against the intoxication of success. In today's highly complex world, this book serves as a barometer for the true standard of greatness and gives inspiration to do what is right, instead of what is popular. A 'must read' book if you want to stay at the top in the long haul!

Ms. Ihsan Mulia Putri
Director and Shareholder, Kapal Api Group, Indonesia

Dr. John Ng shares his personal anecdotes and has obviously put in a great deal of thought and research to compose a formidable tool box; to enable you to discover your WHY and to help you navigate the WHATS that so often make us stumble in our respective journeys for significance.

We all want to get to the point when we can actually feel God's pleasure when we do what we were created to do well. We can use a little help to get us to this point. That's what this book may do for you.

Mr. Arthur Kiong
CEO, Far East Hospitality, Singapore

I was riveted by the book and could not put it down until I had finished it. A truly insightful and inspirational book that concisely articulates the formula to turn a good company into a great company. A 'must read' book for those who are starting a company, and those who are already running an enterprise.

Mr. Kwee Liong Tek
Chairman, Pontiac Land Pte Ltd, Singapore

I first heard John speak about three years ago in China. He caught my attention as another teacher because of his knowledgeable and very pragmatic approach which makes it very easy to resonate and hence, apply to our daily lives. He is no different in person: approachable, humble and discerning. His latest book is again very aligned and easy to read. I love a leader who practices what he preaches. This is a highly recommended book on leadership. Thank you John.

Mr. Walter Lee
Father, Chef, Entrepreneur & Founder
Zy Movement Foundation, Thailand

In a society where much emphasis is placed on star performance, promotion, and delivering results, John's latest book is a timely reminder that there is more to arriving at success. John has provided a broad and refreshing perspective on how we can reach our potential with our character and values intact. In our endeavour to achieve greatness, our fears, greed, rage and even past success can easily derail our leadership journey. The book is a compelling compendium of concepts and takeaways for leaders to strengthen their competencies and stewardship, in service of others.

Mr. Lawrence Leong
Former Assistant CEO, Singapore Tourism Board,
Singapore

Another great book from John for all aspiring leaders. It is a comprehensive, candid and practical handbook about leadership development. It talks about the challenges, pitfalls and temptations which may cause a leader to derail and fall from grace. Above all, it shares about what it takes to be a great leader and the concept of self-leadership. To be a great leader is a journey and John has provided the road map.

Mr. Daniel Lim
Chief Executive Officer, Sunway China – Property Development, China

John has masterfully written a great book on Greatness! This book is a 'must read' for those who want to challenge their status quo of normality, raise their bar of mediocrity and recover from their failures!

The Right Honorable Lim Guan Eng
Chief Minister of Penang, Malaysia

Once I started reading the book, I realised, John has written a book that prompts me to reflect on my role and purpose in my family, my business, my community and to myself.

The book has all the examples and questions that start the reflection process. Reading the book and reflecting as I read the book, I realised my actions and certain characteristics of mine had evolved over the years. It quickly made me think of many things that I do which should be modified and/or weaned. Most importantly, I realised that I have a role and purpose to bring positivity to my family, my business, my community and that personally, I should focus on significance rather than success.

Dato Lim Si Boon
Chairman, Bonanza Venture Holdings, Malaysia

It is stated that there is no shortcut to Greatness. The structured points, thought-provoking questions and valuable real life examples of great individuals not only reveals achievements, but also drastic downfalls and rebounds. This book is a great reminder and guide for me to perceive greatness, and really stirs deep thoughts on how important it is to achieve greatness.

In this book, John also uses his wife and children's experiences as examples. They are very heart touching and can inspire everyone.

This book has certainly inspired me and it will certainly be a blessing to everyone.

Mr. Arnold J. Limasnax
CEO of E-motion Entertainment

Wow. My mouth is wide open. After I started this book, I couldn't stop reading. Neither will you when you get your hands on this book. Each chapter has thought-provoking insights that create a best-selling book.

Dr. John Ng, endowed with what seems to be photographic memory and a genius mind, has condensed his lifelong study of greatness, and distilled it into gem-like principles that are powerfully and convincingly illustrated with real-life, oftentime front-page headlines. No one can argue against his principles.

I highly endorse the book without any reservation. In fact, every person, every family, every study group, every office unit, and every manager should not only read, but spend time studying, discussing and internalizing the content to learn from this great mind.

Dr. Andrew Liuson
Property Developer, Philippines

To attain certain successes in life is likely. To live a life of success is challenging. To maintain the greatness in a successful life is tough. Money, power and sex are three common factors that will bring a person down from greatness. John's book is a 'must read' for those who have attained success in life, and who wish to maintain their greatness and leave a good name behind.

Mr. Paul Low Hong Ceong
Chief Executive, Manulife Wealth Advisors
Manulife Holdings Berhad

John Ng guides along the path to great success, and the first step on that path is reflection about what authentic success entails. Readers will be challenged, informed, and affirmed by this book.

Dr. Chris Lowney
Author of *Heroic Leadership: Best Practices from a 450-Year-Old Company that Changed the World*

This book is both powerful and profound. Based on years of real world experience and extensive research, John Ng communicates with both clarity and conviction about what can rob us of our greatness and how to overcome these common traps to achieve greatness. If you're after a book simply to make you 'feel great', I'd search elsewhere. However, if you want a book that focuses on character and helps you to 'be great', then this is without question the book for you. Read it. Digest it. Then live it. The world has a desperate need for people to discover their greatness and then use it to help others. This book will show you how.

Mr. Paul McGee ('The Sumo Guy')
International speaker and bestselling author of *S.U.M.O. (Shut Up, Move On)*, England

Leaders face temptations and have struggles. The best of leaders have motives that are often mixed. They can make wrong judgments and bad decisions. Credible and effective leaders may be seduced by their success. Leaders are also lonely. Who dares to confront a leader regarding the struggles in their personal lives? Leaders know that the most difficult person to lead is themselves.

Dr John Ng has written a book that exposes the issues of the heart that a leader faces. He provides sound practical wisdom that every leader should heed. This is a book that every leader needs to read regularly, reflectively and prayerfully. I highly recommend it to every leader who wants to serve for the long haul and to finish well.

Professor Neo Boon Siong
Canon Professor of Business and
Dean, Nanyang Business School, Nanyang Technological University, Singapore

The phrase "Leaders are made, not born" offers a new meaning when one is a self-made leader. Unleashing the Greatness in You is a book of priceless gems masterfully gleaned and woven together from the success of self-made leaders. It offers pearls of wisdom on D-I-Y success — how anyone can be a self-made success story. I wish I'd had this book when I started out. It is a 'must read' for every self-starter who believes all hard work reaps a profit and that learning from the mistakes of others paves the path to success.

Dato Peter T S Ng
Founder and Group CEO, UCSI Group, Malaysia

In this book, all the pitfalls and "boobytraps" on the journey of life are well-articulated in the principles by John. Leaders often assume they are above all these challenges and are often over-confident, especially when they have tasted success, and sad to say, I was one of them. John has covered almost all aspects of the challenges in the principles he has put forth and they are totally relevant and timely, especially for the next generation. This book is not meant to be read once. Rather, I would strongly recommend using it as a reference to constantly check on our moral values, integrity and attitude throughout our journey. I believe that if you adhere to these principles, you will leave this world a better place than when you arrived. Then you would have unleashed the greatness in you.

Datuk Dr. Edward Ong
Founder of Sutera Harbour Resort

I have known Dr John Ng since we were 14-year-old schoolmates. And I have witnessed his unwavering commitment to his Lord with "greatness" transformation into who he is today. John's humble background and career epitomize how he has "unleashed greatness" and is now living it daily. This has rubbed off onto his children, whom he is justifiably proud of! This book is loaded with words of wisdom distilled from John's extensive research from the lives of many. I highly recommend that you read this book and be inspired and filled with hope to know that "ordinary people can be great!" and that you can embrace this choice and journey to achieve significance and greatness for your life.

Dr. Peng Chung Mien
CEO, The Farrer Park Company, Singapore

In his latest book, Dr. John Ng has prepared a trove of inspiring insights and experiences from thought leaders across a range of industries that can be useful for anyone, young or old, to push the boundaries of their potential and cultivate the self-belief necessary to motivate others. I personally felt empowered reading this book and would strongly recommend it to anyone who wants to strengthen their leadership capabilities.

Dr. Stephen Riady
Executive Chairman, OUE Limited

A true leader is a role model who inspires others to follow. Creating an environment with mutual trust, admiration and respect can be the basis to motivate team members to achieve success, often greater than they thought possible. Empowering the team to take on more tasks by interactive communication. When a team is unified, the collective accomplishments far exceed what individual members are capable of achieving alone, which is what makes great leaders inspiring and visionary. This is the thought-leadership of Dr John Ng's latest book.

Ms. Roosniati Salihin
Group COO, Panin Bank, Indonesia

John Ng has once again successfully captured the essence of working towards one's full potential in his newest book. He has a deep understanding of the human strengths and weaknesses, which enables him to give us a guided tour on how to unlock our unique potential. By helping readers to recognize and face the challenges of daily life, John looks to sustain and renew our faith in each new day, encouraging us to fulfill the endless possibilities within ourselves as well as to spread the greatness forward within our respective communities and the world.

Mr. Edwin Soeryadjaya
Chairman, Saratoga Capital, Indonesia

I have had the pleasure of working with John for over 18 years, primarily in motivating staff in the organization to transform themselves from just doing a job, to working as a team. John's forte is in engaging staff to realize their own potential to work together to create a spirit, which delivers much more than the individuals could.

In this latest book, John documents this process of "Unleashing Greatness" in his usual "Dim Sum" way whereby morsels of wisdom are delivered in a ten-course fashion. Enjoy the journey as the results have been proven in much of his work to date.

Mr. Mervyn Sirisena
Former Senior Vice President,
Singapore Airlines Engineering Division Consultant/Partnership Management Division
SIA Engineering Company, Singapore

One of the greatest obstacles to an individual's progress in his career is the lack of insight into his own flaws and weaknesses. This book by John Ng offers readers tools to deal with these challenges. He tackles the issue of self-leadership and self-awareness in his usual no-holds-barred approach. John uses personal anecdotes and that of well-known personalities and ordinary folk to effectively illustrate his points. I recommend this book for those who are serious in wanting to move from good to great in both their personal and working lives.

Dr. Tan Boon Yeow
CEO, St Luke's Hospital, Singapore

Many people desire greatness and significance in one form or another, but few know how to find it. In this book, John unravels what greatness means and how one can obtain it through timeless and practical principles. Discover what it takes to be great while remaining grounded, pursuing the right things, espousing the right values, and following the right models, as written in this book.

Dr. Peter Tan-Chi
Senior Pastor, CCF, Philippines

John offers a perspective about life for anyone who aspires to be great — not just in their performance but in their character, not just in doing but in being. John challenges you to believe, encourages you to strengthen your values, motivates you to develop your competence, and helps you to recover from failures. There is certainly much food for thought in these pages. It is definitely well-worth spending a few hours reading and reflecting on what it means for us all.

Mr. Tan Chuan-Jin
Minister for Social and Family Development, Singapore

Dr. John Ng is a highly experienced executive coach. In this latest of his many books, he shows that greatness is not about success but about character, humility, relationship and developing one's potential. Using stories of well-known leaders and athletes, he describes how even the 'mighty have fallen' when one or more of these elements are missing. Conversely he tells stories of lesser-known individuals who have achieved 'greatness' through perseverance and humility. There are nuggets of wisdom here for everyone.

Dato Dr. Kim Tan
Chairman, SpringHill Management Ltd.

Brutally honest, courageous and with authentic sharing, Dr John Ng has packaged a full-course meal. Sometimes after reading other books, I feel I was only served one course. However after reading this book, I felt very well-fed. Add to this the delight of recognising myself in his words and nodding in agreement, and being gifted with the recipe and tips to overcoming and achieving greatness. I feel empowered to spot the potential in others too. The result: I am inspired, grateful and confident that I have the power to achieve greatness!

Ms. Rosemary Tan Mei Leng
Past Global Chair (2013–2014) of Entrepreneurs Organisation
Creative Director, Tungling Group of Companies, Malaysia

Dr John Ng has done it again. You will never want to put this book down once you flip open the cover. It's full of insights on what it takes to be a great leader. It's full of real-life examples of great leaders who have overcome their challenges as well as those who sadly have been derailed. Most of all, it's full of his own personal journey to be as great a leader, husband, father and friend that he can be. It's indeed a great 'must read' book!

Mr. Michael Tan
President, Eagles Communications, Singapore

With his well-written book, John will be able to help many people, especially young working adults, to journey through their life with minimum pitfalls that many will face on their own. Good illustrations and testimonies of everyday people that we are familiar with make reading easy and digestible. A 'must read'!

Dato George Ting
Executive Chairman, Impress Eight (Malaysia) Sdn Bhd,
Malaysia

In this book, Dr John Ng, a veteran consultant and mentor, inspires us with stories, not only of grandiose accomplishments but also of everyday greatness. Studded with gems of insight, he offers keys to unlocking greatness and at the same time warns of what can derail us from greatness. But best of all, with candor and reflection, he reveals how against all worldly wisdom and advice, he supported his son's and daughter's quests in their chosen vocation and helps bring out the greatness in them. Illuminating and touching. This book will pick you up and propel you towards your own greatness. I commend it to you as a rare treasure.

Mr. David H Y Wong
Former Advisor to Tupperware Corporation, Asia Pacific; Managing Director of
Tupperware Malaysia & Singapore & Area Vice President South East Markets, Malaysia

Unleashing the Greatness in You

THE POWER OF SELF-LEADERSHIP

Dr John Ng

Meta Consulting

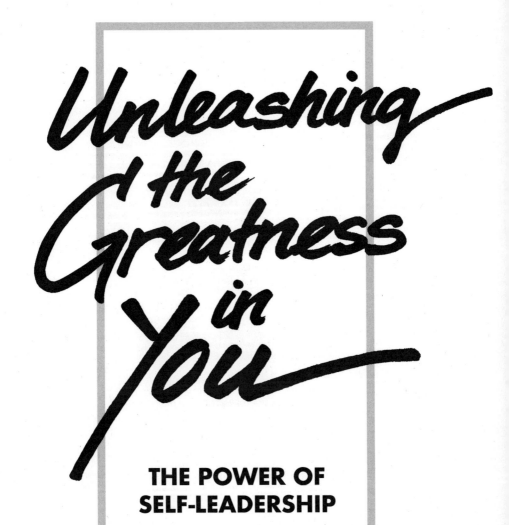

Unleashing the Greatness in You

THE POWER OF
SELF-LEADERSHIP

 **WS Professional**

NEW JERSEY · LONDON · SINGAPORE · BEIJING · SHANGHAI · HONG KONG · TAIPEI · CHENNAI · TOKYO

Published by

WS Professional, an imprint of
World Scientific Publishing Co. Pte. Ltd.
5 Toh Tuck Link, Singapore 596224
USA office: 27 Warren Street, Suite 401-402, Hackensack, NJ 07601
UK office: 57 Shelton Street, Covent Garden, London WC2H 9HE

Library of Congress Cataloging-in-Publication Data
Names: Ng, John, 1954–   author.
Title: Unleashing the greatness in you : The power of self-leadership / John Ng
   (Meta Consulting Pte Ltd, Singapore).
Description: 1 Edition. | New Jersey : World Scientific Publishing, [2017]
Identifiers: LCCN 2017027737 | ISBN 9789813228849 | ISBN 9789813230255 (pbk)
Subjects: LCSH: Leadership. | Self-actualization (Psychology) | Success.
Classification: LCC HM1261 .N514 2017 | DDC 155.2--dc23
LC record available at https://lccn.loc.gov/2017027737

British Library Cataloguing-in-Publication Data
A catalogue record for this book is available from the British Library.

Desk Editor: Shreya Gopi

Typeset by Stallion Press
Email: enquiries@stallionpress.com

Printed in Singapore

CONTENTS

FOREWORD

The Power of Self-Leadership
in an Ego-Driven World

Self-Leadership: In a world that's becoming more and more about "me," the concept of "self-leadership" is an idea whose time has come. The advent of social media has been a major factor in the increasing narcissism of today's culture.

Studies reveal a wide range of implications of living in the social media bubble:

- A college student today without a significant number of social media followers often feels like a failure.
- Social media has contributed to the breakdown of personal relationships, leading to isolation.
- It's been a major cause of the polarization we're seeing in global politics.
- People are using social media to boost their self-esteem.
- Individuals will say things on social media they would never say to people face-to-face.
- Studies reveal growing narcissism in regular users of social media.

The list goes on and on. In fact, in a shocking story in June 2017, a group of high-achieving students who had been admitted to Harvard University were discovered to have private Facebook pages where they regularly posted violent, profane, and sexually explicit messages. In an embarrassing step, the university was forced to cancel their invitation for admission. Keep in mind this is one of the most prestigious universities in the world, which only admits the finest and most qualified students.

Yet, it discovered that even with elite young people today, there is a powerfully compelling dark side.

It's time to awaken the principle of "self-leadership."

Today, leadership books fill bookstores, catalogs, and websites. Everyone seems to be an expert these days, and the leadership gurus crank out online blogs, conference events, and personal coaching sessions. That's all fine because I'm a great fan of leadership, but the problem is, when a leader hits a wall, faces a challenge, or has to make a difficult decision, all those experts, seminars, and consultants can seem so far away.

That's why this book matters.

As any great leader can attest, leadership is often easy – until you hit a wall. When that happens, leadership is often a lonely job, and without resources and inspiration that come from inside us, the options are few.

That's why when Dr John Ng speaks, I listen. I've had the opportunity to share the stage with John at major global conferences, and I've seen first-hand his attitude toward leadership. He's guided major executives through incredibly challenging times, and helped millions through his books, articles, and live events.

When he first spoke to me about the idea of "self-leadership" I was fascinated because my world is *media* – movies, television, digital and social media. In that context, I've seen the shift from leaders who spent their lives working face-to-face in the trenches to a new generation of leaders that want an instant payoff, instant gratification, and instant results. The shift to today's digital world has brought about wonderful advances, but it's also created monsters of our own making.

For instance, our culture today lives with a mobile phone in our hands day and night. 71 percent of people say they sleep with or next to their mobile phone, with 3percent saying they sleep with the device in their hand – in fact, 25 percent of users have fallen asleep with their smartphone. 35 percent of people check their mobile phone the moment they wake up, and only 17 percent even take the time for a cup of coffee before they check it. It's been reported that the typical adult checks their phone more than 125 times a day, with school children checking theirs 85 times a day.

And it will get worse. As a media professional, I'm seeing the global movie and TV industry completely realign their projects for use on a mobile phone. In fact, the saying today is that if it can't be viewed on a phone, then it's not worth producing. And as a media producer myself, I see the point. A recent Federal Communications Commission study from the United States indicated that 22 percent of the African-American audience is engaging with media programming *on a mobile device only.*

That kind of behavior has consequences. As people move from large groups watching a movie together, or a family sharing a television program, we're becoming more and more isolated by focusing on our phone for so much information and entertainment. I regularly take plane flights sitting with people who never speak, but stare at their phones for up to 4 hours without a break playing games, answering email, or checking social media.

And don't get me started on "selfies."

As a result, we are growing leaders in isolation. Men and women who don't know how speak publicly, motivate teams, or engage personally with their employees. One recent survey indicated that today's generation can't read emotion or attitudes from other people's faces because they've spent their lives looking at screens.

I could go on and on, but take it from me: It's time we learned how to manage ourselves, and discovered the power of self-leadership that will help us break the growing addiction of isolation and learn to reach out and engage today's culture.

John Ng's book could not have come at a more important time. This is the moment we need to create a new leadership culture that is inclusive, embracing, and engaging.

A culture that is *driven* from us, not *focused* on us.

A leadership culture that will stand the test of time. John Ng is the man who knows how to make that happen, and I believe this book is a launching pad for a new direction in leadership.

Phil Cooke
Ph.D., filmmaker, media consultant, and author of
One Big Thing: Discovering What You Were Born to Do

June 16, 2017

FOREWORD

"You can be great!" — that's what I read in the opening lines of John's new book. "Seriously?" I thought to myself. "Making companies/countries great again" is a phrase that is overused these days by business and political leaders. I am skeptical about whether they can really deliver what they have promised. It was with this curiosity that I thumbed through John's book, *Unleashing the Greatness in You: The Power of Self-Leadership*.

I met John as the Honorary Chair of Eagles Leadership Institute and have worked with him on several leadership training programs and conferences. He has impressed me with his passion and dedication in equipping the next generation of leaders with the right set of values and skills. I admire his restless effort in helping them to be "the best they can be" and connecting them with a network of like-minded young leaders, coaches and mentors in the region.

In this book, John shares his wisdom from years of research and interviews with thought leaders in our time, and gives a systematic guide to "greatness", from defining it to re-discovering one's self. The book is easy to follow and logically arranged.

I hope you will find the book useful and that it will inspire you to fulfill your destiny and dreams.

Lucas Chow
Former CEO of Orchard Parade, MediaCorp
Former Chairman of Health Promotion Board

IN HONOR OF THESE GREAT PEOPLE

Alison, my wife who believes in me and shares with me the joy of our three children, Meixi, Shun, and Meizhi, whose paths to greatness continue to inspire me.

Peter, Michael, and William, my great companions, who are my role models for greatness over the past five decades.

Chua Hong Koon, the Publishing Director of World Scientific, who never stops encouraging me to write great books. Shreya Gopi, my editor, whose meticulous proofreading and editing helps make my book great. Once again, I thank Alison, my very patient wife, and Tao Ai Lei, my good friend, whose unstinting support in cleaning up my final proofs makes this book greater.

All my great partners who have thoughtfully endorsed the book - it is a gesture that I deeply cherish and I treasure their friendship.

Ang Bee Lian, George Ang, Husodo Angkosubroto, Bey Soo Khiang, Peter Chao, James Chia, Chris Chiew, Kobchai Chirathivat, Chatree Duangnet, David Fung, Ho Peng Kee, Tina Hung, Ihsan Mulia Putri, Arthur Kiong, Kwee Liong Tek, Walter Lee, Lawrence Leong, Daniel Lim, Lim Guan Eng, Lim Si Boon, Arnold Limasnax, Andrew Liuson, Paul Low Hong Ceong, Chris Lowney, Paul McGee, Neo Boon Siong, Peter T. S. Ng, Edward Ong, Peng Chung Mien, Stephen Riady, Roosniati Salihin, Mervyn Sirisena, Edwin Soeryadjaya, Tan Boon Yeow, Peter Tan-Chi, Tan Chuan-Jin, Kim Tan, Rosemary Tan Mei Leng, Michael Tan, George Ting, and David H. Y. Wong.

David Jusuf and Evan Jaccordine, who creatively and painstakingly designed the cover, and Farhana, for her most exquisite sketch of Lee Kuan Yew and his wife, Kwa Geok Choo, making this a truly attractive book.

Lucas Chow and Phil Cooke, whose insightful and astute forewords are reflections of their great leadership. Their affirmations mean very much to me.

Most of all, to my great God, whose greatest sacrifice of His Son, Jesus Christ, made me the person I am today.

Preamble

YOU CAN BE GREAT!
(What you must digest)

"Every human is endowed with the seed of greatness
and is designed to contribute."

Dr. John Ng

My son, Shun, is a professional artiste, a finger-style guitarist. At the age of 14, he picked up his first guitar, which I had bought for him as a Christmas present. Since that day, he has taught himself the guitar and has honed his skills by watching all the incredible guitarists and musicians on YouTube. He is truly fired up. Guitar and music have become his passion and obsession.

He has been nominated for the International Artiste of the Year for four consecutive years at the Boston Music Awards since 2013, and won it in 2015. Nominated by the people in the music industry, he was Buddy Holly's Hall of Fame Holly Prize winner in 2016.

Shun was talent-scouted by the legendary Quincy Jones, who organized a concert for him in Los Angeles. Today, he lives in Boston and is eking out a living as an artiste. Many of my friends have enjoyed his music, compositions and the story of how a boy with dyslexia and ADHD (Attention Deficit Hyperactivity Disorder) found his passion in music.

Those who have seen Shun play admire his incredible dexterity with the guitar and great voice. Some called him a musical genius. Many think he has achieved greatness in music. In one of my conversations with Shun, we discussed the concept of greatness. He acknowledged that he has come very far and that he is far from perfect. Then, he commented, "Actually, everyone can be great. It's just that their talents are undiscovered or get snuffed out when they are young. So, they never achieve greatness." That struck for a while.

I believe he is right. That started my journey of exploring the concept of greatness.

I believe everyone can be great. You too can be great.

I have been researching, studying, listening, discussing, and exchanging ideas about greatness with thought leaders and leading thinkers over the past 25 years.

We all came to the same conclusion: Greatness exists in all of us!

Despised, deprived or discarded,
You don't have to stay that way.
You can live a great life.
This is not an illusion.

First, start believing again,
Take charge of your life.
You must want to change.
Nobody can do that for you.
You must want to unleash your greatness so badly that you will do whatever it takes
to get there.
Hit rock bottom in your life
Be so sick of your own mediocrity that you want to turn it around.
Or remain in the doldrums of despair.

You must be committed.

This is not a self-help book.

This is a book about YOU and how you can unleash your greatness.

— You can be great again and be the best you ever want to be.

— You can move from the ordinary to achieve greatness.

— You can chase your own dreams and fulfill them.

— You can make your own history.

This is a book about Being, not just Doing. In this book, you will learn about:

— How you can develop your character and values while society seeks
   to derail you.

— How you can change your perspective about yourself and develop
   greater self-awareness and self-management.

— How you can earn the respect of people, even those who don't
   believe in you or who oppose you.

— How you can find your own voice and drown out the noises that
   distract and discourage.

— How you can discover your flow.

— How you can nurture your passion and drive to do what you are called to do.

— How you can be emotionally healthy.

— How you can sustain your energy and lead for the long haul.

— How you can learn to recover from moral failures and restart your life.

I am a realist. I know there are many challenges and hindrances to greatness. I want to deal with issues that most books are loathe to deal with, like sex and greed. Unless we confront these obstacles, we can never become great because we will be derailed by them. Many of us don't become great because of:

- The Deceitfulness of Self-Deception
- The Molding of Moral Decay
- The Dark Side of Success
- The Web of Weakness
- The Challenge of Fit
- The Sensuality of Sex
- The Grip of Greed
- The Fear of Fear
- The Tyranny of Toxicity

I believe that you can overcome these issues if you are honest about them, confront them and rise from ashes like the proverbial phoenix.

I believe that no matter how high you have fallen; no matter how long you have been locked up in your own closet of self-disbelief; no matter how much you have been betrayed; no matter how painful your past may be; and no matter how deep your despair has been, you can strive towards greatness!

Many others have done it. So can you.

Why do I believe in this so strongly? Because...

— I have met incredible people who have been crushed, mangled and twisted, and yet somehow, they managed to turn around and unleash their greatness.

— I have interviewed leaders from different countries and heard them articulate principles of greatness.

— I have read, listened, and analyzed much research and synthesized them into simple core beliefs and intentional practices to becoming great.

— I have discussed this with many thought leaders and they have laid out these same principles of greatness.

— I have coached and supported many different individuals to reach their potential and achieve their own greatness.

— I have the distinct honor and opportunity of working with people of all ages, statuses, cultures, ethnicities and personalities, and help them fulfill their dreams to greatness.

— I have seen my own children unleash the greatness in their lives.

— I am a recipient of God's grace, despite my checkered past and many failures, and have a loving, caring community of friends, who believe in me and help me on the journey to greatness. I am still a work in progress.

So I hope you are ready to unleash the greatness in you…because there is HOPE for you.

At the end of your journey, you will discover that your Creator, God has entrusted, enabled, encouraged and empowered you with the gift of greatness so that you can reflect His character and image of a Great God.

Part 1

WHAT IS **GREATNESS?**
(What you must comprehend)

Chapter 1

WHAT IS GREATNESS?
THE TEN INGREDIENTS OF GREATNESS

"Success without successors or
a successful system is not success."

Dr. John Ng

*"Greatness is a lot of small things
done well every day."*
"You must remain focused on the journey to greatness."

Les Brown

Greatness needs to be redefined. Without a proper definition, you can be misled, your priorities misplaced, your efforts misdirected, or worse, you may end up in a life of misguided legacy.

Allow me to share ten facets of greatness.

1. Greatness is Nurturing Character

If you define greatness by position, status, size, power, influence and wealth, then you are short-changing yourself. The first facet of greatness has to be character. Throughout history, truly great people are people of great character. We think of Martin Luther King Jr, Mahatma Gandhi, and Nelson Mandela.

Character has to do with integrity. As my good friend Edward Ong, founder of Sutera Harbor, opined, "The world has no shortage of creativity, but of integrity."

Integrity is 'talking the walk, walking the talk and walking the walk.' It is the moral courage to do the right thing constantly in the midst of conflicting and confounding voices.

As author Zero Dean puts it, "Greatness takes persistence. It takes determination. It takes facing our own fears and doing that which is hard and necessary, instead of what is quick and easy. It takes skipping the mystical shortcuts and using your imagination as a map and preview of life's coming attractions."

This becomes more difficult when we are faced with constant pressures to meet shareholders' expectations and bosses' pressures to deliver results year after year.

For Edwin Soeryadjaya, the founding partner of Sarotoga Capital and heir to the Astra Group, a household name known for its integrity, greatness means voluntarily selling off Astra to repay creditors and depositors in full.

In China, it was a kindly lady, Grandma Chen, a garbage collector, who stopped and rescued Yue Yue, a two-year-old toddler, who had been run over by two trucks, after 18 passers-by had done nothing. When her compassion made headlines in China, many donated money to her. She gave it all away to Yue Yue's mother for her daughter's hospital bill. Unfortunately, Yue Yue did not survive the accident. Grandma Chen did what was right and showed moral courage. When interviewed, she was asked why she had done it, and she simply replied, "I just did it because it was the right thing to do." That is greatness in action.

2. Greatness is Enjoying Healthier Family Life

I am reminded of my pro-bono work in mediating between divorcing couples. The story keeps repeating itself.

I was mediating between a multi-millionaire property developer husband and a high-flying banker wife. During the caucus session, the wife confided, "My husband keeps telling my son and me, 'I work very hard. I am building all these empires for you.' Now he has built the empires but we are no longer there to live in them!"

The common justification for making business our number one and chief priority — "I am doing it for the family" — has left too many people family-less.

One young engineer went berserk after his wife decided to end their five-year marriage. They had a three-year-old son. He was so devastated. He wept uncontrollably and in-between sobs, told me, "I worked so damn hard, working overtime every night, so that we could move from public housing to a private condo. Now I have no one to live with. I neglected my wife and family. The price is too high to pay."

In recent years, we have seen how great men and women have fallen because of failures in marriage and family.

- Oscar Pistorius, who pushed through a double-leg amputation and earned gold medals in the Athens, Beijing, and London Paralympics for his track and field events. On 14 February 2013, he was found guilty of killing his girlfriend, Reeva Steenkamp.

- Ng Boon Gay, the former Central Narcotics Bureau chief in Singapore, lost his job because of alleged corrupt practices for his sexual impropriety with one female Oracle IT executive. Although he was acquitted of the charge, he was retired from the Public Service Commission.

- Michael Palmer, Singapore's former Speaker of Parliament and a senior partner of a prestigious law firm, stunned the nation when he made the surprising announcement that he was involved in an extra-marital affair with a divorcee named Laura Ong. This brilliant lawyer, caring Member of Parliament and fair-minded Speaker had to resign because of his affair.

How tragic! Certainly, greatness cannot be measured merely by economic terms, career greatness or material success. But I also believe in recovery. These men can regain their greatness when they turn around.

3. Greatness is Nurturing Friendships

Jim Baker, former US Secretary of State, once said, "The fleeting aspect of power causes us to understand the importance of lasting personal relationships — friendships." Sometimes, past experiences of corporate betrayal scar a person's desire to develop friendships.

People are also fearful of others exploiting their friendships for business. Great leaders are able to distinguish between professional relationships and personal relationships. They tread this line carefully.

Dr. Robert S Weiss, a psychiatrist who has studied the social choices of executives, reports that friendship is an extremely wide discretionary area for the successful executive. Many executives make no time at all for friendship or see this area of their lives as "totally optional."

Friendship has to be cultivated. We have to make time for friends, something many of us find difficult to do in this day of social media, short messages, and emails. My one piece of advice for young people is to make time for friends. Good friends are willing to be honest with you and are not afraid to challenge you.

The Late Prime Minister and Founding Father of Singapore, Mr. Lee Kuan Yew, paid Dr. Goh Keng Swee, his former Deputy, whom he describes as a good friend, the greatest tribute when he retired from politics: "Your biggest contribution to me personally was that you stood up to me whenever you held a contrary view.

You challenged my decisions and forced me to re-examine the premises on which they were made. Thus, we reached better decisions. This benign tension made our relationship healthy and fruitful."[i]

I have the honor of sharing my life with a group of friends since the age of fourteen. We belong to a non-profit organization called Eagles Communications. And we have been together for almost five decades — a relationship that is priceless. You can read about this in a later chapter.

4. Greatness is Doing your Best Through Values and Results

Phillip Capital Chairman, Lim Hua Min, described the twin 'Doing the Right Thing' and 'Delivering Results' as the two dimensions of trust, which are the 'Alignment of Value' and 'Ability to Deliver'.

For trust to grow, both these aspects must be present. There must be a constant alignment of values on the one hand and the ability to deliver on the other hand. This trust relationship will grow and be sustained 'over time' rather than at 'just a point in time'. This builds consistency and trust over time.

Whether you are a musician, doctor, business owner or athlete, greatness means being the best that you can be through values and results. There is no short cut to greatness.

Joseph Schooling is a great example of a world-class swimmer. You must combine passion with commitment and diligence with perseverance.

Joseph Schooling has pursued his Olympic dream since he was six.[ii] The seed was sown when he had a conversation with his granduncle, Lloyd Valber, Singapore's first Olympian in 1948.[iii] Since then, he plunged into swimming, each time imagining himself behind chased by a shark. He opined, "I just need to stay focused and keep finding ways to get better. My goal is to be the best in the world and I train every day to put myself in that position."

---

[i] Vikram Khanna. "The Practical Visionary". The Business Times. 15–16 May 2010. P 5. Singapore Press Holdings, Singapore.

[ii] Alvinology. "7 things we all can learn from Joseph Schooling's Olympic win". 13 Aug 2016. Yahoo News. Available at: https://sg.news.yahoo.com/7-things-learn-joseph-schooling-035546665.html.

[iii] Chua Siang Yee. "Pain Behind the Glory". The Straits Times. 21 Aug 2016. SPH, Singapore.

He continues: "I like having people chase me. I like being the fastest... I tried to make a statement with the other guys saying 'you (want) to catch me, you have to come and take it.'"[iv]

Bob Buford, a well-known cable television executive and owner, once said "It's just like a tennis match. When I play, I play my best. I just do."

Being the best is a two-edged sword. It can also drive us to physical and emotional collapse. Former financier Michael Milken worked twenty-hour days and expected the same of his co-workers. He was commonly reported to be ruthless and intimidating when securing a deal.

In this example, there is no concept of temperance. The only motivational banner is "More!" For Milken, the desire for power was limitless, causing him to place no constraints on either his ambitions for growth or the means of achieving growth. It is important that in our striving for excellence, our efforts must be tempered by having good values.

Greatness is finding alignment in "can, want and should." "Can" refers to our competence and talents. "Want" has to do with our motivations and passion. "Should" applies to our values. This will be discussed in the chapter on Finding your Fit.

Becoming the best is the constant commitment to develop our competency, discovering and rekindling our true passion and shaping our core values. When our "can," "want" and "should' are aligned, we are most fulfilled.

5. Greatness is Developing People

People development must be your top priority. This is not just propelled by the functionality of performance but it must be a personal value of every leader, regardless of the employee's loyalty.

Parents don't just develop their children for them to perform. They do it for the sake of their children. Similarly with teachers, coaches, and mentors. This must be in our DNA. This is our human stewardship.

You must place a high premium on developing human potential. This is the concept of dignification: treating employees as human beings rather than as cogs in a

---

[iv] Chua Siang Yee. "Coping with Life in the fast lane". The Straits Times. 21 Aug 2016. SPH, Singapore.

money machine, providing them with opportunities to develop skills to accomplish meaningful jobs, and nurturing human potential at every level.

My friend Edward Ong has this philosophy of people development worth emulating:

> We provide staff with lots of training. We are not afraid when other hotels poach them. We are delighted because we can train more people and send them out. That's our mindset. We cannot put people under our bondage. We employ 2,000 people. If they have potential for higher positions in other hotels, we bless them. Those who want to stay, we know their hearts. If they go and leave because of money, so be it. We export our staff to the industry.

Unfortunately, some leaders and organizations are not willing to develop and train their people because they feel that they will leave anyway. They see people development as a waste of time or feel exploited by employees.

Being great takes a different approach. As Dr. Edwards Deming, American engineer, professor, and consultant once said, "Did you hire them like that or did you kill them?", with regards to hiring and training individuals.

6. Greatness is Developing Successors and Successful Systems

One of parents' greatest joys is to see their children become better than themselves. Fulfillment for teachers is seeing their students excel and develop into men and women of character and competence. One of the greatest accomplishments for any business leader or politician is to build a system for leaders to thrive in; leaders who are able to sustain and develop a better organization than the one the leaders leave behind.

Tom Jones of Epsilon defines success in three ways: "For me, in this company, my success would be to have left three legacies: One, someone to replace me so that the company is not at risk; two, a solid value system that will transcend both them and me in terms of what the company stands for; and three, economic soundness and stability."

Success without successors or a successful system is not success.

7. Greatness is Recovering from Failures

Research done by the Center for Creative Leadership shows that most leaders learn leadership lessons from crises and failures. Certainly, a key success factor of greatness must be resilience.

Recovery involves confronting our own realities head on.

For Hsieh Fu Hua, Chairman of UOB Bank, a leader should lead from the front in a crisis. He feels that the leader must be more proactive, demonstrate control, galvanize the people and maintain his sense of perspective and make the final call.

Leaders should not play the 'blame-game'. "During such tough times, a leader should confront the problems head-on rather than confronting his people," he said.

During his first stint as CEO of Bangkok Hospital, Dr. Chatree Duangnet confessed he failed miserably as a change leader. He wanted to push through changes in the hospital but found that no one was following him. He had a big ego and a big vision.

He had to change. In making his comeback to Bangkok Hospital a few years later, he did things very differently. He intentionally enabled his key leaders and ensured that they were with him in the vision and transformation. In short, they have to "cross the river together with me", he said. "A leader is successful only when his followers are successful."

Tom Gernedas, a Holocaust survivor who founded a company that pioneered new methods for controlled temperature testing, saw failure as a very human-centered notion: "When we fail in spite of doing our best, it could turn out to be a step towards better things we cannot see at the time of apparent failures."

By his own admission, Edwin Soeryadjaya started to work only at the age of 42. In fact, people despised him, saying, "You are a playboy, and you don't know how to run a company." According to him, "It was the biggest slap on my face. It was a wake-up call. That was the turning point of my life."

He had to relearn, recoup, recover and rebuild from the crisis. He could not save Astra. But he rose from the ashes of the family's loss in Astra to become one of the most respected and successful entrepreneurs when he started the Saratoga Group.

8. Greatness is Being Humble

When you have gone through crises and failures, they will keep you humble. Cultivating humility involves being constantly aware of your own background, foibles, strengths, weaknesses, vulnerabilities, insecurities, setbacks and inadequacies.

The outworking of our humility is to serve others rather than serve the self.

Greatness is the ability to keep our egos at bay, especially during the pinnacles of success and triumphs. Most successful people become insensitive, believe that normal rules don't apply, and begin to treat people as pawns in their game of life. Success after success can make us arrogant.

Humility is hardest to maintain when you are at the top. That is why most of the time, organizational setbacks, personal crises and health scares help us remember that we are human.

The late Dr. Goh Keng Swee exemplifies this trait, even though he would not tolerate mediocrity. "He was a rigorous mentor, demanding, never stood for any sloppiness in work or argument. But he taught me how to identify an issue from its fundamentals,"[v] said Dr. Tony Tan, President of Singapore.

He was one who liked to get to the root of a problem because he wanted to get feedback from the ground himself. Many will recall that he would cut through red tape and engage the lower ranks. He was famous for spending more time with the frontline managers than the directors and chief executives. He would often pick up the phone and call a line-manager or technician directly to get their feedback.[vi]

But he confessed that he was also demanding, "I expect every request for finance from me to be properly presented, well argued, with figures to substantiate," Dr. Goh said.[vii]

Humility is not sloppiness or mediocre. It is about maintaining high standards but yet being willing to listen and be open to feedback.

9. Greatness is Leaving a Legacy of Great Values

How we end is more important than how we start.

This is true for family, organizations and communities. I want to pass on these tenets of greatness to my children, to the organizations that I lead and to the leaders I have the privilege to coach and mentor.

---

[v] Nur Dianah Suhaimi. "A rigorous, demanding mentor". The Sunday Times. 16 May 2010. P 8. SPH, Singapore.

[vi] Vikram Khanna. "The Practical Visionary". The Business Times. 15–16 May 2010. P 5. SPH, Singapore.

[vii] *Ibid.*

You must embody these values and inculcate these values in others if you are truly great. This is perhaps the most arduous challenge for each one of us.

This is the legacy that the late Prime Minister, Lee Kuan Yew left behind for Singapore[viii]:

> Give clear signals — don't confuse people.
> Be consistent — don't chop and change.
> Stay clean — dismiss the venal.
> Win respect, not popularity — reject soft options.
> Spread benefits — don't deprive the people.
> Strive to succeed — never give up.

His story and legacy will be shared in my last chapter, The Greatness of a Great Leader.

I like the founder of Herman Miller, Max De Pree's definition of legacy: "A legacy results from the facts of our behavior that remain in the minds of others, the cumulative informal record of how close we came to the person we intended to be." This is so true in the life of Lee Kuan Yew! I also hope to leave this kind of legacy of greatness. I am sure you want to do the same, and you can.

10. Greatness is Caring for the Community and the Environment

Our greatness is never complete if it is self-focused or even family-focused or organization-focused. It was Bill Gates who said he was struck again and again by how important it is to improve the human condition. He demonstrated it by investing most of his wealth in the Bill & Melinda Gates Foundation.

In addition to making sure the loved ones in his life are happy and cared for, the second critical component of success for Gates is to make the world a better place. Gates writes, "It is also nice to feel like you made a difference — inventing something or raising kids or helping people in need."

- In 2000, he set aside US$1 billion to help 20,000 young people afford college.

[viii] Zuraidah Ibrahim and Andrea Ong. "Remembering Lee Kuan Yew: A life devoted entirely to Singapore". The Straits Times. 24 March 2015. SPH Singapore.

- In 2002, he installed 47,000 computers in 11,000 libraries in all 50 states in USA.

- In 2010, Melinda Gates, Warren Buffett, and Bill Gates launched the Giving Pledge, a commitment by the world's wealthiest people to dedicate most of their wealth to philanthropy.

- In 2010, Bill and Melinda Gates challenged the global health community to declare this the Decade of Vaccines. They pledged $10 billion over the next 10 years to help research, develop, and deliver vaccines for the world's poorest countries.

- In 2013 Bill Gates helped launch a $5.5 billion effort to eradicate polio by 2018. India was certified polio-free by the World Health Organization, leaving only three countries that have never been free of the disease.

To demonstrate his commitment to greening the environment, in 2006, Bill Gates helped launch TerraPower, a company that aims to provide the world with a more affordable, secure, and environmentally friendly form of nuclear energy. He also created a new fund, Breakthrough Energy Venture (BEV), in 2016 to invest in clean energy breakthroughs.[ix]

For all that, I have the highest respect for a man like Bill Gates. Truly, as is said, "Great words come from great minds. Great minds come from great hearts."

1. Which aspect of greatness captures your imagination? Why?

2. What is one aspect of greatness that you want to work on?

Action Steps

[ix] Gatesnotes. The blog of Bill Gates. Available at: https://www.gatesnotes.com/globalpages/bio

Chapter 2

UNLOCKING THE
GREATNESS IN YOU
THE FIVE KEYS TO GREATNESS

"Greatness is a Choice. Desire, burning desire
or holy discontent is the beginning of change to
achieving anything beyond the ordinary."

Dr. John Ng

*"You have to fall in love with the process
of becoming great."*

Anonymous

I have been studying the subject of greatness for a long time.

But, I am also dismayed that many people do not achieve greatness. Some haven't the faintest idea of what greatness is. Others choose to under-achieve. Still others decide to stay ordinary. Many start well but are derailed along the way.

But I believe that all of us, especially children, aspire to greatness. Children are curious. They have aspirations. They want to experiment. But somewhere, somehow and someone, often a parent, suppresses or supplants their passion.

I am also disappointed by the many leadership fallouts, especially among high-profile global leaders, who were once lauded as role models in our world.

We see this in the US, where we have the late Kenneth Lay and Jeffrey Skilling of Enron. They were leaders in what was once extolled as the most innovative energy company but which became the biggest corporate fallout in the history of America.

Others like Anthony Weiner, the savvy Democrat Congressman, who was found guilty for 'sexting' and sending nude photos, or Chaka Fattah, Congressman from Philadelphia, who was sentenced to 10 years for racketeering, money laundering and fraud, and William McCormick of CMS Energy, which was found to have questionable practices, also fell in the leadership journey.

The misconduct of the financial industry including the Libor scandal (in the fixing of interest rates) by the world's leading banks has become too familiar and so widespread that it has made corruption the No. 1 problem in the world. When a chief executive of one of the world's biggest and most reputable banks was asked why this was so, his nonchalant excuse was, "We did not do it as bad as the others!"

In Asia, Thaksin Shinawatra, business tycoon turned Prime Minister of Thailand, was ousted in a coup and jailed two years for alleged corruption. He then became a fugitive. Most recently, the top Thai monk, the Acting Supreme Patriarch Somdet Phra Maha Ratchamangalacharn, better known as Somdet Chuang, was also investigated by Thai police for alleged corruption.

In Indonesia, President Suharto, the former President of Indonesia, left a controversial legacy. In January 2017, Ex-Garuda Indonesia CEO, Emirsyah Satar, was charged by Indonesia's KPK (Corruption Eradication Commission) on corruption charges involving the purchase of Rolls-Royce engines for Garuda during his stint as chief executive. This was part of the British investigation into one of Rolls-Royce's executives for paying bribes to secure contracts in countries that include Thailand, Kazakhstan, Azerbaijan, Angola and Iraq.

In China, Zhou Yongkang, who was once part of the Chinese Politburo Standing Committee (the highest political decision-making body), became the most senior official ever convicted of corruption and economic crime.

Bo Xilai, Governor of Chongqing and his estranged wife, Gu Kalai, were sentenced to life imprisonment for the murder of a British subject and for massive corruption. Chen Liangyu, former Governor of Shanghai, was removed from office and charged for misappropriation of a social security sum of US$400 million.

In Korea, the ex-President Park Geun-hye was impeached and had to resign from her presidency. She has since been charged formally for 18 criminal charges including coercion, bribery and abuse of power. Together with her was the Chairman of Lotte Group, the largest retail conglomerate, Shin Dong-bin, who was on trial for corruption, and the third-generation scion of the Samsung Group, Lee Jae-Yong, was also on trial for giving bribes to Park.

In India, Vijay Mallya, the tycoon who called himself the 'King of Good Times', was arrested in London for an avalanche of unpaid bills and allegations of fraud.

Even companies like Siemens, JGC (Japan), Snamprogetti (Netherlands), VW (Germany), Sharp (Japan), Samsung (Korea) have not been spared.

Sport has become big business, involving millions of dollars. That is why sportsmen like Lance Armstrong cheated (the seven-time Tour De France champion executed the greatest cheat in cycling history) and Nelson Piquet Jr. succumbed (the Renault F1 driver was ordered to crash so that his team member Fernando Alonso could win the race).

Almost every sports association is tainted with corruption today: FIFA — Federation Internationale de Football Association, the most powerful and influential sport organization in the world; UCI — Union Cycliste International, the world cycling association is still recovering from the Lance Armstrong scandal; and most recently IAAF — the International Association of Athletics Federations, is reeling from the doping scandal in Russia, with alleged systematic and state-sponsored corruption and bribery practices.

Sixty-two percent of Americans believe that corruption is widespread across corporate America. According to Transparency International, an anticorruption watchdog, nearly three in four Americans believe that corruption has increased over the last three years.

The temptation to bend the rules is probably highest toward the end of an economic upswing, when executives must be the most creative to keep the stream of profits rolling in. Company executives are paid to maximize profits, not to behave ethically. In the US, the most toxic, no-documentation, reverse amortization, liar loans flourished toward the end of the housing bubble. And frauds are typically discovered only after the booms have turned to bust.

As Warren Buffett famously said, "You only find out who is swimming naked when the tide goes out."

What is most disturbing and frightening is that no country is spared from this scourge and no industry is untouched by this plague. Fraud, bribery and corruption seem to be the new 'normal' for business, politics, and religious organizations. This list of rogues goes on and on. No country, no sport, no organization is spared.

The fallout affects the political, business, and religious sectors in all countries. People are losing trust in government leaders, judges, politicians, athletes, corporate leaders, non-profit organizations and religious leaders.

How do you combat all of these?

First, you must have the right perspective on life and the ingredients for greatness.

I would like to share the Five-C model of greatness with you. Whether you are a parent, teacher, athlete, artiste, banker, engineer, fashion designer, biotech specialist, architect, fin-tech specialist, manager or leader, this model applies to you.

The Five-C model is a model of great leadership, comprising five critical components: Centeredness, Calling, Competency, Character and Community.

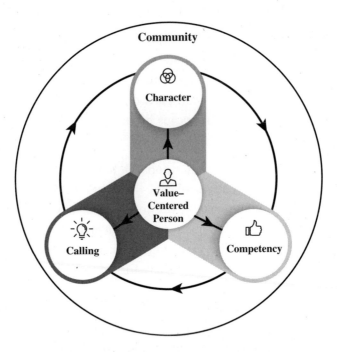

Centeredness (Value of Other-Centeredness)

"Being deeply loved by someone gives you strength,
while loving someone deeply gives you courage."

Lao Tzu

One core aspect of greatness is to be Value-Centered. Values serve as both the gyroscope and thermostat in our lives. The gyroscope provides stability and a reference point to our lives. Values, like the gyroscope, serve as your stabilizer and keep you on the right path.

Value-centeredness is like a thermostat, not a thermometer. Thermostats regulate the temperature. Similarly, your values help you set the tone and regulate the texture of your life and organizations. Unlike the thermostat, thermometers merely follow the environment.

Values keep you in balance and guide your decision-making. The 'Who' comes before the 'What'. In other words, 'Being' comes before 'Doing' and your 'Doing' results from your 'Being'. The values you hold determine the way you lead.

At the core of this value is to be Other-Centered. From this springs respect, honor and honesty, gratitude and generosity. If you want to be great, you have to love people. The great heart is one that cares for others.

Most of the great people we know are Other-Centered rather than Self-Centered.

We have the highest respect for people who are selfless. We admire teachers who care and spend that extra time to help us through our mathematics examination. We remember the manager who coaches us, develops us and pushes us to greater heights in our career. We value parents who work long hours to eke out a living so that they can pay your school fees. We appreciate young people who are willing to give up lucrative jobs to help the poor and impoverished.

My eldest daughter, Meixi, has lived out this value of Other-Centeredness.

She has lived and worked in Mexico City. She applied for and obtained a place in the Princeton in Latin America Fellowship, which selects and matches recent graduates to work for a year with non-profit organizations in Latin America. Through the fellowship, Meixi had the great privilege of working with Dr. Gabriel Cámara, one of the world's foremost educationists, and his team of teachers, who helped transform 9,000 of the poorest schools and communities in Mexico, using the *Tutorial Relationship* (TR) pedagogy.

The key concept is to encourage the kids who have mastered or are passionate in a certain topic to tutor other kids. The teacher serves as a coach, friend and facilitator of learning throughout the school. (www.fiftyfold.org)

Meixi was offered a fully-paid scholarship to do her Ph.D. at Cambridge University. But she wanted to go to Mexico City and learn TR from Dr. Camara. Mexico City conjures up all kinds of negative images for me: Mafia-style kidnappings, murders, rapes and robberies. Of course, for my wife Alison and me, the decision was a no-brainer: She should do her Ph.D. at Cambridge!

But her heart was with the poor in Mexico City and she wanted first-hand experience working with Dr. Camara.

A good friend, Professor Low Guat Tin (who has since retired as a professor in educational leadership from Nanyang Technological University) persuaded us to allow Meixi to go to Mexico. She had heard of Dr. Cámara's work because she knew Pablo Freire, one of the founding fathers of social justice education, who had gone to Mexico and worked with Dr. Cámara. Taking her advice, we reluctantly relented.

Rather than being self-obsessed, I am glad that Meixi is making others a core center of her life.

Calling

Calling creates passion. Author and educator Stephen Covey calls it "finding your own voice." It is finding purpose, meaning and fulfillment in your life. It means understanding yourself, your passion and your destiny.

Calling is your God-given ability to do the job and your God-given enjoyment in doing it. You have a passion in doing it. Of course, passion can be dissipated and has to be nurtured to keep its flame burning.

Michael Novak, in his best-selling book *Business as a Calling*, describes four characteristics of a calling:

- A calling is unique to you. You find yourself. It is self-knowledge, self-identity and self-fulfillment.
- A calling requires talent. According to Logan Pearsall Smith, "The test of a vocation is the love of the drudgery it involves."
- A calling reveals its presence by the enjoyment and renewed energies we get when we practice our craft.
- A calling is not easy to uncover. But when you find it, it drives you and your desire to achieve greatness.

Meixi's calling to work in one of the world's toughest communities in Mexico was first fired when we sent her to Hyderabad, India. She was 11 then and went with her brother, Shun, on a trip with a mission organization named Operation Mobilization, under the supervision of my good friend, Rodney Hui.

When Dr. Cámara asked her what motivated her to work in Mexico City, she recalled her trip to India. She said, "The kids in Hyderabad had so much joy even though they were so poor. That made me question why I could not enjoy my own school, even though I was so privileged."

That trip also made an indelible memory in her mind and created compassion in her heart. Since then, she has gone every year to Chiang Rai, Thailand, to be with the Lahu children and learn from them. After completing her undergraduate studies at Northwestern University, her calling drove Meixi to become the best in her field and she is pursuing her Ph.D. in Education Science at the University of Washington, Seattle, specializing in leadership education for the indigenous people.

She is so committed that she finds time and space to be with her teachers and students in Thailand, organizing workshops for them, empowering them to excel and applying her studies and research to real-life learning communities. She literally has to fly around half the world to do what she does, two to three times a year, while she is pursuing her Ph.D. That's what calling does for you.

But calling is not enough. When you find your calling, you will do anything to hone your skills and to achieve your goals.

Competency

Competency is the accumulation of knowledge and skills in what you do. It comprises both professional competency and leadership competency. It involves both hard and soft skills.

Hard skills have to do with the professional or technical aspect of the business. If you are in the banking industry, you need banking competency, like financial analysis, banking regulations, and business accounting. If you are in retail, you need retail knowledge and skills, like selling, negotiation, and product knowledge. You must have a working knowledge of the business.

But technical or professional knowledge itself is incomplete and insufficient. We need leadership competency, which is the softer aspect of the work, which may include a combination of influencing, coaching, team leadership and people management skills.

Using Meixi as an example, for her to master her craft in TR was not sufficient. While she was in Mexico, she had to travel to many cities and villages to learn to relate to people from different villages, cities and communities. She had to learn to work with students, colleagues, local teachers, community leaders from diverse cultures and ethnicity.

Often, she has to travel alone on buses to the remotest of regions and at times, to the most dangerous of villages so that she can immerse herself in their cultures and learn to be culturally sensitive to experience the transformative nature of TR. TR will not be effectively executed if she lacks people management skills.

Her calling was matched by her desire to learn and work with people of diverse cultures and different strata of society. This is the soft part of competency.

After returning from Mexico, she started a non-for-profit organization, Fiftyfold, with the intent of bringing TR, whose motto is 'Loving to Learn and Learning to Love', to schools in Chiang Rai and Pisanaluk, cities in Thailand.

For the past three years, the result has been stupendous — not only did the local tribal kids enjoy the learning so much, but for the first time, they were empowered to share their learning with their peers. It is her unique combination of both hard and soft skills that make TR so effective.

Character

Character describes a person's integrity and morality. The word 'character' comes from the Greek word, *kharakter*, a stamping tool. It describes a person's quality, a distinguishing mark, feature or trait of a person. Two aspects, integrity and morality, are often the missing pieces in greatness.

Most people associate greatness with power and wealth. If you make these two aspects the stamping tool of your life, then you will be defined by them. You become what you worship. That is why, I believe, there is so much derailment and fall-out. It makes you lose perspective and bearing. It makes you short-sighted.

The other aspect of character is integrity. Integrity is wholeness. It is being real and authentic: What you see is what you get.

I have seen how Meixi develops her character. She really loves her work and she really loves to teach. When she conducts TR sessions with teachers and students, she is full of love and joy. She speaks and writes Spanish so that she can communicate with the Mexicans. She learnt how to speak and write in Thai so that she can communicate with the people in Thailand. This has made her so loved and accepted by the Mexicans and the Thais.

She interacts with them sincerely, is always willing to listen and learn from them and always ready to impart her knowledge and skills. She doesn't care how much she is paid, where she stays, and what she eats. The money she raises from a philanthropic foundation in Thailand goes towards organizing retreats, resources for the students and paying for her basic travel expenses. One teacher commented, "She's the real thing!"

She has one consistent practice: 'contemplation in action' or *examen*, a Jesuit tradition. I noticed that she spends much time reflecting and journaling, which are evident in her blog and website posts. This practice has helped her become more focused in what she is doing.

Beyond her reflections, she puts what she has learnt into action. Everything she learns, becomes part of her and her action plan, which she regularly practices and refines until she has perfected the art. That is integrity — being whole and walking her talk. To her, every failure was a learning discovery, every success a gift of grace.

She personifies Zero Dean's perspective of greatness: "Greatness takes persistence. It takes determination. It takes facing our own fears and doing that which is hard and necessary, instead of what is quick and easy. It takes skipping the mystical shortcuts and using your imagination as a map and preview of life's coming attractions."

Community

To be in community is to have friends: true and honest-to-goodness friends, who will stand with you while others fall away. Having a community of friends will keep you real and accountable. Over the years, I have recognized that friendship is truly important.

To last the long haul and be truly great, you have to cultivate true friendship. It starts with you. You have to be a friend first. Unfortunately, in our fast-paced, time-is-money world, friendship is in short supply.

What does true friendship look like?

In four different studies, using samples from Britain, Hong Kong, and Japan, Dr. Michael Argyle and Dr. Monika Henderson, professors from Oxford University, have established five rules of friendship.

Argyle and Henderson Relational Intimacy Scale
(Rules of Friendship)

Please look at each item and circle the number
(1 – Almost never, 2 – Very seldom, 3 – Somewhat true,
4 – A great deal, 5 – Almost all the time)

I disclose things that are personal and important to this person.	1	2	3	4	5
We hold many common attitudes and values.	1	2	3	4	5
I show my true feelings and behave naturally when I am with him/her.	1	2	3	4	5
I strive to make him/her happy whenever we are together.	1	2	3	4	5
I feel very happy whenever I hear of his/her success.	1	2	3	4	5

20 – 25	Strong, healthy friendship with spouse
11 – 19	Fairly good friendship with spouse: focus on areas to develop
5 – 10	Poor, badly strained friendship with spouse: discuss with spouse on how to rebuild the relationship

---

Try doing this survey, see how many true friends you have. If you do not have many, you should start investing the time to cultivate this type of relational intimacy, where…

…you can disclose personal and important things.

…you share many common attitudes and values.

…you can show your true feelings and real self without feeling that you are being judged or condemned.

…you strive to make the other person happy.

…you genuinely and truly feel joyful when you hear of his/her successes.

Meixi has a penchant for friendships. She makes time for them. Whenever she comes home from the US during her vacation, she will make it a point to connect with friends from high school, her former college mates, the teachers/students from Shuqun Secondary School where she taught for a year, and her mentors in education. She spends time hanging out with them, be it singing karaoke or going out for salsa dances. It helps that she is an extrovert.

To her closer friends, she can be herself and she can share her dreams and fears freely and openly. She discloses herself with them. They do the same with her. There is reciprocity. No wonder she is well-loved by her friends.

But it is not just social. For her work in Thailand, she engages with her staff and board members. She treats all of them as equals, regardless of educational qualification or rank. She discusses ideas and issues with them. She is open and receptive to their suggestions.

She has built a culture of trust and forged very strong relationships with each member of the team, keeping them informed and including them in much of the decision-making to ensure co-ownership of problems and solutions. She interacts well with both the old and the young, treating everyone as friends.

She truly has a community!

Each of these five features of greatness is important. Allow me to articulate what I mean, using the following diagram:

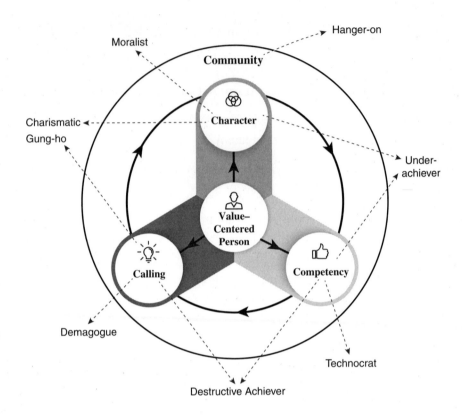

If you have competence, without calling, character and community, you become a technocrat — a functional expert bereft of emotional intelligence.

If you only have character, without calling, competence and community, you become a moralist — dispensing spiritual advice and moral platitudes to your followers, with little credibility because you lack passion and competence in what you do.

If you have calling and competence, without character and community, you become a destructive achiever. I am sure you can cull out examples of this kind of person. The wheeler-dealer investment bankers during the financial crisis of 2008 are fine examples of such people. They are extremely passionate in what they do and they excel in what they do but they lack character (integrity and morality). Hence, they become destructive to the organization, to others and to themselves.

If you have community, without centeredness, calling, competence and character, you are just a hanger-on: a friendly but useless bump.

If you have character and competence, without calling and community, you become a demotivated under-achiever.

If you have character and calling without competence and community, you become a charismatic gung-ho. You are an eager beaver unable to contribute to people and organizations.

If you have centeredness, calling, competence and character without community, you become a lonely solo performer and have no one to share your success or failure with, which is not sustainable in the long run.

Centeredness, calling, competence, character and community: These five features are not techniques or strategies but a frame and perspective that govern your way of life to achieve greatness. All these factors are important.

The real power of greatness lies in the holistic integration of all these five aspects of life.

You must also remember that greatness is a choice and a journey. You must remain focused on that journey to greatness. There is no short cut. At different times, you may lose focus and fail, but you must not give in and give up. It's a long arduous journey worth pursuing and persevering.

You might say I am asking you to bite off more than you can chew. I have this to say: I would rather choke on greatness than nibble on mediocrity.

1. Which aspect of these five factors (Centered, Calling, Competence, Character and Community) is your strength? Why?

2. Which aspect of these five factors (Centered, Calling, Competence, Character and Community) is your weakness? Why?

Action Steps ▼

Part 2

HOW GREATNESS CAN ESCAPE YOU
Ten Ways You Can Be Derailed
(What you must avoid)

Chapter 1

HOW YOU CAN
DECEIVE YOURSELF
THE DECEITFULNESS OF SELF-DECEPTION

"Anyone who has ever tasted the 'good life'
of power, fame and materialism will always
be tempted to justify themselves."

Dr. John Ng

"If you want to cheat, you will always find a way.
You might get caught, but many don't. And every time they don't,
the tyranny of self-deception gets stronger."

Daniel Vasella, former CEO, Novartis

Consider all these individuals.

- **Lance Armstrong — Champion and Cheat**

  Seven-time Tour de France Champion. Even after being diagnosed with testicular cancer, he was crowned Tour de France Champion and founded the Livestrong Foundation to fund cancer research and fight the dreaded disease. When charged and found guilty of the largest dope scandal in sports, Armstrong declared, "As long as I live, I will deny ever doping."

  What was most disturbing was Armstrong's conversation with Oprah Winfrey on her show, after the scandal broke[x]:

  Winfrey: *Was it a big deal to you, did it feel wrong?*
  Armstrong: *No. Scary.*
  Winfrey: *It did not even feel wrong?*
  Armstrong: *No. [That was] even scarier.*
  Winfrey: *Did you feel bad about it?*
  Armstrong: *No, [that was] the scariest.*
  Winfrey: *Did you feel in any way that you were cheating? You did not feel you were cheating taking banned drugs?*
  Armstrong: *At the time, no. I kept hearing I'm a drug cheat, I'm a cheat, I'm a cheater. I went in and just looked up the definition of cheat and the definition of cheat is to gain an advantage on a rival or foe that they don't have. I didn't view it that way. I viewed it as a level playing field.*

  Armstrong confessed that his 'win at all costs' mentality, shared by many champions and aspiring athletes, was a flaw. His strength had become his weakness.

---

[x] "Lance Armstrong & Oprah Winfrey: interview transcript" Available at: http://www.bbc.com/sport/cycling/21065539

- **Rod Blagojevich — "Vain, Vindictive and Mad"**

American politician Blagojevich won the governor's seat by voting for reform after his predecessor, George Ryan, was convicted of racketeering. Even though he was recorded on tape flaunting his greed ("I want to make money"), he threatened to withhold $8 million for pediatric care until one particular officer donated $50,000 to his campaign fund. He was charged in 2008 for selling the Illinois Senate seat, which President-elect Barack Obama had vacated. "I've got this thing," he said of it. "It's ****ing golden... I'm just not giving it up for ****ing nothing."

One state senator revealed how, when he refused to vote for a bill, Blagojevich went ballistic "like a ten-year-old" and threatened to ruin his political career, while hovering over him with his fists clenched.

To some of his fellow politicians, Blagojevich was vain, vindictive and slightly (or entirely) mad. Yet, he refused to resign and had to face an impeachment.

On 5 December 2009, the *Chicago Tribune* reported that the FBI was wiretapping Blagojevich as part of a long-term investigation into state corruption. However, he proclaimed the next week: "I don't believe there's any cloud that hangs over me. I think there's nothing but sunshine hanging over me."

- **Bernard Madoff — The Sophisticated, Likeable Ponzi-Master**

Many of former American stockbroker Madoff's biggest investors believed that getting him to manage their money was like gaining admittance to a 'Who's Who' club. You had to know somebody to get in.

Somehow, he promised them 12 to 13 percent returns a year, come rain or shine. And he didn't charge them any fees! As Barton Biggs wrote, "They ignored one of the oldest adages: If it sounds too good to be true, it probably is too good to be true." What is most scary is this: people who knew Madoff maintained that he was modest and unassuming.

Bernard Madoff, the most sophisticated and charming huckster of all time, could mingle socially (may I add, unconscionably) with his fellow members and their guests at the very exclusive Palm Beach Country Club, even as he was taking their money.

- **Ramalinga Raju — IT Genius and 'Enron' of India**

  Raju's Satyam network covered 67 countries and employed 53,000 IT professionals serving over 600 global companies, 185 of which were Fortune 500. He had been conferred the Ernst & Young Entrepreneur of the Year Award in 2007, and the Golden Peacock Global Award for Corporate Governance 2008. When caught, he confessed that he had falsified accounts. "It was like riding a tiger, not knowing how to get off without being eaten," he said. Analysts called it 'India's own Enron'.

How else can you explain the above?

The world watched in dismay and disbelief over all these scandals. I kept wondering how all these could have happened, and how such dishonesty and deceit could have gone undetected for so long.

I am fascinated with the phenomenon of self-deception — how people can fool themselves into thinking they can get away with their wrongdoing. The leaders listed above are just a few examples showing us how self-deception has become a common feature among those in power today.

It is not just them: many of us also have it. The answer is the deceitfulness of self-deception: Why do you keep deceiving yourself?

1. Personal Conditioning

This is the 'Boiled Frog' effect, whereby a frog is slowly boiled to death without it escaping when it is in a beaker of water and the heat is turned up slowly.

Similarly, Madoff was so successful in conning his friends and clients that he did not know how to stop. As journalist Daniel Gross opined, "There is something Gatsby-esque about the whole story. Madoff is a clear proxy for Meyer Wolfsheim, the vulpine, self-satisfied criminal seducer."

Armstrong had become so accustomed to cheating in order to win that he convinced himself and his team-mates that this was the right thing to do. This became business as usual.

Blagojevich had become so conditioned by the power he could wield anytime and in any way to get what he wanted. It was difficult to stop.

Raju's story was a true rags-to-riches one. He began with a modest IT company of 20 employees, which grew rapidly until he was getting contracts from US companies. Yet he overstated its cash reserves of US$1 billion, and siphoned away most of it for himself. He confessed that he had become so accustomed to the good life and the accolades, he could not imagine living the ordinary life.

2. Self-Justification

Anyone who has ever tasted the 'good life' of power, fame and materialism will always be tempted to justify himself or herself.

You will succumb to self-justifying beliefs. I have heard it so often that I even tend to believe it when people say:

- 'Everyone is doing it.'
- 'That's how business is done.'
- 'We are not as bad as others.'
- 'If you don't do this, you will not succeed.'
- 'There's no other way than this way.'
- 'Don't be so self-righteous. You can't survive if you don't do it.'

You will face these self-justifying and self-convincing phrases. Unless you have a moral compass, you will succumb.

3. Peer 'Conspiracy'

In comparing the Madoff case with the collapse of our financial institutions, American economist Paul Krugman writes:

> The vast riches achieved by those who managed other people's money have had a corrupting effect on the United States society as a whole... While Madoff was apparently a self-conscious fraud, many people on Wall Street believed their own hype...

At the crudest level, Wall Street's gains corrupted and continue to corrupt politics, across both political parties. From Bush administration officials, like Christopher

Cox, chairman of the Securities and Exchange Commission, who looked the other way as evidence of financial fraud mounted, to Democrats who still haven't closed the tax loophole that benefits executives at hedge funds and private equity firms, *politicians have walked when money talked.*

People influence each other into believing things, for good or ill. Be it a peer 'conspiracy' or an unintended consequence, you begin to believe the unwitting 'propaganda' that we give one another.

4. Entitlement Mentality

Many have fallen because they cannot have anything less than what they believe they are entitled to. In each of us, there is a little 'Madoff', 'Raju' or 'Blagojevich'. Before you point an accusing finger or become judgmental, you should look at yourselves in the mirror and recognize that you can begin to feel entitled especially after you have experienced the good life.

Daniel Vasella, former CEO of Novatis, warns: "An individual can be corrupted by what's going on around him, and if you're not careful and suspicious of our own strength, then you will fail... If you want to cheat, you will always find a way. You might get caught, but many don't. And every time they don't, the tyranny of self-deception gets stronger."

Abraham Lincoln got it right: "You can fool all the people some of the time, and some of the people all the time, but you cannot fool all the people all the time." To that, may I add: "But you can fool *yourself* to all people, all the time."

> 1. Who can you think of in your life who has succumbed to the deceitfulness of self-deception?
>
> 2. Which of the four aspects of self-deception are you most susceptible to?

Action Steps ▼

Chapter 2

HOW YOU CAN BE CHOKED
BY SOCIETAL VALUES
THE MOLDING OF MORAL DECAY

"My ambition when I was young was to
be the greatest cheat and not be caught!"

Dr. John Ng

"Do not think lightly of evil, saying, 'It will not come to me.'
By the constant fall of water drops, a pitcher is filled; likewise,
the unwise person, accumulating evil little by little, becomes full of evil."

Buddha, verse 121 of the Dhamnapada

Why has greatness fallen by the wayside? Chief among the reasons is a set of societal values that militates against greatness.

1. You Can Be Fascinated By Evil

Some of us admire people and worship leaders who reach the pinnacle of success through dubious means and are drawn inescapably to leaders whose characters are flawed by low morals.

I can understand why. I came from such a background.

My parents used to own a grocery store in a crowded neighborhood near the Singapore General Hospital. Much of our income came from illegal gambling. I was brought up in a culture where cheating and deceit were part and parcel of my life.

When I was six, I learnt the craft of making money through illegal means. I remember selling 'tikam-tikam', a game where kids will buy slips of paper, with hidden prizes (sweets or cash). Their luck came from picking the right slip of paper with the prize in it. But I took out all those slips that had cash prizes to ensure that nobody would win but me. In this way, I would maximize my profit.

I went a step further in cheating. With those same prize-winning slips, I would go to a 'mama store' (Indian stall) and with the same 'tikam-tikam' pattern, would pretend to buy the ticket, make a quick switch, show my ticket and claim the cash prizes. By doing this, I won both ways: one from cheating my customers and the other from cheating stall owners. I never thought I was cheating. I thought I was the smartest six-year-old in the neighborhood! Further, when I told my brothers my evil scheme, they applauded my ingenuity!

That was how I was raised. And I always admired business people who could make more money in scheming and unscrupulous ways. My ambition when I was young was to be the greatest cheat and not be caught!

As Os Guinness, a visiting Fellow at Brookings Institute, writes, "So, we do not seem dismayed by evil heroes. Indeed, we have a streak of fascination for our fellow creatures with the audacity to transgress."

2. You Tend to Focus on the Bottom Line

Another societal value that militates against greatness is, as Guinness writes, "*as long as they deliver the results, character does not matter.*" I know of friends, who are sales directors, working for corporate companies and Multinational Corporations. They would fudge their sales numbers or do forward sales bookings to achieve their bottom-line.

Recently, I returned from China and was told of some other 'creative' ways of reaching sales targets:

- Shopping mall owners make cash payments for renovation work done to lure premier brand name companies to be anchor tenants. These companies would keep on expanding their stores without the accompanying sales volume to sustain their growth. In fact, they are loss-making companies, but in order to sustain their cash flow, the mall owners keep opening up more and more stores to obtain cash for renovation. They succeed in two ways: They give the false impression of profitability by their expansion and they get more cash to roll without making their sales targets.

- Business owners create fake invoices by recording fabricated sales numbers in their books to boost the revenue figures, so that they can attract investors. In this age of capital markets, some businesses focus on making the books look great to attract capital rather than focusing on the actual effort of making their business good, productive and viable!

  With these inflated accounts, they then can borrow more from banks and private investors. Bank managers are part of this scheme as they are bribed to do so. They look good, the bank looks good, the bankers look good, the stall looks good, and the business owners look good. But it is all a bubble, waiting to burst.

- Another creative technique is delayed or non-payment of goods. Business owners refuse or delay payments with their suppliers and vendors. They squeeze them for longer terms, though they know they have no means of payment. Lawsuits are common. Courts are so overwhelmed with cases that they take years to review the case. So, for many of them, going to the courts is a lost cause. They would have been bankrupted by the time the case is finally heard. Worse still, judges are bribable as well.

Even worse, many of these business owners have no qualms continuing such practices, maintaining that this is 'smart business' and 'creative negotiation'. In the meantime, they enrich themselves with extra bonuses, live the high life, and spend on personal items as though there is no tomorrow!

So, you applaud and buy into Gordon Gecko's philosophy as portrayed in the movie *Wall Street* that "greed is good and greed is legal."

3. You Prefer Short-termism

Short-termism has become the norm today. Dan Vasella, former CEO of healthcare company Novartis, in an interview with *Fortune*, calls it the "tyranny of quarterly earnings". He admits, "Failure, or the prospect of failure is what keeps CEOs up all night. But I would argue that there is another, less talked-about risk that may be more treacherous in the end. That is success. Or rather short-term success — what chief executives and Wall Street analysts call 'making the quarter.' The idea of delivering quarterly results becomes an intoxicating one."

It is this preoccupation with short-term success that can hamper long-term performance and lead you to manipulation.

He asserts, "There is nothing inherently wrong with delivering results — quarter by quarter... but the tyranny of the quarterly earnings is a slippery thing... Once you get under the domination of making the quarter — even unwittingly — you start to compromise on the gray areas, that wide swathe of terrain between the top and bottom lines."

4. You Can Do Whatever You Want

As Os Guinness pointed out most poignantly, "Character has become the victim of modern liberalism's double emphasis on secularity and self-interest." Relativism becomes the new norm: Everyone is right. No one is wrong. It all depends. You can always explain any misconduct.

You subscribe to the dictum: When in Rome, do as the Romans do. Don't ask and don't tell. You have to adapt to survive. Self-interest comes first. You prefer to do your own thing. You do whatever feels right. You do whatever is right for yourself.

Unfortunately, narcissistic behaviour is on the increase. According to the US National Institute of Health, "The incidence of narcissistic personality disorder is nearly three times as high for people in their 20s as for the generation that's now 65 or older. More college students score higher on the narcissism scale in 2009 than in 1982."

This seems to be more acute in China because of the one-child policy, which has created a generation of over-confident and self-absorbed children. According to journalist Joel Stein, even the poor millennials have high rates of narcissism, materialism and technology addiction in their ghetto-fabulous lives.

Joel Stein adds, "If the baby-boomers are the 'Me' Generation, the Gen Y are the 'Me, Me, Me' Generation." This self-absorption is evident in the 'selfie' or 'wefie' movement of photo-taking.

5. You Can Be Obsessed With Power

Of course, power is important. It empowers you to make things happen, influence people, and transform organizations. But sometimes, unfettered power and the craze for power can and often does lead to abuse.

As Guinness once again commented most mournfully, "Winning friends and influencing people is only the kindergarten course. At graduate levels, all of life can come under our 'control' and be ours to 'exploit'. 'Masters of the Universe' are power wielders par excellence. People are reduced to pawns to be pushed around on a chessboard as life is reduced to power games."

We see this most acutely in the sporting world, where influence and power become the name of the game. Leaders in sporting organizations are not just leading organizations. They are powerful individuals. They are movers and shakers in the sports world. They influence decisions, make policies, and discard leaders who oppose them. They consolidate their power base and build their own kingdoms. Sports leadership has degenerated into an extensive patronage and a highly political system.

6. You Want to Look Good

This is what I call the addiction of looking good.

Jean Baptiste Colbert, chief financial advisor to King Louis XIV, was the architect of France's "domination through fashion". He championed, "With our taste, let us make war on Europe and through fashion conquer the world." French haute couture has been legendary ever since. Colbert's influence had widespread impact: the promotion of style and image had become the currency of modern politics and leadership.

Vogue's editor Diana Vreeland's motto was, "Fake it, fake it... Never worry about facts. Project an image to the public. The art of success is to create a world as you feel it to be, as you wish it to be, as you wish it into being." As a result, greatness becomes the casualty.

Young people are also caught up with this obsession. I know of receptionists, clerks, waitresses, etc. working overtime and saving up to buy the latest Gucci bags, Patek Philippe watches, Dior designer dresses, or Jimmy Choo shoes. There is nothing wrong with wanting designer goods, so long as it doesn't become an obsession. Everyone has a certain unique interest, be it music, bags, dresses, cars, etc.

You may end up paying the price by having an overworked and overstretched work life, leading to emotional breakdown, poor health, and neglect of marriage and family. You suffer from burn-out and depression.

You can also become infatuated with your own reputation and face concerns, which can hold you captive. Vasella recognizes, "You can find yourself in a situation where you worry more and more about your reputation and become its prisoner... One day the glitter will be gone anyway. Only once you are unencumbered by that will you become free to do the right things as leader of your company. Otherwise you'll always have to do what others expect of you. Or what you believe is expected of you. If you have a reputation as a consistent performer and you are worried about losing the status... you become a slave to the master of public opinion."

In Asia, the idea of keeping up with the 'Wongs' and 'Chens' and looking good in the communities has become a major concern. Parents want their children to dress right, appear in the right magazines, eat at the right restaurants, party at the right night-spots and be seen with the right company. This is exacerbated by parents who match-make for their children to ensure they marry into the right families, with the right economic status or right standing in the society. This has become a subtle obsession.

7. You are Inclined to Hide the Truth

It is increasingly harder to be truthful, especially with the pressure of quarterly performance. Exaggeration and rising unrealistic expectations may lead to falsehood and falsification. With fearless candor, Vasella puts it this way, "If we say exactly how much we will earn in the next quarter or the next three quarters — and then hit it each and every time — it means that we are playing with the numbers."

He confesses, "To me transparency means that I will communicate truthfully what I do and don't know about my company's performance and prospects, the doubts that I have, and the things that I don't doubt. The goal of transparency is to give the shareholder an opportunity to form an opinion about you, to make a judgment."

He continues, "That's not to say one has to be naïve and publicly share information that will harm your company from a competitive standpoint... it has to be transparent to a degree that allows fair judgment of both the company and the strength of the underlying business."

Like with Vasella, truth-telling is a constant struggle for many. The most recent case is the German car-maker Volkswagen (VW): It's been dubbed the "diesel dupe". In September 2015, the United States Environmental Protection Agency (EPA) found that many VW cars being sold in America had a "defeat device" — or software — in diesel engines that could detect when they were being tested, changing the performance accordingly to improve results. The German car giant has since admitted cheating emissions tests in the US.[xi]

"We've totally screwed up," said VW America boss Michael Horn, while the former group's chief executive, Martin Winterkorn, said his company had "broken the trust

---

[xi] "Volkswagen: The scandal explained". Available at: http://www.bbc.com/news/business-34324772

of our customers and the public". Winterkorn has since resigned and was replaced by Matthias Mueller, the former boss of Porsche. "My most urgent task is to win back trust for the Volkswagen Group — by leaving no stone unturned," Mueller said on taking up his new post.[xii] This means getting to the truth and practice truth-telling again.

The culture of today's world is lies, half-truths, fake news and cover-ups. Truth-telling is a rare commodity.

8. You Can be Corrupted by Materialism

Again, the lure of wealth is most evident and accentuated in the world of sports. Sports used to be a game of passion and healthy competition. But today, positions of leadership are not just positions of influence.

They are door-openers to marketers, government funds, advertisers, and alliances, which have become conduits for wealth generation. These networks are fast becoming money-making machines, which are addictive opiates.

French former football player Michel Platini thought nothing wrong when he asked for two million Swiss francs for consultancy work he did which was nine years late. He thought nothing wrong when his son, Laurent took a job with a sportswear firm owned by the same Qatar sovereign wealth fund that owns Paris Saint-Germain, 12 months after he voted for the tiny Gulf State to host the World Cup 2022, even though he had initially leaned towards voting for the US. Similarly, he had no issue commissioning his former son-in-law to write the Europe League theme song.

It is unfortunate that professionalism in sports has degraded into a money-generating, power-consolidation and corruption-laced machinery.

The idiom 'You scratch my back, I scratch your back' is the order of the day for many of these sports leaders. Soon, all will suffer from back sores!

Certainly, having money is not wrong. Being materialistic is part and parcel of our material world. But both money and materialism have a conditioning effect. The

---

[xii] *Ibid.*

more you are used to the materialistic lifestyle, the more difficult it is for you to cope with less.

Some of us cannot imagine not having a 10,000-square-metre penthouse, swimming pool, a Bentley, suite-class flight privileges, etc. Unfortunately, as Vasella confesses, "The more money I made, the more I got preoccupied with money. It corrupts the mind."

9. You Emulate the Wrong Role-Models

The moral degradation is compounded by the fact that there is a dearth of role models, which has created a vacuum. Instead, today's role models and super stars are sex-scandalized football stars and character-deficit actors/actresses, earning obscene wealth, parading their well-sculptured bodies or sexy-outfits, Botox-manicured bodies, admired by millions of fans.

Even in the corporate world, very little is written about humble leaders of great character. More space is given to outstanding CEOs, who made the quickest bucks with little concern about how unethically they have acquired their wealth, or how they have neglected their families in the pursuit of material wealth.

To sum it up, greatness is about your moral values — values that will stand the test of these temptations. As Vasella asserts, "I truly believe my ability to keep shareholders' faith in our company depends in the end not on whether I make the quarter but on who I am, what my guiding principles in life are, my behavior. What counts is who you are personally."

I have these four questions for you:

— How much longer can you continue at this pace of relentless growth?

— How long can you afford to take shortcuts to maximize your material gains, sacrificing your morals in the process?

— How often can you silence your material desires and still be happy, especially as economic conditions yield less prosperity in the years ahead?

— How often have you checked your innermost hidden motives and asked why you do what you do?

In short, moral values and moral courage are at your essential core and will help you stay on course and guard against succumbing to moral degradation.

1. Which of the above societal values do you think have caused most people to fail?

2. Of the four questions asked at the end of this chapter, which one is most pertinent to you? Why?

Action Steps

Chapter 3

HOW YOU CAN LOVE THE DARK SIDE OF SUCCESS
THE SUBTLETY OF SUCCESS

"The connections of success tend to feed into your ego and you isolate yourself from common human existence."

Dr. John Ng

*"Everything is built to reinforce the ego of the CEO.
The wallet full of platinum cards, the 'other' entrance to the building.
Everything implies you're more important than everyone else.
You get to believe it."*

Tom Jones, former CEO of Epsilon

Success is a two-edged sword. Everyone wants to be successful. Everyone yearns to be successful. Everyone applauds success and successful people. Yet, there is a dark side to success.

1. Success Breeds Infallibility

Success after success can breed a false sense of infallibility. You become larger than life.

Success is a good servant but a bad master. You attract followers who enjoy your success and flatter the successful you. You begin to believe in your own propaganda. You behave almost god-like.

Worse still, our successes can make us arrogant. But arrogance leads to blind spots and blind spots will lead to blindness. The process is frightening — first, we assume that we can do no wrong. If we do fail, we think it is an aberration. Second, we become less and less open to feedback. Third, we react negatively and defensively when people give us feedback. Fourth, others stop giving us feedback. We build up our weaknesses gradually until they lead to our downfall.

Our 'house of cards' is not built in a day. Best-selling business author Jim Collins has written about the crisis of business ethics in the wake of the bankruptcies at Enron and WorldCom. He describes how some business people went wrong:

Some business executives were a part of the malleable masses. These were people who, in the presence of an opportunity to behave differently, got drawn into it, one step after another. If you told them 10 years ahead of time, "Hey, let's cook the books and all get rich," they would never go along with it. But that's rarely how most people get drawn into activities that they later regret.

When you are at step A, it feels inconceivable to jump all the way to step Z, if step Z involves something that is a total breach of your values. But if you go from step A to step B, then step B to step C, then step C to step D... then someday, you wake up and discover that you are at step Y, and the move to step Z comes about much easier.

2. Success has High-Powered Connections

No one will dispute that in today's business environment, we need connections. Cultivating this kind of connection is both necessary and dangerous because it places you in touch with the world of perks and privileges. With this comes status and connections. With it also comes a belief that normal rules don't apply to you; you are not subject to any regulations, and act without any checks or balances.

Connections can also make you selective about who you talk to and who you spend time with. Because time is money. As one businessperson suggests, "I attend the right functions to make the right connections to get the right deals." The right cocktail parties become important. You want to be seen in the right crowd. If they are of a certain status, they might help you. Otherwise, no status, no access.

These connections of success tend to feed into your ego and you isolate yourself from what is now seen as common human existence. You belong to the *avant garde* rather than the *hoi polloi*. Subsequently, you lose touch with the realities of the common. You forget your roots.

3. Success Makes You Egoistic

This is the dilemma of leadership. Having an ego is important as it builds self-confidence. Being egoistic is a different matter. Success both builds your ego and can make you egoistic. As former Harvard professor Laura Nash explains, "A person needs a certain amount of ego, or self-confidence, in order to have the stability, decisiveness, ambition and independence of mind to be an effective leader... So the problem with ego is not with having an ego but with losing one's proper perspective."

Ego has many bright sides: It brings drive, it gives excitement and it provides a sense of satisfaction when things go well.

It has many dark sides as well: It needs to be massaged; it makes us feel that we are bigger than we are, and finally, it leads to self-aggrandizement and pride.

Tom Jones, former CEO of Epsilon, puts it insightfully, "Everything is built to reinforce the ego of the CEO. The wallet full of platinum cards, the 'other' entrance to the building. Everything implies you're more important than everyone else. You get to believe it."

Our identity is often wrapped up in our vocation and our work is measured in monetary terms so that success in our career boosts our ego and failure deflates it.

We lose perspective when you develop a hyper-inflated self and a deflated regard of others and their contributions.

4. Success Makes You Feel Permanent

Power, the high life and the lifestyle of successful people have an intoxicating effect. You are made to feel that you can't live without them. You create a deepening and insatiable desire to make them permanent.

Jim Baker, the former US Secretary of State, sounded this warning in a conference: "Someone asked me what was the most important thing I had learnt since being in Washington... I replied that it was the fact that temporal power is fleeting." He recalled driving through the White House gates and noticing a man walking alone down Pennsylvania Avenue. Baker recognized him to be someone who had held his position in a previous administration.

"There he was alone — no reporters, no security, no adoring public, no trappings of power. Just one solitary man alone with his thoughts. And that mental image continually serves to remind me of the impermanence of power and the impermanence of place." Tom Peters, a business writer, mentions this frequently about success: "If it ain't broke, it soon will be."

5. Success Makes You Self-Reliant

Self-reliance is both a virtue and a vice. We are often told that in this dog-eat-dog world, one cannot depend on others. If you don't help yourself, no one will help you. Hence, the need to be self-reliant.

Self-reliance is a plus because it helps you achieve your economic objectives, teaches you to be creative and encourages you to accomplish the organization's goals.

On the other hand, self-reliance can make you over-confident and too self-assured. You fail to consult with others and are reluctant to admit your own mistakes.

Success after success can lead to self-reliance and then to arrogance. When arrogance exceeds intelligence, you've got trouble. *Arrogance not only leads to blind spots, it also leads to blindness.*

On this topic, Harvard professor Morgan McCall writes: "The bright light of their own achievements can blind successful executives; immensely talented people tend to fly too close to the sun, like Icarus."

At the extreme, arrogance feeds on a belief that a person is immune to any consequences. Arrogance erodes the effectiveness of leaders by creating a perception that normal rules don't apply to them, that they can bend the rules. Eventually, they see themselves living by a different set of standards.

Once-effective people become increasingly out of touch and less effective. Arrogance blocks out any room for growth. As author Croft Pentz says, "A conceited person never gets anywhere because he thinks he is already there."

The first corruption of successful people is the corruption of judgment and perspective. They attribute their success to themselves.

Marshall Goldsmith, who is regarded as one of the world's most effective executive coaches, writes: "One of the most mistaken assumptions of successful people is, 'I am successful. I behave this way. Therefore, I must be successful because I behave this way.'" Successful people tend to believe that they are successful because of themselves. They feel that they have done many things right or think that they do many things right.

James Collins, in his best-selling book, *Good to Great*, used two imageries to describe two types of leaders: the Mirror and Window. For the first type of leaders, whenever there is success, they look at the mirror and attribute the success to themselves. But whenever there is a failure, they look at the window and attribute it to others and to circumstances.

On the other hand, the second type of leaders — the great ones — look at the window when they experience success and recognize the contribution of others and the situational factors. But when they face failures, they look at the mirror and evaluate what they have done wrong and seek to correct them.

Goldsmith asserts that successful people tend to be delusional about their success. The truth is that they are successful in spite of some behavior that needs to change and because others have contributed to their success.

6. Successful People Consistently Overrate Their Own Performance

An ongoing research by Marshall Goldsmith has found that successful people tend to overrate their own performance.

In the US, when professionals are asked how they rate themselves relative to their professional peers, 80 per cent to 85 per cent of all successful professionals rate themselves among the top 20 per cent of their peer group. This is statistically impossible. It simply shows that we have the tendency to inflate our own performance.

In my seminars with leaders in Asia, the survey result is similar.

Professor Nash comments that it is no wonder that the extreme visibility of the CEO's position gives rise to over-personalization and megalomaniacal conceptions of success.

Jack Trout, one of the most famous names in the world of marketing strategies, sums it up well: "You don't find success inside yourself. You find success outside yourself." It is because of the "other-person" in our lives: a boss, friend, peer or family member, that success is made possible.

7. Success Can Become an Over-Utilized Strength

In his landmark book, *High Flyers*, Professor Morgan McCall traces the derailment factors of chief executives. The main factor is what he calls "The Darker Side of Strengths." He describes how strengths could become weaknesses.

- Track record? This can be misleading: Other people or events may have had more to do with the success than the executive would care to admit. Success may have been achieved in destructive ways, or the executive may have moved too fast for the negative consequences to catch up.

- Brilliance? This can be intimidating to others. Brilliant people sometimes dismiss people they think are less brilliant than them or devalue other people's ideas or contributions.

- Commitment? Over-commitment may lead to defining one's whole life in terms of work and expecting others to do the same; being willing to do anything, including questionable activities to achieve success or treating people as the means to an end.

- Charm? Charm can be used selectively to manipulate others.

- Ambition? Ambition darkens when people do whatever it takes to achieve personal success at the expense of others or the organization.

Robbie Ftorek, former Head Coach of the NHL Hockey Team Los Angeles Kings, illustrates a different angle on strengths becoming weaknesses. He was described as technically good and a good teacher — strengths perfectly suited to the Kings when they were a struggling team with a lot of young, inexperienced players.

As the team matured and acquired veteran players, including superstar Wayne Gretzky, Ftorek's teaching style was no longer so well received. The more he attempted to tell the veterans how to play, the deeper his former strengths got him into trouble.

The problem with strengths that have led to success is a result of the success itself. It is difficult to abandon what has worked, even when circumstances change, and it may be nearly impossible to give up old patterns if no new skills have been developed to replace the old ones.

8. Success Makes You Less Open to Feedback

Because there is self-attribution in success, successful people don't respond very well to feedback. Why should they listen to others when they have been so successful?

Marshall states, "Overrating their own performance (relative to their peers) can lead to a decrease in their desire to learn and change...The challenge is to help successful people realize that less successful people can still have valid opinions."

One *Fortune 100* CEO observes, "Success can lead to arrogance. When we are arrogant, we quit listening. When we quit listening, we stop changing. In today's rapidly moving world, if we quit changing, we will ultimately fail."

The point is that most leaders find it difficult to accept feedback, especially negative feedback. When you are not open to feedback, you build up a large blind spot — most people know your weaknesses except you.

The higher you climb in the corporate world, the less willing people will be to give you the feedback that you need to stay humble and accountable.

As Bob Dylan, the intrepid songwriter and Nobel Prize Winner once said, "Even the President of the United States sometimes has to stand naked."

1. What has success in your life taught you, positively or negatively?

2. Which aspect of the dark side of success are you most vulnerable to? Why?

Action Steps

Chapter 4

HOW YOU CAN IGNORE
YOUR WEAKNESSES
THE WEB OF WEAKNESS

"You and I are bound to fail, unless you put in
the time and effort to prevent it."

Dr. John Ng

"After being married for over 37 years,
I showed extremely poor judgment by
engaging in an extra-marital affair."

General David Petraeus, former CIA Director

I can say that Your Weakness Matters.

General David Petraeus, former CIA Director, Commanding General of the Multi-National Force in Iraq and Allied Commander in Afghanistan, is a classic example of a highly intelligent and successful leader who, in a moment of weakness, fell from grace. He had an affair with biographer Paula Broadwell and confessed: "After being married for over 37 years, I showed extremely poor judgment by engaging in an extra-marital affair."

The irony is that during his brilliant military career, General Petraeus had to constantly make extremely good *professional* judgments, but he confessed that he showed indiscretion and made extremely poor *personal* judgments. We wonder how this is possible.

The former Prime Minister of Italy, billionaire Silvio Berlusconi, was ousted and formally charged after a parliamentary revolt against his scandal-tainted rule, which included having sex with an underage prostitute, tax fraud and selling state secrets.

For a long time, I have subscribed to this dictum of Peter Drucker: "Leverage on your strengths until your weakness becomes irrelevant." Our weakness never becomes irrelevant, however. We have to deal with it.

Having studied, researched and examined many leaders who have fallen, I began to realize we all have weaknesses. And your weakness matters. Many men and women have fallen because of particular weaknesses in their lives, whether it was:

- The late pop icon Whitney Huston (drugs)
- Tiger Woods (affairs)
- Former New York Stock Exchange chairman Richard Grasso (corruption)

Examples abound, but they have one thing in common: Their weaknesses have become their downfall. Allow me to share two perspectives about weaknesses.

1. We All Have Weaknesses

"Be you ever so high, the law is still above you."
Thomas Fuller,
British historian

It is unfashionable to admit that you have weaknesses, especially in our Asian culture. You have to be strong, or at least appear to be strong. Admitting weakness is a sign of weakness; it is to lose face, even when your failures are exposed. We often deny them and deflect the blame. Allow me to emphasize this: You will fail and falter from time to time but more importantly, you need to recover.

There are four types of weaknesses. Each one of us suffers from one or more of them:

- ***Personality weakness***

  "Where does personality end and brain damage begin?"

  Doug Copeland

This weakness arises from an over-utilization or over-indulgence of a particular personality trait. For example, those of us are more introverted tend to fall into 'paralysis of analysis' syndrome — endlessly examining a situation without taking action. On the other hand, extroverts can overwhelm people with 'verbal diarrhea', especially when they dominate discussions at meetings.

As an extreme extrovert, I have the tendency to talk and I am a poor listener. This is not helped by my recent discovery that I have hearing loss, especially when there is a chatter of voices or noises.

- ***Competence weakness***

This weakness comes from untrained, undeveloped, or unmanaged weakness resulting from your over-utilized strength. For example, I am spatially challenged. I forget where I parked my car. I am very poor with directions. Sometimes, I can't tell left from right, north from south.

I am also weak administratively. I tend to miss out the details. It can be very embarrassing when you make presentations with the wrong slides or with the names misspelt. This can frustrate my colleagues who are working with me and are anal about details. So, I can compensate my competence weakness by ensuring that I have someone who is stronger administratively or in details to proofread my work.

The other more serious competence weakness is an over-utilized strength that has led to your success. An over-utilized strength is a weakness. This is the flip side of every strength.

I am more of an entrepreneurial positive thinker. I know no fear. I see only the doughnut rather than the hole. Often, I am charging alone without realizing that my people have a hard time catching up with me. At times, because of my lack of detailed planning and execution, I fail in the execution of my strategy.

- ***Emotional weakness***

   "Negative thoughts are like termites that chew up and spit out happiness."

Another type of weakness has to do with our emotions such as anger, fear, lust, or jealousy. Usually, these weaknesses and lack of self-control in these areas can wreak havoc in our lives.

It can result in becoming a way of behaving, usually hidden from others except our closest family members and colleagues. These are activated by trigger words, situations and people and are aggravated when you are over-stressed, anxious and are experiencing a lack of sleep or rest.

These emotional weaknesses reside deep in your psyche. They are usually suppressed and repressed until triggered. Some of these emotional angsts have deep-seated psychological needs associated with deep rejection, unresolved bitterness and traumatic past experiences.

I have a foul temper, which I have denied for a long time. On the surface, I seem like a very nice amenable guy. Only my family knows how I can break out into a rage. I remember an incident when my daughter, Meixi was six years old. She was behaving badly in the car. I tried to stop her. I gave her repeated warnings but that made it worse.

I threatened her, saying, "If you don't stop crying now, I am going to stop the car and drop you off until you stop crying." Obviously, she didn't stop. I jammed on the brake, opened the door, dragged her out of the car and left her on the side of the road in the middle of the night. All the pleadings from my wife, Alison, and Meixi did not work. She was wailing to no avail.

I literally drove off. I was in a rage. After driving for about 200 meters, Alison scolded me and demanded that I returned to pick her up. Fortunately, common sense prevailed, and I drove back and picked her up. She was still sobbing away.

There were other incidents that made me realize I have uncontrolled anger. It was really scary. I realize now that this rage is triggered when I am over-tired and when I cannot get my way. I also realized that part of my rage is a result of my family history and learnt behaviors from my father, who also had a terrible temper.

- ***Character weakness***

> *"I am flawed. Deeply flawed. I think we all have our own flaws."*
> Lance Armstrong

This weakness stems from a character flaw in your life. It is deep-seated within the individual. These are areas in your life that you struggle with. These weaknesses, left unchecked, will derail you. For example, Tiger Woods developed an unusual habit of satisfying his sexual urges through indulging in escapades. As my colleague Michael Tan declared, "We don't have character flaws – *all* characters are flawed."

As mentioned, one of my earlier character weaknesses was cheating, which I accepted as the norm. From a young age, I had learnt the art of deceiving others and wanting to win at all costs. The worst part is that I thought I was clever. I lived the earlier part of my life trying to get the better of others. And didn't think it was wrong. I thought I was smart. Thankfully, after becoming a Christian and being surrounded by good friends, my flawed character began to remold and my hard-wired values and behaviors started to be rewired.

2. You are Bound to Fail

Not only do you and I have weaknesses, you and I are also bound to fail, *unless* you put in the time and effort to prevent it. Your inherent pains, your subtle family values, your parents' unrealistic expectations or your dysfunctional upbringing push you away from becoming great.

You become even more vulnerable when character weakness is coupled with the anonymity and accessibility of quick-win schemes, anonymous pornographic websites or association with friends who endorse your behaviors. The increasing pressure of life, the higher expectations from society, the inevitability of conflict escalation in this competitive world and the relentless pursuit of perfection will expose your weaknesses and make them even more apparent.

Worse still, you are made to believe that you can get away with it. You think you can hide and can never be exposed.

And it's hard to admit your wrongs even when you know you are wrong. This is certainly another aspect in the web of weakness.

Although your strengths and weaknesses are twins in the same womb, it is never too late to master both of them for the betterment of yourself and society. As the Roman philosopher Seneca reminds us, "Every night before going to sleep, we must ask ourselves: what weakness have I overcome today and what virtue did I acquire?"

1. How much do you agree with the statement, "We are bound to fail unless we put in the time and resources to prevent it"?

2. What weakness have you overcome today?

Action Steps

Chapter 5

HOW YOU CAN
BECOME A MISFIT
THE CHALLENGE OF FIT

"If you want to unleash your greatness
at work, you need to find your fit."

Dr. John Ng

"Everyone is a genius. But if you judge a fish by its ability to climb a tree, it will live its whole life believing it is stupid."

Albert Einstein

Albert Einstein wasn't able to speak until he was almost four years old and his teachers told him he would "never amount to much."

People are not engaged in their work; they don't seem to enjoy what they are doing and don't stay long in their jobs these days. According to the US Department of Labor:

- One in four workers has been with his current employer for less than one year.

- One in two workers has been with his current employer for less than five years.

- It is estimated that today's learners will have 10 to 14 jobs by their 38th birthday.

If you want to unleash your greatness at work, you need to find your fit. For the employer, retaining talent is indeed a great challenge for organizations today. It often boils down to the elusive concept of "fit."

1. Job Fit

Finding the right job to fit the right person has become a much sought-after skill. Headhunters and recruitment managers tasked with the job of recruitment have not found it easy. They find that interviewees today are better trained in giving politically correct answers.

Many interviewees have gone for interview training and are better equipped to answer questions from interviewers. Some are armed with impressive track records and even testimonials designed to sweep interviewers off their feet. Others are now interrogating their employers, demanding their terms and perks.

It is therefore not easy to find the right person for the right job.

Another challenge in a tight labor market is that you do not dwell too much on a person's soft skills. It is almost a truism that you hire people for their competency but your fire them for their relationship and personality. Finding the right job fit has indeed become a real challenge.

2. Team Fit

However, just having the right job fit is not enough. Even if a person has a good job fit, the next factor is team fit.

Some people have resigned or have been asked to leave because they can't fit into a team. To get staff members to give the extra discretionary effort, team fit is equally important.

Sue, a Canadian woman, had joined an advertising company as a sales manager. She really enjoyed her work. However, she had much difficulty with her peers. She was unable to adjust to Mohan, the Indian administration manager; Tan, the Chinese public relations manager who had a completely different personality from her; and Tony, the Canadian finance manager who had quirky work habits and communication styles. Sue finally quit her job.

You have to spend time building relationships, adjusting to and accommodating the different work styles and habits of others. Learning to relate and work well is another important step to achieving greatness. You need that extra emotional quotient to help them fit into a team. A Gallup Q12 study has found that having a best friend at work is an important factor that will raise engagement level.

3. Boss Fit

Another factor to greatness has to do with Boss Fit. The oft-quoted statement, "staff don't leave bad organizations, they leave bad bosses," is a truism. Your ability to work with bosses is an important factor to unleashing your greatness. But this is not easy because bosses have idiosyncrasies. They come in all shapes and sizes.

Jack is a visionary leader in an event management company but he is, to put it mildly, rather disorganized. He is not into and does not like details. A one-page executive summary will do for him. But he drives his personal assistant crazy because she is hard-nosed, task-oriented and detail-loving. After three years, she quits.

Other bosses are meticulous and enjoy massively detailed information. They get frustrated with staff who are more fun-loving and creative, and not into the nitty-gritty. These bosses can make life difficult for others as well.

There are other bosses who are very direct and aggressive. The soft-spoken, more sensitive staff may take negative comments personally. These clashes can drive staff away.

Hence, boss fit is another reason why some people do not stay long in their jobs. But your ability to relate to, work with, and learn from different bosses is a tremendous asset to greatness.

4. Organizational Cultural Fit

Every organization has its own culture. Values are best seen in behavior. We can claim to be generous but if we are calculative and money-pinching in our treatment of resources, people will heed what we do rather than what we say.

Similarly, organizational culture is not reflected in nicely printed words framed on a wall. An organization's culture is seen in the behavior of its leader and people.

This is one factor that may cause you to resign. You may like what they do, enjoy the team, like your bosses but somehow feel that the culture does not fit you.

If you have been working in a global organization like Citibank, you may find it difficult to fit into a family-based, or a hierarchical organizational culture like the Civil Service.

Some organizations thrive on driven-ness and creativity. If you are stodgy and the rule-abiding type, you will not survive very long in more dynamic organizations. Hence, it is important that you discover your fit and also learn to work with different organizational cultures to discover where you thrive best.

One thing is for sure, an organization's culture is hard to change. It is easier for you to adapt and change rather than the other way around.

5. Life Style Fit

Some people have a particular life style that is important to them. I know of people who enjoy meeting people and love working in jobs in the hospitality industry because they like this kind of life. Others are more inclined to a steady nine-to-five set up. They would rather spend time having fun or taking care of their young children. The latter would rather sacrifice their career for the sake of family.

My wife was a banker who was fortunate to have a boss who understood her family constraints. The boss made her responsible for corporate services. She lost out in terms of fast track promotion but both sides were happy with the arrangement.

You have to decide what kind of life style you want. You have to make personal sacrifices. If you are posted overseas, you have to make adjustment to family demands and find ways to connect with your children.

6. Life Stage Fit

In my years of consulting with organizations and executive coaching, I have found yet another factor that makes someone quit their work: "Life Stage" fit.

There are some of you who have had enough of corporate life and prefer a more sedentary and meaningful work life. You can join a non-profit organization to pursue "a higher calling." Some call this a "half- time" call so that they can lead a life with more meaning and balance.

Recently, I had a good friend, Lee, who left his job of 25 years in a global drink-packaging company, to teach English to a group of Lahu children in northern Thailand.

Or Jane, who really liked her job as the PR manager in a hotel, loved her colleagues and bosses, and enjoyed working in the hotel; but quit her job because she wanted to spend more time with her children.

To me, this is the best reason for quitting. It is unfortunate that an organization has to lose staff for this reason but it is a lifestyle choice that you are making. And usually, there is nothing the organization can do about it. A good leader will allow you to pursue your dream.

In short, finding your fit is definitely an important aspect in unleashing your potential.

1. How well fit are you in your present job? Why?

2. What is one area of fit that you should work on and two things you can do to improve?

Action Steps ▼

Chapter 6

HOW YOU CAN BE
LURED BY SEX
THE SENSUALITY OF SEX

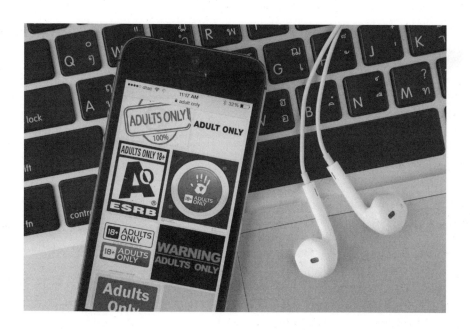

"With the connectivity and anonymity of the
internet, pornography is readily available
on computers, smartphones and tablets; you
can find sex anywhere, anytime and anyhow."

Dr. John Ng

*"Sexual temptation is where we are
held least accountable and where we can
fall fastest."*

James MacDonald

In early 2012, an infamous sex case captured the attention of many Singaporeans. *The Straits Times* broke the story: '44 men charged with having paid sex with underage girl'.

This case shocked many Singaporeans. The accused ranged in age from 21 to 48 and include a former principal, a police superintendent, a military officer, a lawyer, businessmen and bankers. In Singapore, prostitution is not against the law — but having paid sex with a girl under 18 is.

Who could have ever imagined that Jimmy Saville, a BBC presenter and a devout Catholic, could have gotten away with sexually abusing children as young as eight for over 50 years? He was never found out until after his death!

Peter Lim, former chief of the Singapore Civil Defense Force (SCDF), faces 10 'sex for favors' charges. He has been found guilty for corruptly obtaining sexual gratification from three women, who worked in senior positions at IT firms. Two of them are married.

Sexual impropriety, sexual assaults, sexual trysts and sexual deviations have become a norm. Some people are caught and some are not.

Pornography websites are the No. 1 most visited sites on the internet with an estimated revenue of US$97 billion a year. It is estimated that one in five mobile searches is for porn sites.

Recent research suggests that having a profession that involves caring for people also poses a higher risk of marital break-up. According to Dr. Michael Aamodt, an industrial psychologist at the Virginia-based Radford University, these are the top four 'high-risk' groups:

- Dancers and choreographers: 43 percent
- Bartenders: 38 percent
- Nurses, psychiatrists and in-home health caregivers: 29 percent
- Entertainers, performers, sportspeople and related workers: 28 percent

Commenting on the study, Dr. Dai Williams, a member of the British Psychological Society, said:

> What is interesting is that those involved in caring professions experience a high level of break-up. This might be because they spend too long caring for other people at the cost of their own families or because they are naturally sensitive people who are more vulnerable and sensitive in their relationships.

Some psychiatrists have called this 'emotional transference', whereby a client in a therapy session transfers his or her feelings of affection to a therapeutic third party, such as the therapist. That is why even in the Church, where such counseling often takes place, we hear of scandals.

Why is sex so alluring?

1. Sex Starts Innocuously

It starts with an innocent glance, a casual conversation, a peek at pornographic sites, a visit to a singles bar, a drink at some sleazy club or a night out with your clients. Soon, you get sucked into a series of illicit encounters and events. Before you know it, you are hooked.

This becomes more tempting when marital relationships are strained or have broken down. This then provides the emotional connection with a sympathetic client or a caring secretary. When you are emotionally disengaged with your spouse, loneliness sets in.

That the grass is always greener on the other side is ever so true in marital infidelity. You begin to compare your spouse with the 'young thing'. Coupled with sexual dissatisfaction with your spouse, you tend to look elsewhere for sexual satisfaction. Sexually deprived people are hungry people.

2. Sex is Pervasive

No one is exempt. As long as you are human with sexual libidos and drives, you are vulnerable. It releases dopamine and feeds on the pleasurable feelings. From sports figures to high-powered politicians, from pilots to flight attendants, from principals to teachers, from grandfathers to teenagers, from decorated CEOs to construction workers, sex drives and pleasures are real.

These sex drives are also hard to contain and easily satisfied. One episode of the popular Singapore documentary *Get Real!* featured the sexual trysts of Bangladeshi construction workers and Filipino maids. One Filipino woman confessed that she was driven to have an affair due to the loneliness of being away from home and then discovering that her husband was having an affair back in the Philippines. Her rationale: "If my husband can do it, why can't I?"

3. Sex Seduces the Powerful, Rich, Good-looking and Famous

Powerful people are more susceptible to sexual temptation. There is a lot of temptation directed at the powerful, good-looking, rich and famous. Whether they are men or women, people want to get close to them.

Other rich and famous figures caught in sexual trysts have included former International Monetary Fund Chairman Dominique Strauss-Kahn, golfer Tiger Woods, footballers Wayne Rooney and Cristiano Ronaldo, and basketball player Kobe Bryant.

The *New York Times* has reported:

> In July (2011), Xu Maiyong, the former vice-mayor of the capital of Zhejiang Province, Hangzhou, was executed for bribery and embezzlement worth more than US$30 million. Nicknaming him "Plenty Xu", the Chinese press reported that he kept dozens of mistresses.

In another bizarre case, "an official in Hubei province was detained in December, 2010, on suspicion of strangling his mistress — then pregnant with twins — and dumping her body in a river after she demanded he marry her or pay her US$300,000."

It looks like China is set for more tragedies fueled by lust. The *New York Times* summarizes it thus:

> As China has shed its chaste Communist mores for the wealth and indulgences of a market-oriented economy, the boom has bred a generation of nouveau-riche lotharios yearning to rival the sexual

conquests of their imperial ancestors... Judging from the embarrassing revelations to emerge in recent months, such arrangements appear to be commonplace among corporate titans, rags-to-riches entrepreneurs and government officials whose inordinate and sometimes ill-gotten gains can maintain one or more lovers — many of whom are sustained through stipends, furnished apartments, and luxury sports cars.

— Powerful people are greatly admired

Some men and women are enthralled by charming, intelligent, and wise leaders, especially those who are in a high position or authority, and in the limelight. Being admired feeds into their ego. These women would love to hang around such leaders, compliment them, and be photographed with them.

— Powerful people are more vulnerable

When their egos are massaged by glamor, adulation and admiration, they believe in their self-importance and self-propaganda. They think they are super-men/women. They let their guard down. They become more susceptible to ladies'/gents' charm. Clients, suppliers and vendors win favours from them by bringing them out for entertainments. Sexual favours are part of the deal.

— Powerful people believe in their invincibility

Absence makes our hearts wander not fonder. They spend more time with their clients than their spouses. They become too engrossed with their business. Busy-ness gives us a sense of self-importance. In the process, they ignore their spouse and neglect their relationship.

They are spending more time with other men/women. They enjoy their company and vice versa. Soon, acquaintance becomes attraction. Attraction becomes friendship. Friendship becomes romance. Romance becomes an affair.

— Powerful people are emotionally exhausted

Because of super-busy schedules, exacting demands, unrealistic expectations from clients/friends, over-achievement tendencies, and hyper-drive, powerful people are often exhausted. We tend to make mistakes and lack personal judgments.

When another person sympathizes with your emotional emptiness, you feel emotionally connected with her. You end up becoming sexually involved.

I asked my wife, Alison what she thought of the *New York Times* article. She said, "All people are the same. It's just that these men make sensational news." I guess she has a point.

Extra-marital affairs can happen to anyone. You are all admired in different ways. Remember: Beauty is in the eye of the beholder!

Sex feeds your ego, big-time.

4. Sex is More Accessible, Available and Anonymous

Once I was in Shanghai, walking along the Bund during winter. I was approached by two very attractive, scantily-dressed young girls. "Do you feel cold?" one of them asked.

"Of course, I do!" I said.
"Do you need to be warmed?" she asked.
"Of course I would, but not with you!"

With that, I walked away. But they kept pressurizing me until I reached my hotel!

This has become a routine temptation for me whenever I travel alone. Whether it is to Bangkok, Shanghai or Kuala Lumpur, men and women on the streets are trying to accost you with sexual favors. I must say they have become more blatant over the years, which is why I try to travel with at least one of my colleagues. The only way to deal with this is to say a firm "No."

In Singapore, when the government tried to restrict prostitution to certain streets in the Geylang area, it only drove the practice underground. It is easily available with just a phone call and on many websites. Camouflaged as massage parlors, they operate in almost every housing estate offering 24-hour services. They are blatantly advertised and solicited online.

With the internet, you can watch pornography in the privacy of your home, office, hotel and anywhere you want it. With the connectivity and anonymity of the internet, pornography is readily available on computers, smartphones and tablets; you can find sex anywhere, anytime and anyhow.

I had joined a chat group of old friends. Some of them would send pornographic material almost daily. It could become so alluring that it would make me vulnerable. For this, among other reasons, I decided to remove myself from the chat group.

5. Sex is Pleasurable

The *dopamine effect* after sexual encounters is well-documented. When dopamine, a neurotransmitter associated with pleasure, binds to the receptors in our nerve cells, a jolt of pleasure results. There is a region in the brain that rewards pleasurable activities like eating and drinking. Having sexual feelings and engaging in sex have powerful dopamine release.

Having sex feels good, but it will take more encounters, done more often, to sustain the pleasures. That is why one pleasurable feeling and encounter will lead to another. It is difficult to stop.

6. Sex Leads to Hiding and Lying

How did Tiger Woods keep his affairs with other women going for so long? By hiding and lying. Lying can be addictive because the thrill of lying emits adrenaline. Lying is relentless once it gets started because one lie leads to a second, a third and so on. We cannot stop at just one lie. When we succeed in deceiving others, we find it even more thrilling to keep doing so; to cover our tracks and conceal more skeletons in our closets.

I agree with the sex addiction expert Sharon O'Hare's conclusion about Woods: "The biggest problem with sex addicts isn't necessarily the issue of sex. It's the issue of lying." How else can we explain the golfer's stable of other women, even when he had married the gorgeous Elin Nordegren and had two beautiful kids?

7. Sex Enslaves you Slowly but Surely

An adulterous affair does not happen overnight.

In the study of extramarital affairs, Henry A. Virkler, professor of counseling and an author, underscores the stages and process leading to such shenanigans:

Stage 1: Desiring. Having enjoyable interactions with and developing attraction for the other party.

Stage 2: Repressing. Suppressing growing romantic feelings.

Stage 3: Rationalizing. Justifying spending inordinate amounts of time with the other party — "I am doing my professional duty."

Stage 4: Denying. Denying our frustration with the present emotional hollow marriage or denying our personal need for relational and sexual satisfaction.

Stage 5: Deepening. Involving more intimate interactions, leading to secret get-togethers and greater physical contact.

Stage 6: Deceiving. Needing concealment, desiring to hide, telling half-truths or lies, and giving in to self-deception.

Stage 7: Dichotomizing. Living a double life, separating work from sexual impropriety, and/or have a dichotomized sexual relationship with one's spouse and the other party.

Stage 8: Habit-forming. Having a full-blown adulterous relationship leading to an uninhibited, unashamed and accentuated adulterous affair.

Before we point an accusing finger at all these men or women who have been caught, it is advisable to look deep into ourselves, and recognize that we too are vulnerable to the temptations that ensnared them. They have been caught and we have not. But the damage to our lives and families is really not worth the risk!

In the next section of this chapter, I want to focus on why women are attracted to men, especially powerful men.

1. In Asian societies, sex is still a taboo subject. Why is this so and how can you make yourself accountable for your sexual behaviors?

2. When are you most sexually vulnerable? What is one thing you can do about it?

Action Steps ▼

Section 6a

HOW NICE WOMEN ARE ATTRACTED TO POWERFUL MEN

"No one can make you feel inferior without your consent. Finding our self-respect vicariously through others is a sure way of losing it."

Dr. John Ng

"It's good to have money and the things that money can buy,
but it's good, too, to make sure that you haven't lost the things
that money can't buy."

Anonymous

Men are often blamed for sexual trysts. Where do women fit into the picture? What role do women play in luring men, especially powerful men, to sexual infidelity?

1. Pining for Financial Security

From a status-conscious lawyer: "I don't want to just survive. I want a better life; I don't mind being a mistress if my man can provide me with a nice house."

In a world where money speaks louder than anything, some women feel they need more money to live comfortably. They want to be financially secure, which is one of our most fundamental needs. They don't just want to survive, but to have a sustainable life free from worries about money.

A retail manager confessed, "My mom is chronically sick with a hefty hospital bill to pay. I met this businessman in a bar and we hit it off on our first date. We had sex that night, and what I thought was a one-night stand became regular sessions in bed. He gave me S$5,000 after I shared about my need... Actually, I feel guilty after learning that he is married. But what can I do? That's the only way I can think of to get out of my financial dilemma."

When women face financial crises in their lives, it can be another strong push towards having an affair with a powerful man, who can raise the money they need. Affairs are thus seen as an unfortunate necessity, a means to an end.

Younger foreign women working in Singapore have found their security in old men with the financial means to support them. These lonely neglected older men spend their evenings in coffee shops, drowning themselves with beer. Beer serving waitresses entertain them by 'coffee-shop chats' and by serving their needs. Sometimes, they end up in affairs.

Other younger women ply their trades in 24-hour massage parlours, strategically placed in public housing areas. One-night stands become a common phenomenon. This has become a social problem in Singapore.

In fact, another social phenomenon is the rise of matching agencies, dedicated to helping older men find young Vietnamese or Indonesian brides. This has become a lucrative business.

2. Hankering for a Branded Lifestyle

From a lifestyle-conscious air stewardess: "I love beautiful things and branded goods. In the beginning, I had to save for one year to buy my first LV (Louis Vuitton) bag. Since I met this tycoon, he buys me what I want. Do I enjoy his company? Honestly, no. But who cares? I get what I want and he gets what he wants."

It is not enough to have the basics. Many women want more and powerful men can amply provide that. This is the fast track to a 'branded' lifestyle.

The pull to pursue material wealth and join the rich and famous is strong. Look at any glitzy magazine or any lifestyle website, you'll see persuasive articles and enticing photos of successful women being defined by the finer things of life. The message: We need this and we should live like them! What is a more effective way to reach these dizzy heights than finding the right men, who will generously dispense these luxuries on us?

Nowadays, women have become more conscious about the clothes they wear, the restaurant they patronize, the type of homes they live in and the brand of cars they drive. They want to be seen wearing the 'right' things, eating and drinking at the 'right' places, and living in the 'right' districts.

That's why high-end bars, glitzy nightclubs and lovers' lounges usually attract women on the prowl for a better life. They want to find wealthy men who can sustain their lifestyles and move from one bar to the next in search of them.

These things validate their lives and status. If they haven't been able to find that approval in their marital or family relationships, they'll seek it in material things. As someone once said, "It's good to have money and the things that money can buy, but it's good, too, to make sure that you haven't lost the things that money can't buy."

3. Fulfilling their Esteem Needs

From an image-conscious personal assistant: "I enjoy all these cocktail parties my rich boyfriend brings me to. I feel so good hanging around all his friends. It makes me feel important. And it's fun, drinking free wine and great food."

A person's self-esteem is often equated with what you have, how much you earn, what position you hold and more significantly, whom are you seen with. Nothing is more alluring than for nice women to be seen with the right crowd. This provides the self-respect that a woman desperately needs. Their mantra: "It's the company you keep, stupid!" They believe that people will treat you well if they hang around powerful men and they are seen with the right company.

The truth is that no one can make you feel inferior without your consent. Finding our self-respect vicariously through others is a sure way of losing it.

4. Yearning for Emotional Connections

From an overworked banker: "I work so hard every day till 8 pm. I get so tired. It's good to hang out and be emotionally connected with people. I found this famous politician. He was so kind and nice, seemed so understanding. One thing led to another. We became sexually attracted to each other. Very soon, we were hooked!"

Loneliness is the bugbear of many high-flying professional women. Emotional connection is more important for women than men. Without it, they feel lonesome and neglected. Many of them have discovered that loneliness is not simply a feeling of being alone; it is a feeling that no one cares when you are alone.

Our workloads have only gotten heavier. It has become more and more difficult to connect with our loved ones and find the emotional support we need. Married women may not feel emotionally connected to their husbands if both become engrossed and absorbed in their work. They simply don't have time for each other. In short, they become emotionally disconnected. But, the deep need for connection is very real.

After a hard week of work and when these women spend time in bars to let their hair down, it is not uncommon for them to find their emotional connection with suave, smooth-talking and understanding men.

Being low-spirited, having a one-night stand and then slowly progressing to affairs becomes a natural consequence. These women see this as a cure for their loneliness and emotional neglect. Of course, connecting with men of means and power is a bonus.

Unfortunately, after a few years of finding happiness in these short-term relationships, many of these women discover that they are done with trying to have it all and ending up with not much at all.

This makes them feel depressed and leaves them in despair. They soon discover that they have lost their personhood, self-worth and true relationships. But getting out of this pattern of life is extremely difficult, until they hit a crisis.

5. Exchanging Sex for Money

From an underpaid accountant: "I do it primarily for money. It's simply transactional; they want my body and sex. They have to pay for them."

This accountant sells herself for sex on the side. Her clients include wealthy businessmen and powerful politicians, whom she services discreetly at 5-star hotels. When she first started, she felt dirty and guilty — but soon became accustomed to it after servicing a few well-paying clients. For her now, it is a purely business transaction. Her friends and family are not aware of her double life.

For some women, they are attracted to and develop an attachment to powerful men. They are prepared to be their weekend mistresses. They soon realize that offering sex for money is not a profession that glorifies women and may cause marital break-ups. Deep down they know it is a confession of their desperation, alienation and loneliness. But, alas, it is an addiction that is difficult to get rid of.

In summary, the need for money, a branded lifestyle, self-respect, emotional connection and sex are what drive this trend. This is exacerbated by how the world defines our self-worth based on our status and by the pressures at work, which keep us from emotionally connecting with our significant other.

Before we judge these women, we need to look deep into ourselves, our values and how our society champions success. These women, like us, have real needs that are not met in real ways.

6. Being Attracted to Physical Looks

From a beautiful young doctor: "I love cute men — hunks with the looks. I'm naturally attracted to men with great bodies."

The hunk has an additional aura. He is tall, dark and handsome, with great abs and a look to admire. He is the man other men want to be.

Although beauty is in the eye of the beholder, most beholders have a stereotype of what beauty actually means.

Different women are attracted to different parts of the male anatomy, and might point out their idols' angular faces, smiling eyes, well-groomed hair, prominent eyebrows, well-proportioned body shape, or chiselled abs.

It seems that men like Paul Newman, Johnny Depp, Godfrey Gao and Hrithik Roshan have the perfect combination of good looks, musculature, wealth, influence and impeccable fashion sense. Throw all those things in, and such men become the total package.

In the same way that men like 'hot' women, women like 'hot' men. They represent ideals that are rarely realized in daily life.

7. Admiring the Aura of Wisdom

From a driven beauty salon owner: "I adore men who are wise. My pastor was such a person, and I become attracted to him. One day, I went to him for advice. He gave me such good counsel and before I knew it, I was going to see him almost every week. Soon, from platonic friendship, we became soul mates and then secret lovers. Until his wife found out…"

Another group of women is attracted to men of wisdom and insight. To them, learned men such as professors, counsellors, psychiatrists, motivational speakers, clergymen, doctors, philosophers and others are prime targets, because they must be self-confident, intelligent and good communicators to succeed in their fields.

Women seek those qualities in their ideal men, and before long, admiration turns into hero-worship and outright attraction. When such 'heroes' give these women their attention and share their knowledge, they connect on an emotional level as well.

If care is not taken and boundaries are not set, they invite sexual attraction —
especially when both parties' emotional and mental needs become intertwined.

8. Charmed by A Suave Conversationalist

From a lonely restaurant manager and single mother: "I enjoy talking to men who
can carry themselves and speak well. This businessman I met is well mannered,
speaks well and has a great sense of humour. He is not the 'ah-beng' type, uncouth
and rough. I am really attracted to him and every time we date, we connect. He
makes me so happy."

Women want good conversations, and are attracted to men who can provide them.
Some of these powerful men are great communicators who know how to make
others comfortable in their presence, through humour and insightful conversation.

Many women enjoy their company and want to be their friends.

A friend of mine put it well: "Panache and refinement, which wealth and social
exposure allow these men to cultivate, make them very attractive to lonely women."

It's a slippery slope. A female friend has rightly pointed out that many of these
women start on this road innocently, not knowing what they are doing. They find it
easy to get in, but difficult to get out.

They don't set out to cheat or wreck their marriages and those of the men they are
attracted to; many simply want a fix for an urgent need. But close relationships have
a way of enmeshing our material and emotional needs, giving us pleasure and the
feeling of being wanted and loved.

This is why illicit relationships hurt so much, and why marriages and children suffer
as a consequence. But they carry on regardless and are almost impossible to break
out of, unless one hits rock bottom — materially, socially, emotionally or spiritually.
When this happens, some people do find the courage and strength to change things
and put them right, while others spiral into depression or worse, kill themselves.

We search for many things: Financial security, a good lifestyle, approval from
ourselves and others, good-looking partners and wisdom, and we think they will
make us happy and secure.

None of these are bad in themselves. But too often, we set our quest for those things above our values, our regard for others and the nature of society itself. There are too many tragic stories of broken affairs and broken families to make this worthwhile.

One of these is the story of Tiger Woods, which I would like to use in the next section as a tragic story worth telling and analyzing.

1. Which of these eight reasons above can you identify with the most?

2. What can you do to prevent yourself from being derailed, either as a victim or as a protagonist?

Action Steps

Section 6b

HOW TIGER WOODS FELL FROM GRACE: HIS TRAGIC STORY

"We never stop at one lie."

Dr. John Ng

"In some ways, the same quality that allows
you to reach Herculean heights can also
work to destroy you."

Stan Teitelbaum

When the news broke out that Tiger Woods was a sex addict, I was devastated. *No way!* I thought. It sounded too bizarre. I was in denial. Simply unbelievable!

The world was shocked to learn about Woods' dalliances. What began as a home-rescue from a wrecked car by a sympathetic wife turned out to be the event that triggered the revelation of a string of extra-marital affairs by the 'squeaky-clean' Woods.

I have admired Woods ever since he came on to the world stage at a young age, showcasing his amazing golf talent. Besides being the most incredible golfer the world has ever seen, he has been among the highest-paid professional athletes around, earning an estimated US$110 million from winnings and endorsements in 2008.

Above all, he appeared to be a model of goodness. Only 34 years old, Woods had already won 14 professional major golf championships, the second highest of all time after Jack Nicklaus. He was the youngest player to win the Grand Slam, and the youngest and fastest to win 50 tournaments on tour.

According to *Golf Digest*, Woods made US$769,440,709 from 1996 to 2007, and the magazine predicted that by 2010, he would pass US$1 billion in earnings. In 2009, *Forbes* confirmed that he was indeed the world's first athlete to earn over a billion dollars in his career.

In a seemingly made-in-heaven marriage, he wed the beautiful Swedish model Elin Nordegren. They have two lovely children, Alexis and Charlie. Woods was touted to be a loving father who would spend time with his children.

When he came on stage with his winsome smile, I thought that at last we had a great athlete who could become a great role model to millions of kids around the world, especially after having read stories of insanely rich soccer players with sexual appetites as large as their passion for the game. Alas, it was not to be.

From being the most marketable sports personality and one of the most endearing golfers, Tiger Woods has become the epitome of shame and embarrassment for the golfing world. Almost immediately after his confession, a number of well-known companies such as Accenture, TAG Heuer, Gatorade and Gillette cancelled or suspended him from their product endorsements.

This entire episode of his sex addiction left me feeling despondent and sad. Another great athlete had fallen from grace. These questions keep bugging me:

- Why did he waste it all?
- Didn't he realize that what he had done would devastate his mother, his wife and his children?
- Didn't he know that it would ruin his golf career?
- Didn't he know that he would lose millions in endorsements with his indiscretion?
- Didn't he care about his reputation?
- How could he have hidden those shenanigans for so many years?
- Why did he need other women when he had such a beautiful wife?

Let me attempt to put the pieces together.

1. Temptation is All Around — No Place is Safe

It has now become well known that the golf circuits are filled with stories of lewd come-ons and nightclub visits that end in hotel rooms. Just by playing with Tiger Woods in the first round of the US Open, Australian golfer Michael Sim found propositions in his locker.

Even in the Asian golf circuit, post-game sex parties seem to be fairly common. Singapore golfer Mardan Mamat confessed:

> Of course, there is no doubt there is plenty of temptation... It's up to the individual. If you have a family already, and you want to play around with another girl, it's up to you... Of course, if I want to be wild, I can be wild, but for me, I have to keep myself fit and healthy to play my game.

Without a doubt, temptations are all around even in the golf circuit, which many once considered to be a haven for good sportsmen.

2. Arrogance can be Destructive — Your Strength is Your Weakness

From the time, he took up golf and was handed a miniature golf club, Woods was told by his father Earl that he was 'the chosen one'. As Nick Pitt of the *Times of London* said, "And now he has no choice but to continue, trapped like a monarch, not by divine right, but by his talent and celebrity."

When he lost to South Korea's Yang Yong Eun at the PGA Championship, Woods scowled and walked off the green when Yang had yet to putt out, which was pure arrogance. As one critic said, "It was the end of an era." At the Australian Masters, he hurled his driver away, endangering spectators. He failed to apologize, though he still won the event.

Highly driven and successful people, like Woods, can often become arrogant and feel a sense of entitlement. Former US President Bill Clinton probably said it best. When asked to explain his behavior regarding the scandal with then-intern Monica Lewinsky, he answered, "Because I could."

Professor Herbert Samuels, an expert in human sexuality, said: "I think there are some men in positions of power who have a sense of entitlement that the rules of the game don't necessarily apply to them."

"In some ways, the same quality that allows you to reach Herculean heights can also work to destroy you," writes Professor Stan Teitelbaum. The author of *Sports Heroes, Fallen Idols*, has coined the term, 'toxic athlete profile' to describe the mix of arrogance, grandiosity and entitlement that some athletes possess.

3. Loneliness at the Top — Running on Empty

It's always lonely at the top. At tournaments where his fellow competitors stayed in hotels, Woods had the use of a private, guarded mansion. As Nick Pitt wrote:

> ... the gilded cage can be a privilege or a prison and long before the scratches, the three-iron through the car window, and all the revelations that have kept us aghast, there were signs of emotional disturbance of Woods losing control.

This sense of being unloved may have started with his father and mentor, Earl, who was also a love cheat. According to Woods' high school girlfriend, Dina Parr, he would be devastated, crying and saying, "My father is with another woman!"

Woods loved his father dearly, and that was one thing about his dad that he never got over. The irony is that he has now tripped over the same thing. Perhaps Mother Teresa was right when she said, "The most terrible poverty is loneliness, and the feeling of being unloved."

4. The Rush of Lust — Dopamine defies Logic

Hugh Grant, Jude Law, Prince Charles, Ashley Cole and Tiger Woods have something in common — they all had glamorous, headline-grabbing beautiful wives; yet they have all cheated on them. Familiarity breeds contempt. "It's a fallacy of human nature that we tend to get tired of the old and excited about the new... It's about falling in love and not staying in love," reports Harry Low, a senior counselor at the National University of Singapore Health Center.

It's not about the looks but the needs; Woods' need to maintain his top-ranked position in golf made him all the more susceptible. Dr. Ang Yong Guan, a consultant psychiatrist, recognizes that a fierce competitor like Woods is under tremendous pressure to perform. In his case, it became worse after his injuries. "Someone like him may feel their equilibrium is being affected and so they seek ways to compensate. This could mean testing their limits with risk-taking behavior, like having an affair, smoking or drinking to get excitement," explained Dr. Ang.

Sharon O'Hare, an expert in sex addiction from the US Sexual Recovery Institute and president of the National Council on Sexuality Addiction and Compulsivity, writes:

With athletes like Tiger, there's often an addiction to the thrill and the need for intensity, because in sports, it's the intensity that drives athletes... There's a lot of temptation thrown at you at the top of your game. And if you're good-looking, you have power.

5. The Addiction of Lying — One Lie leads to Another

From porn actress Veronica Siwik-Daniels, who claimed to be Woods' full-time mistress, to cocktail waitress Jaime Grubbs, who carried on a torrid 31-month affair with Woods, Woods had serial relationships with many women for years but was not caught earlier.

How did he do that? By lying. Lying can be addictive because of the adrenaline-filled thrills that the transgressor gets from trying to avoid getting caught. Lying is unstoppable once it gets started because one lie leads to the second, the third and so on and on. We never stop at one lie.

We are then made to think and believe that we have become invincible. This sense of omnipotence and of being able to manipulate others will soon become the source of our downfall. No lie can be hidden that long before it is exposed. It is important to keep in mind Phillips Brooks' warning: "Keep clear of concealment and the need for concealment."

Conclusion

From Tiger Woods' story, you can see that:

- A beautiful wife does not guarantee martial fidelity.
- Golfing greatness does not guarantee moral strength.
- Being charitable minded does not guarantee integrity.
- Being a good father is not to guarantee that one is also a good husband.

It's tough to stay professionally successful yet morally clean. Society condones moral laxity, even moral failure as normative. You are expected to have affairs. That is the price of fame.

Will Woods' darkest hour become his brightest renaissance? Apparently, it might.

On 19 February 2010, Woods gave a televised statement in which he said he had been in a 45-day therapy program since the end of December. He again apologized for his actions:

> I thought I could get away with whatever I wanted to... I felt that I had worked hard my entire life and deserved to enjoy all the temptations around me. I felt I was entitled. Thanks to money and fame, I didn't have to go far to find them. I was wrong. I was foolish.

Woods and Nordegren divorced on 23 August 2010.

At one point, it was heartening to know that Woods has recaptured his past glories at least momentarily. From the lowest point of his golfing career, where he plunged to the fifty-eighth position in the world ranking, he has become Number One again. From two years (2010-2011) of not winning any tournament, he won four in 2013. From the lowest earning of his career at US$660,238 (2011), he earned more than US$5 million in 2013.

But due to injuries, his ranking has plummeted to 108 and with no trophy wins for a few years now. On 18 March 2013, Woods announced that he and Olympic skier Lindsey Vonn were dating. But they have since separated.

Recovery from sex addiction is a long, long road. Only when he is prepared to keep coming clean, accept the 12-Steps of Sexaholics Anonymous, seek forgiveness from those whom he has hurt most (his wife and children), get professional help, find a trustworthy life-coach (just as he has a golf coach), refocus on what's really important and examine the kind of legacy he wants to leave behind, will there be true recovery.

I really hope he can write a new chapter in his life and continue to fight his addiction. Golf is only game. Life is not. Even if he doesn't win any trophy but recovers, I will salute him as the greatest golfer who has ever lived!

1. Which aspect of Tiger Woods' story can you identify with?

2. What can you do to support someone who is a sex addict?

Action Steps ▼

Chapter 7

HOW YOU CAN BE CORRUPTED BY GREED
THE GRIP OF GREED

"Greed lives on the axiom, 'Never enough'."

Dr. John Ng

"When the stakes are high, everybody cheats."

Steven Levitt, *Freakonomics*

The financial crisis gripped the world in 2008. China went through a crisis of its own in 2012, losing trillions of dollars.

During the crisis in 2008, BEAR Stearns, Freddie Mac, Fannie Mae, Lehman Brothers, AIG, Washington Mutuals and Wachovia — all these firms were brought down by the financial meltdown.

Soon after, the contagion also hit the European market: Fortis in Belgium, Bradford & Bingley (B&B), HBOS in England, Hypo Real Estate in Germany and Glitnir in Iceland have all suffered.

Countries like Greece, Portugal and Ireland would have gone bankrupt if not for the European Union rescue packages. Greece, Italy, and Spain are still struggling to get out of this.

Many have speculated on what went wrong. I am not an investment banker, nor am I a financial expert. But I consider myself a keen observer of the world's trends and times and a student of leadership.

After researching and analyzing through a mass of articles and websites, and interviewing some of the best brains, one cannot help but come to the single most important factor that has caused the collapse of all these institutions and countries — *greed.*

When I shared this analysis with a friend who is a venture capitalist, he acknowledged, "Simple but true." As Nayan Chanda, Director of Publications at the Yale Center for the Study of Globalization, writes:

> Sub-prime mortgage-backed securities have turned out to be greed's latest vehicle, a worthy successor to the one-of-a-kind sure-fire 'winners' that came before it, ranging from tulips in the 17th century to North Sea oil and internet start-ups in the 20th.

How else would you explain these phenomena?

- CEOs being allowed to take high-stakes risks and fail, but still getting rewarded. In order to pursue growth and meet quarterly results, highly intelligent, experienced CEOs with the smartest leadership teams in Wall Street could expand beyond their capacity and chalk up impressive profit and loss statements by buying 'toxic assets'.

- Reputable institutions ignoring signs of undercapitalization and financial ratios, but relying on their brand names to collude with Wall Street fund managers to come up with beautifully packaged but dubious funds.

Any one of us can succumb to the same temptations if we put ourselves in similar situations.

What is greed?

Merriam Webster defines it as a selfish and excessive desire for more of something (as money) than is needed motivated by naked ambition.

I define *greed* as an innate, growing, and unbridled desire for the pursuit of money, wealth, power or other possessions — driven by self-interest to maximize short-term gains while denying or minimizing the same benefits to others. But it will finally lead to collapse.

Allow me to examine its anatomy:

1. Greed is growing and global

Whether we are in Delhi, Dubai or Detroit, greed's tentacles spread far and wide and reach deep into every nook and cranny. With clever marketing and packaging, shrewdly disguised low-interest mortgage-loans and seemingly highly lucrative derivatives can tug at our depraved human hearts, which is greed's innate residence.

Everyone, from Wall Street hedge fund managers to average homeowners, went for easy money and short-term profits by investing money they did not have, buying things they did not need and by betting on their future earnings.

As Jonathan Eyal of the *Straits Times*' European Bureau rightly points out:

> And though the current attention is on shady speculators, the reality is that ordinary consumers everywhere must share some of the blame. Some were accidentally sucked into the maelstrom — with unsolicited credit cards, for instance. But many willingly engaged in the credit orgy. Speculating on one's house by borrowing against an existing mortgage — 'releasing equity', as it was politely called, became an honorable occupation in all Western countries.

I mention greed as one of the chief causes of this global meltdown not from the stand of a moral judge, but to show that greed affects everyone. It is easy to look at the speck in another's eye, and forget the log in our own!

2. Greed is innate and unbridled

John McCain, the Republican presidential nominee in 2008, had proclaimed, "We're going to put an end to greed." Personally, I don't think greed can be 'ended'. Even if our actions actually stop greed from causing harm (and that is very unlikely) it will rear its ugly head again sometime in the future. Why? Because we are born with it.

As Chanda writes insightfully, "Greed is the mother's milk of global commerce." Greed is a human inclination waiting to be unleashed given the right opportunity.

A close cousin of greed is ambition. It is very difficult to differentiate between the two. Both are emotional and adrenalin-driven elements that make us dissatisfied with the status quo and keep us creatively engaged, but can also lead us into disastrous decisions.

Look at how, time and again, greed keeps rearing its ugly head and growing into an uncontrollable monster:

— **Regulation**

Following the stock market crash of 1929, the Glass-Stegall Act of 1933 prohibited consolidation of investment, commercial banking and insurance services. It also created the Federal Deposit Insurance Corporation (FDIC) to insure consumer bank deposits. The Act was intended to stop bank executives from steering consumers' deposits into risky investments, and to prevent the collapse of financial institutions.

— **De-regulation**

In 1999, the Gramm-Leach-Bliley Act repealed the Glass-Stegall Act and freed financial institutions by allowing consolidation among banks, securities firms and insurance companies and created competition.

Even Alan Greenspan, the former Federal Reserve Chairman, proclaimed, "American consumers might benefit if lenders provided greater mortgage-product alternatives to the traditional fixed rate mortgage."

— **Industry expansion**

At this point, the greed party started. Commercial lenders began engaging in highly lucrative trading of mortgage-backed securities (MBS) and collaterized debt obligations (CDOs), just like investment firms. The derivative market grew from almost $100 trillion in 1998 to $600 trillion in 2007.

Finally, the **boom and bust** came. With the US Federal Government lowering interest rates, cheap mortgage loans were readily available for consumers, who in turn generated a thriving investors' market for derivatives such as MBS, CDO and other exotic securities. However, as interest rates rose, homeowners defaulted and put derivatives at risk. That was the beginning of the financial tsunami.

My verdict on McCain's statement: Greed can only be *contained*, but never *eradicated*.

I agree with Minister Mentor Lee Kuan Yew of Singapore, who with his pragmatic outlook proclaimed:

> Have we learnt nothing from the last Great Depression? Everybody has read Charles Kindleberger [Manias, Panics and Crashes], what shouldn't be done the next time. I think [the US economy] will pick up again. But does that mean the end of all crashes? No.

3. Greed is driven by self-interest under cover

The Americans are masters of marketing and packaging. Who else could have invented terms like 'sub-prime', 'structured products', 'collaterized debt obligations', 'mortgaged-backed securities', and 'Troubled Asset Relief Program (TARP)'?

Even the phrase *sub-prime* is a cunning invention of the hedge fund managers. As one of my friends commented, "It is either prime or no prime. When do we have sub-prime?"

It is "the sorcerer's apprentices on Wall Street who invented instruments like sub-prime mortgages that hooked the unwary with low teaser rates which would become exorbitant over time." Before the fallout, it was being hailed as part of the genius of American marketing.

Greed thrives on lack of transparency and disclosure — or sometimes, even confusion. Fear, its emotional sibling, prevents corporations from making honest disclosures. Again, Chanda observes, "The absence of transparency that fueled the 2003 SARS crisis was similarly apparent in the case of the sub-prime virus." As Steven Levitt writes in his book *Freakonomics*: "When the stakes are high, everybody cheats."

4. Greed is insatiable and kills the competition

Greed lives on the axiom, 'Never enough'. There is always one more rung on the corporate ladder to climb, one more billion to make and one more company to acquire. Mahatma Gandhi rightly observed, "The world is enough for every man's need, but will never be enough for every man's greed."

It is both intoxicating and insatiable.

Greed thrives under these environments:

- **Cut-throat competition**. Wall Street investors are always ready to pounce on new opportunities. The financial herd is merciless; more than $2 trillion is traded every day in the globalized economy.

- **Long-term integrity risked for short-term gain**. You will face the temptation to abandon the business of real life for the business of financial statements. Looking good and ensuring double-digit growth in profits requires CEOs in financial institutions to creatively engineer growth, and they are especially tempted to fudge the numbers.

- **The tyranny of the quarter**. Almost every staff is required to 'meet the quarter', or post high earnings every three months to ensure strong annual growth. If you don't make two quarters, you are out. "If you can't take the heat, get out of the kitchen," we are told.

Making the numbers is what keeps CEOs awake at night. The idea of cycles of growth and decline seems to have been lost, in favor of growth and more growth. So, board members end up looking at numbers, rather than businesses.

One global CEO confided in me, "Honestly, this is unsustainable; so, we cheat creatively."

5. Greed can make you collapse from hero to zero

Think of Lehman Brothers CEO Richard S Fuld, Jr. He was a hero who became zero.

In 2001, the firm acquired the private-client services business of Cowen & Co. In 2003, the firm aggressively re-entered the asset-management business, which it had exited in 1989. Beginning with $2 billion in assets under management, the firm acquired the Crossroads Group, the fixed-income division of Lincoln Capital Management and Neuberger Berman.

During the U.S. housing boom in 2003 and 2004, they acquired five mortgage lenders, including subprime lender, BNC Mortgage and Aurora Loan Services, which specialized in Alt-A loans (made to borrowers without full documentation). The acquisition seemed prescient and strategic as they showed record revenues in the capital markets unit to surge 56 percent from 2004 to 2006, a faster rate of growth than other businesses in asset management or investment banking.

These businesses, together with the PCS business and Lehman's private-equity business generated approximately $3.1 billion in net revenue and almost $800 million in pre-tax income in 2007. Prior to going bankrupt, the firm had in excess of $275 billion in assets under management. Altogether, since going public in 1994, net revenues had increased over 600 percent from $2.73 billion to $19.2 billion and employee headcount over 230 percent from 8,500 to almost 28,600.

As the credit crisis erupted in August 2007 with the failure of two Bear Sterns hedge funds, Lehman's stock fell sharply. During that month, Lehman slashed 2,500 mortgage-related jobs and shut down its BNC unit. In 2007, Lehman underwrote more mortgage-backed securities than any other firm, accumulating an $85 billion portfolio, or four times its shareholders' equity in the fourth quarter of 2007.[xiii]

[xiii] Read more at http://www.investopedia.com/articles/economics/09/lehman-brothers-collapse.asp

Lehman's high degree of leverage – the ratio of total assets to shareholders equity – was 31 in 2007, and its huge portfolio of mortgage securities made it increasingly vulnerable to deteriorating market conditions. On March 17, 2008, following the near-collapse of Bear Stearns – the second-largest underwriter of mortgage-backed securities – Lehman shares fell as much as 48 percent on concern it would be the next Wall Street firm to fail.[xiv]

These cracks were made worse when the US Securities and Exchange regulators and the New York Attorney General's Office alleged that the firms had improperly associated analyst compensation with the firms' investment-banking revenues. They also promised favorable, market-moving research coverage, in exchange for underwriting opportunities.

This is indeed a warning for you. Greed has a way of doing you in, and the greedier you are, the more likely you are going to be caught.

1. If "Greed is the mother's milk of global commerce", how do we contain it so that it does not become destructive?

2. How do you fight the short-termism and yet be accountable for growth?

Action Steps ▼

[xiv] *Ibid.*

Chapter 8

HOW YOU CAN BE OVERCOME BY FEAR
THE DREAD OF FEAR

"Fear can prevent you from becoming great.
It can discourage your efforts, diminish your
dreams, destroy your trust and dismiss
your aspirations."

Dr. John Ng

*"F-E-A-R has two meanings: 'Forget Everything And Run' or
'Face Everything And Rise.'"*

Zig Ziglar

We are living in troubling times. Four out of ten Singaporeans cited 'losing their jobs' as their top fear in times of recession. In the US, 'being unable to pay their mortgage or rent' was Americans' greatest fear.

The second biggest fear was being 'unable to survive economically'. With rising costs and lowering income, the fear of our inability to pay for health care costs, education, etc. has now hit countries like Singapore, Taiwan, Hong Kong, Malaysia, and European countries.

Fear is a normal human reaction to external threats and internal disequilibrium. It is triggered by your internal perspectives, which usually evoke an emotional response. There are many situations in which fear may come to you:

- **Fear of the future.** The future can be a very terrifying proposition. Parents worry themselves sick about their children's education. Ordinary citizens are worried about safety and security with the incessant reporting of terrorist attacks.

  Business owners are worried about survival with lowering profits, rising cost, increasing competition, and poor business climate. Patients are worried about their prospects of recovery after undergoing major surgical procedures. Displaced people are worried about the threats of death. Refugees worry about their next meals. The future indeed looks bleak.

- **Fear of losing.** Your child not returning home on time despite your frantic calls. Your partner is acting suspiciously and seems more disconnected to you. Your teenage son is partying every night and indulging in unhealthy habits. You feel uneasy when your business partners spend more time with their other businesses than yours. Impending loss can trigger more fears in your heart.

- **Fear triggered by failures.** Failures, especially repeated failures, can be frightening. You fear your ability to raise good teenage children and they seem to be more and more rebellious. You feel numb with fear when you suffer anxiety attacks. Your failure to motivate your staff to do more can break you down.

Your stock prices keep going down. Your investments meet with all kinds of obstacles. Your partnerships are on the brink of collapse. All these will make you question your own ability, talent, position, status and identity.

- **Fear triggered by crisis.** You feel terribly afraid when you or your loved one has been diagnosed with cancer. Your marriage is breaking down irretrievably. Your business collapse is days away. Your closest friendship has become destructive. You feel fear in a deep way. You have no end in sight, no light at the end of a very long dark tunnel.

If we have experienced similar situations, we know how fear can grip and paralyze us if left unmanaged. Worse still, if not managed properly, it will depress us and cause untold damage to our lives.

This was what happened to Karthik Rajaram, an out-of-work financial manager who killed himself and his family in an upscale neighborhood in Los Angeles. Rajaram blamed his actions on economic hardships, seeing his finances wiped out by the stock market collapse. He said in his suicide note that he had two options — to kill just himself, or to kill himself and his family. He had decided the second was more honorable.

LA Police Department deputy chief Michel Moore was right on when he said:

This is a perfect American family that has absolutely been destroyed, apparently because of a man who just got stuck in a rabbit hole of absolute despair, somehow working his way into believing this to be an acceptable exit.

Fear can drive us to do the unthinkable and the horrific!

Fear and how it works

- *Fear is an instinctive, emotional reaction.*

Fear is an emotional response to threats and dangers, external and internal. Reactive fear can prompt us to make irrational decisions, which we will regret later. Why is this the case?

In our brains, a structure known as the thalamus acts as an 'air traffic controller' to keep the neural signals moving. In a normal situation, the thalamus directs the impulses to the cortex (the 'rational' part of the brain) for processing.

However, when we are in a state of panic, the thalamus quickly reacts to the potential threat and sends signals past the cortex, straight into the amygdala — a more primitive part that controls the 'fight, flight, freeze or faint' response. We react instinctively based on previously stored patterns. This is what brain researchers call the 'amygdala hijack'.

I believe this was what caused the Wall Street panic during the global financial collapse of 2008 — when investors and bankers reacted nervously and emotionally based on their survival instincts.

- ### *Fear is relative*

What causes you to fear may not affect another. Take this global crisis for example: if you have not invested in derivatives, property or the stock market, you have little to fear.

Some people respond better than others in a similar crisis. I have a friend who has just lost $25 million, and yet he is able to take it in good stride because he has seen the highs and lows of the stock market.

What you fear most depends on what you value most and what you are most invested in. If your children are all you have, fear will drive you to do everything to protect them. If you have heavily invested in your business and it is about to collapse, you will be stricken with anxiety attacks or even go into depression.

- ### *Fear can be generated by peer pressure*

Personal fears can be compounded by a herd instinct to create mass hysteria. This was what happened when markets across the world tumbled in 2008 and the Dow fell nearly 600 points, the lowest plunge since the 2003 SARS outbreak. The entire world's financial institutions and banking sectors panicked, resulting in massive selling and a big plunge.

Traders only wanted out. "It was a vicious circle. Buyers were in short supply, causing jittery sellers to dump stocks at whatever prices they could fetch."

Your feeling of anxiety can be heightened if you are suffering from cancer when your relatives begin to opine about the deaths of friends who have died from similar cancers. You will feel greater fear when you listen to your friends, who gossip about stories of unmanaged teenagers, who have similarly slipped into drugs and alcohol.

Today, if you listen to the barrage of issues on social media without much discernment, it can lead you to unbridled fears. I know of friends who cancelled their planned vacations when they heard news of terrorist attacks from the social media. In this digital age, fear can be easily and quickly heightened to irrational, emotive panic, although research has shown that the risk of you experiencing a terrorist attack is extremely low, compared to car accidents or major illnesses.

- ### *Fear engenders distrust and panic*

Distrust is both the cause and the consequence of fear. With Triple-A financial institutions such as Merrill Lynch and Lehman Brothers collapsing in quick succession, it is no wonder there is widespread fear that more might collapse.

This contagion of fear, which started from the sub-prime property collapse in the US, later spread to investment banks, commercial banks, insurance companies and other countries — a classic example of fear that is caused by distrust and bringing about even more distrust. Iceland is a classic example of this.

Before her collapse, Iceland was one of the wealthiest nations in the world. With a population of 320,000, Iceland focused on banking and finance as her engine of growth.

But local banks were too highly leveraged, and Icelanders were borrowing too much from abroad. In neither case did the government do enough to dissuade the accumulation of risk disproportionate to the size of the economy. This created distrust between the Icelandic government and Wall Street bankers, due to the proliferation of bad loans. When the financial crisis hit, it clobbered Iceland.

Without proper management and adequate industry oversight, Icelanders grew to distrust their leaders, and the country collapsed. Tion Kwa of the *Straits Times* wrote:

> Iceland's currency has halved in value since last year — prompting the moniker 'Halfpriceland'. Its three biggest banks have collapsed and have

had to be taken over by the state. The spectacular wealth they helped build is dissipating just as spectacularly. The success story that Iceland once was is now shaping up to be a cautionary tale.

Iceland was bracing itself for an economy that would contract 10 percent in 2009 and an unemployment rate that would hit 7 percent the next January. Inflation surged to reach 17.1 percent — an 18-year record!

To many Icelanders at this time, the fear was very real. They believed their government had let them down, and that fear and distrust in turn came from the distrust between the banks and the government. Governments around the world realized they had to restore trust in the banking sectors. This was why they had to inject massive amounts of money — to guarantee that the deposits the banks needed to stay in business would continue.

This distrust in governments, institutions, and organizations has become even more severe today with the spread of fake news and half-truths. The insidious cyber-attacks have exacerbated the situation. Now the fear element has increased as distrust increases.

Fear can prevent you from becoming great. It can discourage your efforts, diminish your dreams, destroy your trust and dismiss your aspirations. Therefore, your first duty is to conquer fear. You must contain it or else you cannot act.

1. What are you most afraid of in your life and business?

2. 'Fear can prevent you from becoming great. It can discourage your efforts, diminish your dreams, destroy your trust and dismiss your aspirations.' How have you experienced this in your life?

Action Steps

Chapter 9

HOW YOU CAN
BECOME TOXIC
THE TYRANNY OF TOXICITY

"For a start, nobody starts out to be toxic. Neither
does anyone aspire to be a toxic leader. Toxicity, like
gangrene, simply grows in you if you allow it to."

Dr. John Ng

*"A man must be big enough to admit his
mistakes, smart enough to profit from them, and
strong enough to correct them."*

John Maxwell

I have always been fascinated with political leaders like Hosni Mubarak.

He was the President of Egypt for 30 years from 1981 to 2011. He started as a military officer with an aspiration to lift Egypt out of economic doldrums and became an international statesman, a trusted Western ally. He was successful for many years by providing domestic stability and economic development even though he ruled with an iron hand. He also survived six assassination attempts.

His downfall began when he started to accumulate immense wealth for his family and inner circle of ministers and political heavyweights. At its height, the personal wealth of Mubarak and his family was around US$40 billion, garnered from corruption, bribes and legitimate businesses.

Political figures and young activists were imprisoned without trial. Illegal, undocumented, hidden facilities were established. The Egyptian government expanded bureaucratic regulations, registration requirements and other controls that fed corruption, which became a significant problem.

He resigned during the Egyptian uprising in February 2011. In 2011, the court found him and his two sons, Alaa and Gamal, guilty of corruption and abuse of power. He was released after serving six years in prison, after the highest appeal court overturned his previous convictions. But in prison, his health declined and he seemed to suffer from depression.

We see similar patterns of god-like behavior in some political and business leaders today. I often wonder why these leaders refuse to face up to their depravities, but continue to believe in their invincibility. They continue to enrich themselves and their cronies in their own corrupt and repressive ways. They use their tyrannical leadership to exploit the poor and disadvantaged. They become toxic as a result.

For a start, nobody starts out being toxic. Neither does anyone aspire to be a toxic leader. Toxicity, like gangrene, simply grows in you if you allow it to. It is a built-up trait. It thrives in a chaotic environment. It surrounds itself with other toxic loyalists and kills off those who don't follow their rules and create hell on earth. The seed of toxicity is in us! It just needs a conducive environment. In other words, you and I can become toxic if we are not conscious of the nutrients for toxicity.

How does one become a toxic leader?

1. You Clamor after Popularity and Power

Unfettered power and unabashed popularity can condition you to believe in your own publicity. You start off wanting to do good and make the world better. You are an activist. However, success and fame eventually get into your head. You become more and more powerful as your followers, having tasted victory, entrust you with greater power. Very soon, your popularity turns into an illusion of grandiose, god-like delusions and fame into infamy.

Pride takes center-stage. You become the spotlight with yourself. Others in the team pale into insignificance or at most, serve as a supporting cast. Toxic leaders believe that they are the "special ones" and therefore untouchable. Peter Drucker, founder of Modern Management, warns against the self-focused leader, "The leader who basically focuses on himself or herself is going to mislead."

"The psychopath has no allegiance to the company at all, just to self. A psychopath is playing a short-term parasitic game," reports Paul Babiak, an industrial psychologist. They live on their followers and the followers live on them. It becomes an incestuous co-dependency.

2. You Can Do No Wrong

"We are an arrogant species, full of terrible potential to behave
like god when given the opportunity."

Dean Koontz

Some doctors in hospitals, professors in universities, super-stars in sports, mega-pop icons, ego-maniac politicians, rank-conscious military generals and even some tiger-moms and dads behave like gods. They convince themselves that they can do no wrong. They rule their turfs like their serfdoms. They rule their subordinates/children like slaves, with muted voices. You can end up behaving the same way.

Your followers make you believe that you can do no wrong. Even if you do, they know how to cover up your mistakes and your misdemeanors are justified. "Anyway, he is our Anointed One!" is the mantra for your coterie of hangers-on.

3. You Will Do Anything to Avoid Losing Power

"It is not that power corrupts but the fear of losing power that corrupts those who wield it and fear of the scourge of power corrupts those who are subject to it."

Aung San Suu Kyi

Lord Acton's famous adage: 'Power corrupts, and absolute power corrupts absolutely' needs to be modified to Aung San Suu Kyi's famous words: "Fear of losing power corrupts those who wield it".

Toxic leaders truly fear the loss of power. This has happened to dictators throughout history, including Saddam Hussein of Iraq and Muammar Gaddafi of Libya. When you lose power, you lose face, you lose your ill-gotten wealth, and your special privileges, with its accompanying lifestyles. Most of all, you fear the loss of your family and even your life because your opponent will want to make sure you suffer what they have suffered.

Hence, the fear of losing power will drive you to all sorts of malevolent and malicious acts against anyone who is a threat to you.

You will even manufacture crises to preserve your power. Crises often offer positive opportunities for you to thrive because you can crystallize the agenda to scapegoating. You will set up bureaucratic obstacles in the name of "survival." Often, you like to keep your organizations in constant crisis mode so that you can perpetuate your reign.

In a cover story called "Is Your Boss a Psychopath?" Alan Deutschman, a senior writer for *Fast Company*, writes, "There's evidence that the business climate has become more hospitable to psychopaths in recent years" and that "...the New

Economy, with its rule-breaking and roller-coaster results, is just dandy for folks with psychopathic traits."

With severe downsizing, restructuring, mergers and acquisitions, fueled by an uncertain economy, you have no difficulty dealing with the consequences of rapid change like chopping off people, cooking the books and displaying uncouth behavior.

Coach and consultant Paul Babiak asserts, "Organizational chaos provides both the necessary stimulation for psychopathic thrill-seeking and sufficient cover for psychopathic manipulation and abusive behavior."

4. You Marshal Resources to Safeguard Your Status

"Arrogance is a creature. It does not have senses. It has only a sharp tongue and the pointing finger."

Toba Beta

Why are some leaders allowed to hold on to power for so long, and continue to wreak havoc on their people, economies and organizations? One of the key factors is because they have amassed enough resources to champion their agenda and silence the stakeholders.

In such a situation, you can use your power and influence to bribe, bully and threaten others. You make compromises to stay in power. When the evidence of evil and corruption is stacked against you, you bully your way through, you make compromises, create fake news, and form unholy alliances to stay in power. You will sacrifice integrity on the altar of self.

You will pretend to give in while you connive your own plots to stay in power. You will even use resources to support or contribute to good causes, as bargaining chips to stay in power.

You use spin-doctors and control the media to manufacture a persona, deny accusations and project a clean image, although today, with the spread of social media, it has become more challenging.

You will even buy over your enemies. As such, your good actions become sinister plots in a game of chess maneuvers. You smooth-talk, cajole, and deceive to stay in power. You will use whatever means you can to retain power. If it involves lying, cheating and conniving, so be it. You become masters of politicking and maneuvering. No depth of treachery and deception is beyond such people in turning situations to their advantage.

As the saying goes, "your right brain has nothing left and your left brain has nothing right."

5. You Create a System of Patronages

Although character flaws begin to surface and loom large, this is often left unchecked. In fact, your weakness is glossed over by your strengths. Professor Alan Deutschman reports that psychopathic bosses are typically likeable. They make us believe that they reciprocate loyalty and friendship. They have developed an actor's expertise in evoking our empathy, which makes it easier for them to "play" us.

According to Michael Maccoby, a psychotherapist, "They have an element of emotional intelligence, of being able to see our emotions very clearly and manipulate them." When we realize that they have been manipulating us all along, we feel betrayed.

Leaders like Hosni Mubarak will 'feed their lovers and starve their enemies'. Many people will continue to support you as long as they can enjoy special privileges and share in the plunder. You also make sure that your followers are kept under your control because you know the skeletons in their own closets. You are ever ready to bring them to light, which will seal their fate. They become enslaved and beholden to you and the system of patronages.

It is ironic that many such leaders have supportive spouses and children who stand by them despite the condemnation they face. In most cases, they have become part of the system and are wielders of power themselves.

With your consolidated power and unchallenged authority, whistle-blowers are very few and far between. Loyalists are recognized and championed. As a result, you have created a system that is almost impossible to dismantle. You have created as a new normal of evil. All your followers become as tainted as you are.

The toxic leaders become puppet-masters in the whole drama.

6. You Destroy your Opponents Systematically

"Arrogance is in everything I do. It is in my gestures, the harshness of my voice, in the glow of my gaze, in my sinewy, tormented face."

Coco Chanel

You will go to extremes to neutralize foes, scapegoat adversaries and invent murderous schemes to silence them. You will use institutions like the courts, the police and the army to do your biddings. To cement your power, you may build up a vast and wide network of cronies, circumspectly cultivating them for your use when needed.

Everything then becomes fait accomplice: You excel in toxic greatness.

1. Research the story of Hosni Mubarak. Why do you think he was a toxic leader?

2. How do you think toxic parents/leaders can breed toxicity in your family and organization?

Action Steps

Chapter 10

HOW YOU CAN BE DESTROYED BY RAGE
The Insanity of Rage

"When you get into a fit of rage, you are totally
oblivious to the injuries it has caused the victims.
The extreme stage of rage is a murderous impulse to
obliterate others."

Dr. John Ng

"If this can keep the communication going and shine the light and keeps us progressing and not regressing, that's the main thing."

LeBron James, four-time NBA
Most Valuable Player, whose home was vandalized.

Rage is on the rise. People are angry. Very angry. Look at what has happened in our world.

- London was under attack with seven people killed and 48 wounded, after a van drove into the crowd on London Bridge and three men jumped out to stab people in Borough Market in June 2017.

- Suicide bomber Salman Abedi killed 22 people in the bombing disaster at a pop concert by Ariana Grande in Manchester in May 2017.

- There was a rampage at the Resorts World Manila casino where 36 victims died in an attack by a lone gunman, Jessie Carlos, in June 2017.

- Marawi, a southern city in the Philippines was under siege by ISIS militants, with thousands trapped and 19 civilians murdered by the militants in May 2017.

- Bryan Moles, a heavily armed man with an AR-15 semi-automatic assault rifle, handgun and ammunition, was arrested at the Trump International Hotel in Washington near the White House in May 2017, which averted potentially another disaster.

- After Donald Trump's election in 2016, protest marches spontaneously erupted in the major cities in the US. Trumpism or "Making America First and Great Again" has driven many to become more xenophobic.

- Britain and France are divided along economically advantaged and disadvantaged, right- and left-wing and for-EU (European Union) and anti-EU lines, resulting in Brexit for Britain, and 33.9 percent voting for the right-wing Marine Le Pen in France. This is symptomatic of the growing dissent and division among fellow citizens.

- In Jakarta, the former Governor of Jakarta, Ahok, as he is affectionately called, was jailed for two years for allegedly blaspheming the Koran in May 2017. This resulted in tens of thousands of hard-line Muslim demonstrations in Jakarta over this incident. The verdict divided the country after he was jailed, but the outpouring of sympathy and love for him was evident as thousands kept vigil for weeks.

- In Singapore, there was the incident of a trio arrested for committing rash acts of throwing bowls, tables and chairs in a Teochew Porridge restaurant over a S$28 food bill in May 2017.

In June 2017, just before the NBA Finals between his team, Cleveland Cavaliers, and the Golden State Warriors, the basketball superstar and four-time NBA Most Valuable Player of the year LeBron James' home was vandalized with racial slurs.

He put it most bluntly: "Being Black in America is tough and we've got a long way to go as a society for us as African-Americans until we feel equal in America. It just goes to show that racism will always be part of the world, part of America, and that hate, especially for African Americans is living every day."

He hopes that this incident could move people closer to ending such hatred by saying, "If this can keep the communication going and shine the light and keeps us progressing and not regressing, that's the main thing."

Why all this rage today? How you can be derailed by rage?

1. Rage is an emotional state triggered by hot buttons and the uncontrollable Amygdala Hijack

Rage is a psychological and emotional state. It is the acute expression of outbursts of unrestrained passion. If anger is a strong feeling of annoyance, displeasure, or hostility, then rage is violent, irrepressible anger. Rage is a vehement desire or passion.

Rage has been described as the ego's big gun by which it tries to restore its feeling of control over others. Rage problems are conceptualized as the inability to process emotional or life's experiences, because the capacity to regulate emotions has never been sufficiently developed or has been temporarily lost due to recent trauma.

The term "rageaholic" is often used to describe people who slip into a fit of rage whenever they need to bolster their sagging ego. You have to watch against this.

When you get into a fit of rage, you are totally oblivious to the injuries it has caused the victims. The extreme stage of rage is a murderous impulse to obliterate others. This may explain the behaviour of Salman Abedi as well as the senseless killings of innocents in Paris, London, Kabul, and Boston.

These rageaholics require psychological intervention, personal counselling, ideological rehabilitation, prolonged therapy and/or jail terms. There are deep hurts, psychological scars and destructive mental patterns that have to be addressed. Seeking professional help is recommended for such people.

In lesser ways, your rage is often triggered by "hot-buttons", which are words/phrases and behaviours that cause the Amygdala Hijack (discussed in Part 2, Chapter 8). The trio who went on a rampage, throwing chairs and tables over a S$28 meal, were probably reacting emotionally to something that was said or done. Of course, they were intoxicated, and that made matters worse!

2. Rage is supplanted by suppressed bitterness, wilful revenge and unbridled hatred

Free, sometimes irresponsible speech, has become a source of this hatred and revenge. The journalists of Charlie Hebdo experienced this first hand when their offices were attacked. Unfortunately, much of this free speech has become irresponsible satire and injurious insults, funded by libertines, business leaders and politicians with hidden agendas.

In the past, the primary function of newspapers and magazines was to inform, and secondarily, to make money. But the reverse is now true. Now, they have to make money first and then inform secondarily.

Whatever sells gets the headlines and repetitions. Professor Timothy Garton Ash, historian and author, puts it most candidly: "So all our newspapers become more sensational, more partisan, more celebrity, more sensationalist, more 'if it bleeds, it leads. If it roars, it scores'". The result: the amount of investigative reporting, non-partisan, evidenced-based, and clear in-depth analysis is drowned out or dried up.

The idea of free speech, which is supposed to be the bastion of democracy, has become a victim of money-making businesses, prejudices, bitterness, hatred and revenge. But free speech has become distorted in our times. It is imperative that you and I are ever-conscious of our prejudices.

In ancient Greek society, they talked about free speech in two concepts. *Parrhesia* was free speech for the public good, not saying whatever comes into our heads. The motivation and purpose was key. Unfortunately, in today's society, the common good has been compromised by personal agenda, self-serving interests, and subgroups with extreme positions.

The other Greek concept is *isegoria*, which means equal speech where everyone has in principle the equal right to speak. This is the idea of open dialogue and debates on opposing ideas, listening to evidence and facts and then coming out with the best solutions. It is American jurist Oliver Wendell Holmes' concept of the hope that the best ideas will win out and best policies will be chosen, based on evidence-based and reality-based discourse.

Sadly, this is hardly the case today. The world is dominated by fake news, superficial short-messages, populist misinformation and extremist propaganda of all kinds. You have to be careful of what you read, how you interpret and the source of the information.

3. Rage is caused by socialized distorted prejudices and ideologies

Undiscerning readers of fake news, distorted prejudices and extreme religious ideologies have become the new normal today. Very few people want to know the truth. Social media allows people to stay in their cloistered bubbles where they don't learn about other, different views and beliefs.

Some 30 to 40 percent of the news Americans get is from Facebook or Twitter. In China, it is Weibo or WeChat. The frightening part is that these pieces of news are repeated massively, colored by readers' own biases and left uncorrected when they are incorrect. You are fed such news hundreds of times every day, purporting to be facts and then re-tweeted, unadulterated.

For instance, a purported message written by Ahok, the former Governor of Jakarta, after he went into prison, was sent to me on WhatsApp by some well-meaning friends. I checked through my sources and discovered that the message was written by a fan of Ahok. I had to inform all my friends of this misinformation.

Misinformation and distortion can be disseminated as though they are from a real person and a real source. Professor Ash warns that "Anonymity has a huge contribution to the level of hate speech and abuse and even death threats online."[xv]

The little gadgets in your pockets — the smartphones in the hands of three billion people, have become the channels through which these instant short messages are spread, without checking for facts or depth of analysis. The internet has become an infinite platform for all kinds of fragmented, distorted and unsolicited news. This has led to cyber bullying, uncensored hate videos going viral, and worse still, socialized extremism.

According to Professor Ash, the result is that it has also become "a very powerful echo-chamber effect… Donald Trump's supporters hear only Fox News and Breitbart and talk radio's Rush Limbaugh and their friends on Facebook. And Hillary Clinton supporters, MSNBC or CNN and NPR and The New York Times, and their friends on Facebook."[xvi]

What I find most disturbing is that even though the internet has served to expose socially poor behaviors and promote greater accountability with instant relays, it has also fanned the flame of hate.

Eventually, you are forced to take sides. If you do not, you are perceived to be narrow-minded or compromising. In so doing, there are more conflicts and greater disunity.

4. Rage is fueled by continual unrealized and unrealistic economic goals

In 2016, 62 of the richest billionaires controlled 50 percent of the world's wealth and in 2017, income inequality is so lopsided that the world's eight richest men

---

[xv] Timothy Garton Ash, 'Answer to populist and fake news might lie in public service media.' Speech given at the St Gallen Symposium on May 7, 2017.
[xvi] *Ibid.*

have the wealth of 50 percent of the world's poorest. Rising inequality and social polarization pose two of the biggest risks to the global economy in 2017.[xvii]

A top corporate CEO earns as much in a year as 10,000 garment factory workers in Bangladesh. The world's 10 biggest corporations together have revenue greater that the 180 poorest countries combined.

According to British-based Oxfam, an international poverty-fighting group, "From Nigeria to Bangladesh, from the U.K. to Brazil, people are fed up with feeling ignored by their political leaders, and millions are mobilizing to push for change. Seven out of 10 people live in a country that has seen a rise in inequality in the last 30 years."[xviii]

Extreme wealth is economically inefficient, politically corrosive, socially divisive and environmentally destructive. Unfortunately, some wealthy tycoons obtain their wealth through "legal corruption" and "exploitative practices". Paul O' Brien, Oxfam America's vice president for policy and campaigns, says "Such dramatic inequality is trapping millions in poverty, fracturing our societies and poisoning our politics."

The rich have become richer and the poor become poorer. The former keep realizing and reliving their dreams while the latter keep faltering and failing in their dreams. This is the "superstar economy" — the returns of the super talented can be super high.

Globalization — a hot-button topic at the 2017 Davos forum — is a double-edged sword. It can be a powerful force to reduce inequalities between countries, although it also can increase inequality within countries at the same time. These unrealized personal or community economic goals make people frustrated and very angry.

Having said that, sometimes the disenfranchised, disadvantaged and poorer people have unrealistic economic goals. The "get rich quick" syndrome is becoming more and more acute. They want stuff fast, without the hard work. Instead, they bank their hopes on gambling, engaging in get-rich schemes hoping for high returns, corrupt practices or illegal trades. When they fail or get caught, they blame everyone

---

[xvii] Oxfam: 8 people have the same wealth at the poorest half of the world. Available at: https://www.usatoday.com/story/news/world/2017/01/15/global-inequality-oxfam-report/96545438/
[xviii] Ibid.

including the corporations, institutions and governments, except themselves. This fuels their rage.

These flocks of listless sheep, who may end up being led by selfish and self-serving extremist religious leaders and political shepherds who are really wolves in sheep's clothing. They challenge the status quo, create populist disruptions and encourage political revolutions by any mean possible, including hate speeches, suicide bombings, and mass destructions.

These leaders jump on the populist bandwagons to champion the poor and the disenfranchised. They seek legitimacy from the masses or even small disenchanted minorities, defined by ethno-centrism like poor Mexicans, fanatical Muslims and miserable Mongs of Laos.

Professor Ash is spot on when he writes "The other thing that populism does is that it quite skilfully aggregates quite different social groups and social interests to create coalitions of the unwilling, everybody who is outside, who is left behind, who is disconnected, discontented for one reason or another." Donald Trump, to me, is the best example of this, matched by his skilful albeit simplistic, heart-tugging oratory.

The divide is no longer between the right and the left. It is between the Nationalist and the Internationalist. It is between the "can-get-more" and the "cannot-get-more".

Hence, when your rage is not reined in, it will distort your perspectives, ostracise you socially, make you emotionally immature and suspicious, destroy your trust in humanity, and finally derail you on your journey to greatness!

1. Of the four factors listed as the cause of rage, which factor affects you the most?

2. How can you prevent rage in your life?

Action Steps

Part 3

HOW TO BEGIN THE JOURNEY TO GREATNESS
The Power of Your Heart
(What you must do)

Chapter 1

STAY AUTHENTIC
GUARDING YOURSELF
FROM SELF DECEPTION

"It's amazing how you and I can have a 'work me'
and a 'home me.' You can't be yourself at both
places."

Dr. John Ng

"Authenticity is the alignment of head, mouth, heart and feet — thinking, saying, feeling and doing the same thing — consistently. This builds trust and followers love leaders they can trust."

Lance Secretan

Lance Armstrong, Rod Blagojevich, Bernard Madoff and Ramalinga Raju — these people seem to have lived two lives. They have a public persona whom you admire and a private life that you detest when you know the truth. They seem to be able to dichotomize their lives into public and private lives.

Before we condemn them, you too may be leading two lives. The only antidote to this is authenticity. It's amazing how you and I can have a 'work me' and a 'home me'. At work, you play a certain role, you behave a certain way, you have a certain personality, because you have to live up to someone else's or the organization's expectations. You can't be yourself.

At home, you can be yourself. You lose your temper, you are easily annoyed, you are honest about your likes and dislikes (and you let it be known), you tell it like it is, you use words at home that you don't use at work or *vice versa*. That's why your children and spouse know that you are a hypocrite.

Unfortunately, you also learn to cover up and live a life of pretence. Your close ones know that you are a person who pretends to have virtues, moral or religious beliefs, principles, etc., that you do not actually possess, or a person whose actions belie stated beliefs.

In Thai, they call courteousness '*Kriang Chai*' and in Chinese, it is called '*Ke Qi*' (客气). At work, you are very 'Kriang Chai' or 'Ke Qi' but at home you are '*Mai Kriang Chai*' or '*Pu Ke Qi*' — courteous no more. You and I are masters at that.

Until you can bring your whole self to work and home, you will always deceive yourself. The key is being and staying authentic through the following:

1. **Authentic and Genuine**. You are genuine: You are not a copy or imitation. Or as one of my friends describes his boss, *"He is solid gold, not gold-plated"*. You are real. What you see is what you get at home and at work.

2. **Authentic Principles**. You are your own guiding compass: You have your own True North (your fixed point in a changing world) and you live by those principles and values at work and home. You live out your values and when you don't, you apologize and make rectification.

3. **Authentic Through Times**. You are the same in good or bad times. You behave the same way in buoyant times or tumultuous times. You are unshakeable. *You are not a 'just-a-time' person but a 'through-the-time' person.* You are rock solid. You can be trusted whether the going gets tough or the tough gets going.

4. **Authentic Ownership of Mistakes**. You take ownership for your wrong decisions and don't play the blame-game or scapegoating. You have the courage to admit mistakes and you share the responsibility for any mistakes. You are not afraid to be corrected. In fact, you invite feedback.

5. **Authentic Creativity**. You have the guts to push boundaries and creativity. You question current status quo and you are willing to defend your position when questioned. You are constantly tested to deliver instant results versus long-term outcomes. You know what you can and what you cannot compromise in the short-term without jeopardizing the longer-term goals.

6. **Authentic Learning**. You are always learning and willing to share the learning with others in order to better yourself and the team. You know what you know and what you don't know, that's why you keep on learning. You are very self-aware of your own inadequacies and areas of incompetence as well as aware of your strengths and areas of expertise.

7. **Authentic Sharing of Resources**. You are willing to share your resources and network with people to enrich them without expecting any returns. You don't expect people to do likewise but are grateful when they do so. You spend time developing people by sharing your values without expecting them to be cloned. You allow them to be themselves in their areas of expertise and career development but guide them towards principles and values that will make them great in the long haul.

8. **Authentic Situational Awareness**. You are very situationally aware. You don't burst out saying what you are thinking or feeling. You exhibit self-monitoring behaviors, understand how you are being perceived and you communicate the 'truth in love'.

You don't embarrass others, or chide people in public (children included) irrationally or reactively. You have good emotional intelligence. You are willing to be objective and applaud the successes of your people (even your enemies) and learn to share your glory with them, without feeling jealous or arrogant.

9. **Authentic Transparency**. You are able to reveal yourselves appropriately in true humility, credibility and trust those around you to do the same. You have created the climate of transparency that people are willing to expose their true feelings in, without feeling judged or condemned.

10. **Authentic Influence**. You influence through your authenticity and compelling influence, not through clever manipulation, 'carrot and stick' strategies or veiled threats. You generate believability by being human. You demonstrate certain vulnerability and at the same time understand your genuine influence on others, without exploiting them for your personal ends or self-interest.

Bill George, *author of Discover Your True North,* a senior fellow at Harvard Business School, and former chair and CEO of Medtronic who coined the term Authentic Leadership, defines it this way, "People of the highest integrity, committed to building enduring organizations… who have a deep sense of purpose and are true to their core values, who have the courage to build their companies to meet the needs of all their stakeholders, and who recognize the importance of their service to society."[xix] I like his definition.

He has found through his massive research on authentic leaders that if you truly want to live a meaningful great life, you need to discover your True North so that when you look back on your life, it may not be perfect, but it will be authentically yours.

All this seems so impossible. But if you begin to understand the different facets of being authentic, you begin the journey of greatness. When you do, you set the gold standard for humanity.

[xix] Bill George. *Authentic Leadership: Rediscovering the Secrets to Creating Lasting Value.* 2003. John Wiley & Sons.

1. Why is it difficult for you to be authentic — to be the same at home and at work?

2. Which aspect of authenticity do you find it most difficult to achieve?

Action Steps ▼

Chapter 2

FOCUS ON INTEGRITY
PROTECTING YOURSELF
FROM MORAL DECAY

"In a world of corruption and compromises,
finding people with integrity is like unearthing
a rare find. When you discover that, you have
found a crown jewel."

Dr. John Ng

"You can't skip the fundamentals if you want to be the best. You can get away with it through the early stages. But it's going to catch up with you eventually."

Michael Jordan

Our society is changing. So are our morals. We have seen how we can be corrupted by wrong values:

- Fascination with evil
- Focusing on the bottom line
- Preferring short-termism
- Doing whatever you want
- Being obsessed with power
- Wanting to look good
- Being inclined to hide the truth
- Being corrupted by materialism
- Obsessing about the wrong role-models

We must get back to the fundamental value that will prevent moral degradation.

Fundamentals matter. Ask any great athlete. The difference between a great athlete and an average performer is in the consistency of execution in the fundamentals. It is this constant and unequivocal focus on the fundamentals that will make the difference. Athletes spend many hours practicing their fundamental routines, be it golf, gymnastics, swimming, or basketball. To achieve greatness involves constant practice of the fundamentals.

Michael Jordan, one of the world's greatest basketball players, puts it most succinctly, "The minute you get away from the fundamentals, the bottom can fall out. Fundamentals are the building blocks or principles that make everything work. I don't care what you're doing or what you're trying to accomplish; you can't skip the fundamentals if you want to be the best. You can get away with it through the early stages. But it's going to catch up with you eventually."

Practicing the fundamental consistently makes the difference between greatness and mediocrity. Edward Ong, Founder of Sutera Harbor Resort, consistently follows the mantra: "The world has no shortage of creativity but of integrity."

What is this fundamental value of life?

Through my interactions with many great leaders, I cannot help but summarize the fundamental value which keeps them great: Integrity.

Integrity is not merely a concept but a practice. It is through integrity that trust is built for the long haul. It is the cornerstone of relationships and the galvanizing force of the organization. It is something so precious that it cannot be bought. Primarily, integrity means "walking the talk and talking the walk".

Some learnt integrity from their parents. Lee Oi Hian, Chairman of Kuala Lumpur Kepong, describes his father as a man of integrity, honesty and hard work. His father demonstrated these values through his dealings with people and taught him from young as Oi Hian observed his life and lifestyle while working for his dad after school.

Lim Guan Eng, Penang Chief Minister, has the same inspiration. His father Lim Kit Siang's indomitable spirit and absolute integrity were a fine example for him to follow.

So, did Edward Ong. His father Ong Chwee Kou told him, "You can lose money, but you cannot lose integrity." It was his exemplary example that Edward has maintained and practiced in all his business dealings.

Ho Peng Kee, Singapore's former Senior Minister of State for Home Affairs and Law, found his inspiration in his father, who started from scratch after the war to build a successful watch business. He was hardworking and determined, a man of integrity. Peng Kee explained that he picked up those traits from him.

Integrity is multi-faceted.

1. Integrity Means Doing the Right Thing

Integrity is having the courage to do the right thing, being willing to pay a personal price and to face the consequences of your actions.

Jaruvan Maintaka, the former Auditor-General of Thailand, is a leader who is 'prepared to die for her integrity'. Her fight against corruption had resulted in death threats to her and her family. For a year, when she was collecting evidence against corrupt leaders and practices in her country, she was protected by five bodyguards armed with M-16s, revolvers and bullet proof vests. Her house was even burnt.

Another example of doing the right thing and paying the price is the family of Edwin Soeryadjaya, founding partner of Sarotoga Capital. Edwin belongs to the Astra Group, a household name known for its integrity and one of the best-run corporations in Indonesia.

As Kwik Kian Gie, the former Indonesia Minister of National Development Planning, writes, "What impressed me most is not what they have done to Astra to make it successful, but rather what they did with Astra when the family's other investment in a financial institution was in need of funds to repay the creditors and depositors. The family's decision to voluntarily sell Astra to repay creditors and depositors in full, shows their integrity in business dealings."

Former Temasek Holdings Chairman S. Dhanabalan was prepared to leave his cabinet position if he felt it went against principle and belief. He was also prepared to remove leaders who had moral defects. In his own words, "Competence cannot trump moral defects in character."

Amnuay Tapingkae, former chairman of Payap University in Thailand, was willing to put his presidential position on the line when the President of the Faculty Association and some faculty members insisted on putting a statue of Buddha at Payap University. He refused because Payap is a Christian university. He challenged them, "I am prepared to die for my faith for this cause. If you are prepared to do the same, then we can talk." They never came back with the same request.

United Overseas Bank chairman Hsieh Fu Hua recounted an incident whereby he had to pay the price for making an erroneous personal investment which he could have hidden but chose to redress. He said: "As a leader, we have a duty to uphold the rules of the game and the rules call for fairness and transparency. These rules must apply to you, even if it is hugely embarrassing. That is the right thing to do."

Lim Guan Eng is a champion of this. He keeps what he does in Penang simple: "Do what is right. Don't steal people's money. Stick to the rules you set."

2. Integrity Means Delivering Results

Whether it is managing a hotel, restructuring a company, being a politician, transforming communities, or being a good parent, a person with integrity has to be very good at what he does.

Idris Jala, chief executive of PEMANDU (PErformance MANagement and Delivery Unit), is an exemplary leader in this aspect. He was personally chosen by the Malaysian Government to turn around loss-making Malaysian Airlines (MAS) based on his integrity and competence when he was serving in the Royal Dutch Shell in Sri Lanka. Within two years, he had turned RM1.3 billion in losses into a RM260 million profit.

This was also the case for Sandra Lee, who became the CEO of Crabtree & Evelyn, and engineered its turn-around when it was undergoing Chapter 11 bankruptcy proceedings. She had to prove her integrity by transforming the company. To do this, she had to lead with passion at Crabtree, which she claimed was easy because as she put it, "The brand was my passion. My vocation was my vacation." Even then, she had to galvanize her team with a clear vision and mission to rebuild the brand and turn it around. She made it profitable within three years.

Edwin Soeryadjaya rebuilt his career and business at Saratoga Group by recognizing that trust was something that money could not buy. He learnt from his father by recruiting trusted, competent people who had a proven track record from Astra to manage his company. He ensured that his company reduced its borrowing cost.

In doing so, he rebuilt trust again by having good governance, executing discipline, and being fair to people. He said: "If more people catch you being dishonest, the more they will not trust you. Mistrust breeds mistrust."

3. Integrity Means Not Accepting or Paying Bribes

Jaruvan Maintaka has been tempted many times to take bribes. She elaborated that each time she was tempted, she would often think about its impact on her family and felt strongly that she could never let her children down. She has this firm belief — "Money is not everything. I had very good chances to get rich easily. I tell myself that if I had taken the money, I would be in jail by now and that would have ruined my reputation."

This aspect of integrity, not accepting or paying bribes, is also seen in the example of Domino Pizza's Chairman, George Ting. For him, "If you pay to one government department, the other departments will know and then it becomes a norm. So, it's better not to start." Edward Ong believes that business leaders must take the lead in the fight against corruption and not wait for the government to eradicate it. He said: "If there is no payment, there is no corruption! We cannot stop the solicitation but we can stop the manifestation."

4. Integrity Means Being Fair

OUE chairman Stephen Riady resolves to be fair when removing people who are not competent and not able to deliver results in their work. Before he dismisses any staff member, he ensures that there are enough evidence and facts. But, at the same time, he has to be sensitive to their concerns and their family's needs. He will never embarrass the employees by disciplining them publicly. He will ensure that they are adequately compensated, even using his own money at times, as well as helping them find alternative jobs.

Running a family business, Francis Yeoh, managing director of YTL Corporation, also ensures that his company practices meritocracy and healthy competition for senior positions. His children had to go through the different levels of work in the organization, earning their stripes and trust along the way. He also imbibes in his children a deep sense of stewardship, not entitlement.

He models compassion and selflessness, ensuring that their rise is based on fairness and their own competence and professionalism in the organization. The children of the Yeoh clan were placed in leadership positions out of merit and not kinship. They have to work hard, perform well, deliver results and be measured objectively. If Francis doesn't do this, he says, "I lose integrity!"

5. Integrity Means Upholding a High Standard of Business Practices

For Roosniati Salihin, deputy CEO of Panin Bank, integrity is the defining value of a banker, as "trust is the biggest asset and reputation". This is the key criterion of being a great and successful banker in the long term. As she puts it, "banking knowledge can be taught and learned but integrity has to be earned".

To put this into practice, she refuses to accept any gift given to her by her clients and makes this practice part of the organizational culture. Whenever a gift is received, she would make all the employees return it to the client with a thank you letter, informing them that this is company policy, and mentioning that providing good service is part of their professional duty.

For Francis Yeoh, maintaining high morals is a choice. It is having the courage to walk away from lucrative business opportunities and from what we consider as expedients, if it means compromising on unethical and illegal practices.

This may mean the company working harder to comply with government regulations, obtaining permits and getting more sales and becoming more transparent in all dealings because they have to reject conventional practices of kick-backs and illegal back-doors. He says, "It also means making business smarter and better to create niches and creating blue ocean strategies for business."

6. Integrity Means Building Trust with your Stakeholders

Ngiam Tong Dow, former Permanent Secretary in the Singapore Ministry of Finance, remembers the words of his mentor, the late Goh Keng Swee, ex-Deputy Prime Minister of Singapore: "Your job as permanent secretary is to raise the competence and standards of your team to a higher plateau." Since then, his mission in any ministry he has led is to raise the bar in all areas for the whole organization.

For George Ting, it even goes beyond the issue of bribery. Integrity means doing everything to comply with the laws and the regulations of the land and even beyond, like paying suppliers faster than your competitors, so that your suppliers will prefer to do your business and ensuring that there is less chance for corruption. In the process, he obtains better prices and services from the suppliers.

For UOB Chairman Hsieh Fu Hua, integrity means building trust between the chairman of the Board and the CEO. He opined: "As the chairman, you help the CEO by showing understanding and listening well to the ground, not micro-managing or interfering. If there are any major disagreements, the issues must be raised directly and not through a third party. The CEO must be given the opportunity to execute and allowed to deliver the goals in his/her own way."

Indeed, integrity is the most outstanding and definitive characteristic you can have to fight the moral degradation taking place in our society. Integrity is all of these: who you are, what you think, what you say, how you behave and how you do your business.

I believe that having integrity will prevent you from derailment.

Integrity is the foundational trademark of your life, family and business. In a world of corruption and compromises, finding people with integrity is like unearthing a rare find. When you have that, you have found a crown jewel.

1. What is integrity to you and how do you practice integrity at home and work?

2. Which aspect of integrity mentioned in the chapter do you find the most difficult to practice? Why?

Action Steps

Chapter 3

REMAIN HUMBLE
KEEPING A CHECK ON YOUR SUCCESSES

"A self-focused individual cannot be humble and an other-centered individual cannot be arrogant."

Dr. John Ng

*"Pride comes when people treat you with
great respect and you enjoy it so much that you
refuse to let it go. Humility is the ability to accept humiliation and not be upset."*

S. Dhanabalan

I had the privilege of interviewing 28 Asian leaders for a previous book, *Heart to Heart with Asian Leaders: Exclusive Interview on Crisis, Comebacks & Character.* What strikes me most about all of them is their humility. Of course, some leaders only became humble after they had been brought down from the pinnacle of success.

Malaysian businessman Dato Roland Wong is an example. His company was primed for public listing. He was associated with the who's who in the Malaysian business and political circles. Failure was the furthest thing from his mind.

He was living the high life — having prominent places at restaurants, privileged seats on important occasions, and premium branded goods. But, all these came crashing down during the Asian Financial Crisis and he almost went into bankruptcy. Friends deserted him.

But fortunately, he found God who gave him a sense of serenity and peace. He managed to persuade his banks to restructure his debt that ran into million of dollars, assuring them that he would clear it all. His perseverance paid off. Today, he lives a humbler lifestyle and is involved in many non-profit organizations.

As I have discussed, success has a way of intoxicating you:

- Bestowing you with the feeling of invincibility,
- Connecting you to a coterie of high-powered community members,
- Feeding your ego,
- Conferring you with a sense of self-dependency and self-reliance,
- Giving you the tendency to over-rate your strengths and success,
- Making you less open to feedback, and
- Seducing you to feel that success is permanent.

1. Humility Means Being Self-aware and Honest about your own Weaknesses

Humility comes from a deep self-awareness — recognizing who you are, remembering where you come from, not taking for granted your strengths and dealing with your own weaknesses. Most of us have more than one.

Everyone I interviewed is ever-conscious of their weaknesses and willing to deal with them, by heightened awareness or by building an 'accountability group' consisting of people who are willing to give candid feedback.

- Paul Chan, former Group Head, Hewlett-Packard Asia Pacific — "Tendency to criticize and seeing the negative aspect of people, not building enough bridges to people."

- S. Dhanabalan, the former Minister of Foreign Affairs, Singapore — "My biggest struggle is pride, when I am not treated with respect."

- Dr. Chatree Duangnet, Group CEO, Bangkok Hospital — "Not spending enough time with family."

- Hsieh Fu Hua, Chairman of UOB Bank — "It is managing one's ego."

- Dato Seri Idris Jala, Chairman, Heineken Malaysia — "Inability to make the trade-offs and who to listen to — the majority or the minority?"

- Puan Sri Sandra Lee, former Group CEO, Crabtree and Evelyn — "Having a Type A personality, I am impatient and quick- tempered."

- Khunying Jaruvan Maintaka, former Attorney-General, Thailand— "Too demanding. When they can't do it, I'd rather do it myself."

- Edwin Soeryadjaya, Chairman, Saratoga Group — "I was raised by indulgent parents, and must admit I in turn indulge my children. I find it very hard to say no to them."

- Dr. Amnuay Tapingkae, former President, Payap University — "Being too quick to judge."

Their successes have made them even more conscious that their weakness can derail them. Many of them protect themselves by having accountability. Some have spouses to bring them down to earth before their egos become too big for their own good.

2. Humility Means Serving the People and the Poor

The outworking of humility is to serve others.

Advisor, Government Investment Corporation (GIC, which is Singapore's investment arm), Lim Siong Guan, who has served as Permanent-Secretary in many different ministries and is the former Head of Civil Service, describes his purpose as "leaving behind a place where people want to be the best."

YB Senator Datuk Paul Low, Minister for Governance, Transparency and Integrity in the Malaysian Cabinet is another example of humility. He is prepared to do menial tasks such as shifting chairs or even cleaning the toilet in church. He is driven by one passion — a constructive engagement to serve the people. He said: "The biggest part of character should be humility. When you are humble, people will connect with you."

This is the same stance for Ngiam Tong Dow, whose ability to remain humble comes from learning to be sensitive to people, having compassion for the poor, reminding himself where he came from and not lording over them.

3. Humility Means Shunning Materialism and Glamor

Dr. Kim Tan, Chairman, Springhill Corporation, a multi-million investment company focusing on social causes, has a policy of flying economy, renting modest cars, entertaining modestly and staying in four-star hotels. When he met his hero, the late Sir John Templeton, an US investor and founder of the Templeton Funds, he was surprised and impressed that he also lived modestly and would fly economy too. Yet, Kim Tan also accepts that everyone has their own set of indulgences. For him, he confessed his indulgence was rugby and became a director/ shareholder of the internationally renowned Saracen Rugby Club. He remains a minority share holder of the club.

People like Dr. Kim Tan lived a simpler lifestyle. Those who are born to privileged positions and have immense wealth like Edwin Soeryadjaya and Sandra Lee, do not flaunt their wealth or their lifestyle. Their children, whom I know, do not behave like spoilt brats. Some of their children are even working for non-profit organizations. They use their wealth to set up foundations to enrich others and help the disadvantaged.

4. Humility Means Adopting a Learning Posture

The person who epitomizes the above is James Chia, Group President, Pico Group. He has made learning a life-long posture. At every phase of his life and from various people — from his cultural heritage, his National Service (Compulsory Military Service), his siblings, his customers, and from being a grandparent, he says, "At different phases of my life, I was blessed to work with very capable people who became my mentors." He is also a voracious reader.

Ngiam Tong Dow, former Chairman, DBS Bank and former Permanent Secretary of Defence, practices humility by his willingness to listen to the "people on the streets besides the Harvard graduates."

Truly, the mark of greatness is humility.

The Chief Minister of Penang, YAB Lim Guan Eng, was most honest when he reminded me of the phrase that kept him going during his two-time imprisonment: "The night is always the darkest just before dawn. Things will get worse before they become better. When you are at your depths, it will pass."

When I asked him how he keeps his feet on the ground now that he is the Chief Minister of Penang, riding on the crest of success, his instinctive response was, "When you are at your heights, it will also pass." It might be fortuitous for him as he faces new charges of corruption.

What stands out for me in these leaders is that their humility is consistently tested. They learn to be other-centered. Looking at leaders who have fallen like Lance Armstrong and Madoff, they fall when they become self-focused. This is what I have found: A self-focused individual cannot be humble and an other-centered individual cannot be arrogant.

Hence it is an ongoing process of discipline living through their learning posture, service to people, passion for the poor, shunning of glamor, and adoption of a modest lifestyle.

Most of all, they discipline themselves by keeping their egos in check, especially when they are at the pinnacle of their success and positions. They do not allow their special status to enslave them and make them victims of an entitlement mentality.

It is this trait that their followers admire them the most for because it impacts them the most.

The dark side of success can be combated by remaining humble.

1. Humility is a constant work in progress. Would you agree that to avoid the dark side of success, one of the most effective ways is to remain humble?

2. How true is the statement *"A self-focused individual cannot be humble and an other-centered individual cannot be arrogant?"*

Action Steps

Chapter 4

CONFRONT YOUR
WEAKNESS
TRANSFORMING YOUR WEAKNESSES

"If the flipside of every strength is your
weakness, the corollary is also true: your
weakness can become your strength."

Dr. John Ng

*"You cannot run away from your weakness. You must sometime
fight it out or perish."*

Robert Louis Stevenson

You have weaknesses and you are bound to fail unless you put in the time and effort to deal with them. To recognize that you *do* have weaknesses and that you are bound to fail should make you more conscious of our failings and fallibility.

As discussed in the chapter on weakness in Part 2 of this book, there are four types of weakness: Competence, Personality, Emotional and Character Weakness.

Most of these weaknesses are inherent in us. Some are cultivated over the years because of ill-disciplined habits, persistently bad practices, or uncorrected values. But how do you deal with your weaknesses?

1. Own your weaknesses

We have to learn to deal squarely with character flaws. Your weaknesses will not go away. If you harbor the emotional weakness of bitterness, it will haunt you. If you don't manage your rage, it will devour you. If you don't confront your addiction, it will destroy you.

Coming to terms with it means admitting the weaknesses, apologizing to those you have hurt, and being willing to ask for help. The last can come from seeking professional therapy, finding support groups, or getting others to hold you accountable. This must be done, no matter how long it takes.

The rewiring of our character or emotional weaknesses may take a long time, but it will be well worth the effort as your flaws are corrected and stop affecting your life.

2. Give people the permission to correct you

It has been said that when you give people the permission to correct your mistake, that takes courage. As you climb the corporate ladder or take on parenting roles, there will be fewer people, especially among your subordinates or children, who will have the courage to correct you. They are less willing to give you candid feedback, instead, they will tell you what you want to hear.

Your egos may take some battering in the correction process, but the long-term result is a stronger, more united family and team. John Maxwell is spot-on when he writes, "A man must be big enough to admit his mistakes, smart enough to profit from them, and strong enough to correct them."

3. Work out complementary relationships

"What we have to do ... is to find a way to celebrate our diversity and debate our differences without fracturing our communities."

Hillary Clinton

None of us have a complete set of competencies and personality types that will suit every situation. You need to find people in your family and work who can accept you for who you are as you learn to accept others for who they are. This complementary relationship, without denying our individuality, is key to greatness. The ability to do this is a unique gift that will help build better teams.

In this way, you learn to work with people who are different. You manage around your weaknesses. At times, it may seem more difficult because we prefer people who are like us. But, in the long run, if both parties can learn to work together, maximizing each other's strengths, the organization will be better and stronger.

Leaders need to be aware that deceit and greed begin with small steps, and unchecked weaknesses keep us on that road until it is too late.

4. Provide the space to fail forward

Deficits in competence, personality, emotion and character have become more prevalent today. Some have tragic consequences and may be disastrous, like deaths of innocent people, prolonged jail terms, etc. This is inevitable. But we must put in place a recovery process to give yourselves and your loved ones the opportunity to fail forward and recover — that is, to give those who have failed chances and opportunities to put in practice the painful lessons they have learnt.

I suggest we put in place a process of recovery when major failures happen. In a commentary on the sex scandals Singapore has experienced, *Straits Times* sub-editor Zuraidah Ibrahim commented, "Over time, Singapore too, may need to strike that balance between condemnation of the act and the redemption for the individual." I can't agree more.

Remember that our weaknesses really matter. And we neglect them in our leadership to our peril.

5. Transform weaknesses into opportunities

In his book *High Flyers*, Morgan McCall cites two critical factors that can derail leaders. First, over-utilized strength can be a weakness; and second, unmanaged weakness will derail you. If the flipside of every strength is your weakness, the corollary is also true: your weakness can become your strength.

The analogy of the mythical phoenix is a great lesson in transforming weakness into strength. The phoenix is a large-sized, strikingly beautiful bird with beautiful red and golden feathers, setting it apart from commonplace birds.

In addition to its remarkable qualities and long lifespan, the phoenix was also immortal, in a way. It would burn itself to death, and only after being totally consumed would a new, youthful phoenix rise from the ashes.

This is a useful mindset to have when we are confronted with your weaknesses and the failures that result.

I will conclude this chapter by sharing with you the lessons I have personally learnt on how to transform my weaknesses into strengths. It is always a work-in-progress in my life. These lessons include:

1. Weakness Helps Me Recognize My Humanity

One of my areas of expertise is conflict management. I have conducted training for literally thousands of mediators and conflict managers. I have researched and studied this subject. I have written research articles, and even have a book on it, *Smiling Tiger, Hidden Dragon*. It is easy for me to advise parties caught in conflict (whether at work or at home), to 'stay calm', 'learn to listen' and 'see the other person's perspective'.

In fact, I have successfully mediated many conflict situations. People often see me as an expert in this field. Eventually, my strength became my weakness. I was arrogant and thought I could manage conflicts all by myself.

But at home, I am an amateur. When I am personally involved in marital or family conflicts, I often lose control, become emotional and react negatively. That makes me realize that I am only human. In fact, I often fail to manage my own conflicts well, and sometimes do it really badly.

It was so bad that at one point in my life, I had to seek professional help. My wife and I went to see a psychiatrist to help us manage our conflicts with our children at home. It was the lowest point in my life. But that was also one of my most important breakthroughs.

I now understand more about the pre-frontal cortex and about the Amygdala Hijack, and the 'flight, fight, freeze or faint' reactions (see my chapter on Harnessing Emotional Energy in Part 4). I realized that when my heart rate rises beyond 100 beats per minute, the Amygdala Hijack would take over.

Thankfully, the sessions with my psychiatrist saved my family and helped me in my own conflicts with my children. It was the beginning of a journey to learn about the brain and see how it can affect the way we manage conflicts. I am now more sympathetic with those who struggle in conflicts with their teenage children. I recognize my own human frailty and others. It made me more human.

2. Weakness Helps Me Accept the Gift of Limits

My weakness helps me appreciate my limitations, and recognize that I am no superman — something most humbling to accept. When I was much younger, I was so driven that I thought I could do everything. But my weaknesses make me recognize that I do have limits.

In the past, I had a 'Messiah Complex', thinking that I was the 'savior of the world'. Nothing was impossible. Today, I recognize I cannot solve every problem, and must leave the 'Savior's role' to God.

In the past, I did not like to hear bad news or receive criticism. I didn't receive feedback well. Nobody likes to be reminded of his flaws. Hence it is natural not to actively solicit feedback for fear that it might be bad. And I did not handle it well. I only wanted to hear compliments or good news.

After delivering a good training session, I would often ask my peers and colleagues: "What have I done well?" I enjoyed being affirmed and applauded. It boosted my ego. It was an emotional need that I had.

Today, I have learnt that feedback is neither good nor bad. It all depends on how I respond. A positive feedback can be bad if it makes me arrogant and proud. A negative feedback can be good if I receive it well, learn from it and make the change.

Now, I have learnt to create a culture of learning among my staff and in my family. After each training or consultation session, we use a four-quadrant system: Do More, Do Less, Stop Doing and Start Doing. We know that in every project or assignment, there are areas we have done well (Do More), areas to improve (Do Less), areas or fatal mistakes we have to stop (Stop Doing), and areas in which we can try new ideas (Start Doing). See the diagram below.

Do More (What we have done well)	**Do Less** (What we can improve)
Stop Doing (Near fatal errors we should stop doing)	**Start Doing** (New, fresh ideas we can try)

We do this almost religiously after each assignment. We get each person to complete this for themselves first before giving others feedback. This has been very useful to create self-awareness, be more issue-focused and create a learning environment for the organization. I also do this with my family.

3. Weakness Helps Me Take Myself Less Seriously

A healthy way of handling our weakness is not to take ourselves too seriously. You need to be able to laugh at yourself more. In fact, I believe that unless you can laugh at yourself, particularly at your weaknesses, you are not emotionally healthy. The principle is to *take God seriously, not yourselves*. This frees you from becoming too obsessed with your needs, idiosyncrasies, pride, and failures.

My daughter Meizhi and I are incredibly clumsy. We trip over things frequently. We have the knack of knocking over drinks and spilling food. People tease us about our ineptitude and lack of motor control, which we admit to. We used to feel embarrassed, become defensive and even angry with them. We would try to justify our behaviors, and beat ourselves up over this weakness. The harder we would try, the more we would fail and the clumsier we would become — and the more people would snigger at us!

Today, we have learnt to accept this 'handicap' as one of our givens in life. We learnt to laugh at ourselves. To comfort both of us, when I trip, she will imitate the trip. When she spills a drink, I spill some too. Just to make us feel better.

4. Weakness Reminds Me of the Need for Accountability

It is very easy for you to follow your own instincts, depend on your own insights, make decisions based on your own intellect and rush into things without consulting. You become the master of your own universe.

I realize that this used to be my cultural value: "Don't depend on others. You can only depend on yourself". It's scary to live like that. I recognize that I do need communities of accountability to support me when I am down, help me see my blind spots, and give me a fresh perspective on issues. This is one of the many blessings of my life.

I belong to a non-profit organization, Eagles Communications. The Founder is Peter Chao and the President, Michael Tan (my buddy since we were six years old), and William Tang is our Executive Vice-President.

We have been serving together for 49 years. Presently, I serve as the Chair of the Eagles Board.

The four of us started working together when we were 14 years old. We often tease one another that there is nothing they would not do for me — and there's nothing I would not do for them. (And for the last 49 years, we have been doing absolutely nothing for each other!)

We share the same passion and values. We are committed to developing leaders, nurturing younger people, and helping the disenfranchised of society. To have survived and thrived in this unique community for this long is truly a miracle. We know each other so well. We literally know what each one of us is thinking before we say it. We have the highest respect for each other. We know our strengths and weaknesses and we support each other.

Peter is straightforward, candid and direct, and razor-sharp in his insights of people. He cuts to the chase when clients and staff try to put up a false front. He was called the 'snake-slayer'. Michael is more thoughtful, slow to anger and less driven to act. He is our 'snake-tamer'. William is a 'snake-healer', he heals the wounds of those bitten. Finally, I am more of a peacemaker, less confrontational and more willing to compromise and seek agreements. They call me the 'snake charmer'.

We deal with conflicts very differently. We listen to one another carefully and take everyone's input seriously. We are not afraid to correct each other and we relate to each other as friends. We are vulnerable to each other. Relationship is fundamental. We will not do anything to jeopardize that.

In major decisions, we are usually unanimous. If there is no unanimity, we will delay our decision-making because we value each other's insights and perspective. But whenever a decision is made, we are in full support of each other. We stand united.

One of the secrets of our synergy is the friendship. Once, I made a critical error in leadership. I reprimanded someone sharply for the way he treated one of our staff. He didn't take it well. I had nurtured him, but he turned against me. William, Michael and Peter were the first to be there to comfort, correct and support me.

Another time, Michael was almost derailed because of a drinking habit he had acquired during his army days. We were there to discipline and correct him. He was also willing to learn and grow. Today, he is the President of Eagles Communications — a loyal and highly competent leader.

William is a most remarkable guy. He is the silent one. He is never on the public front. His main work has been more of a supportive role in the logistics and audiovisual areas. He is always the first one in and the last one out in any event. He has been doing that for the last 49 years! Faithful, loyal, hardworking and extremely relational. All our volunteers love him!

Some leaders in the organization had a fall-out with Peter. There were times he had been too harsh. But he was always ready to listen to us and at times, we had to calm him down and persuade him to give them another chance. But sometimes, after listening to his strong arguments, we would agree with him and support his decision to discipline people who have become toxic to the organization.

It is through these checks and balances that we appreciate and build each other up. The enormous trust we have for each other is truly incredible. Till today, we complement each other so well. We cover up for each other's weaknesses and enhance each other's strengths.

Our weaknesses have helped us recognize the need for friendship and an accountability community.

5. Weakness Keeps Me Humble

In my journey of leadership, I have learnt humility. It has been one of the hardest lessons to learn and most difficult to practice. Succumbing to flattery is one of my major weaknesses.

To cultivate this humility, I have learnt to constantly:

- Become more other-centered
- Learn to accept my own limitations and human-ness
- Admit wrong when I am in the wrong
- Learn to listen more, including younger and lower-positioned staff
- Leverage on the strengths of others in my team
- Manage around my own and others' weaknesses
- Use my strengths and networks to help my staff succeed and grow their potential.

These are the behaviors that I measure myself against, and I have given my team permission to hold me accountable for them.

6. Weakness Helps Me Become More Realistic, Less Judgmental and More Forgiving

One of the benefits of appreciating my own weaknesses is to become more realistic about other people. Now I am seldom surprised, but often grieved by leaders' failures. I have become more conscious of their limitations and human-ness, which has made me less judgmental of others and more tolerant of their weaknesses.

Indeed, weaknesses can become our strengths if we care to acknowledge them, recognize our need to be held accountable and find people to complement what we lack. I live by the dictum that failure is not final unless I allow it to be so.

Allow me to conclude this chapter with the story of Sir Winston Churchill. His ability to bounce back has prompted the writing of the book *Churchill: A Study in Failure* by Robert Rhodes James. His tumultuous career has enthralled many researchers and students in leadership, but this great British Prime Minister began as a poor student (the bottom of his class) with a lisp, a speech impediment. He failed the college entrance examination twice.

On entering the political arena, he lost the parliamentary election of 1899; and as a head of the British Admiralty, he was held responsible for the strategic failure in World War I. He resigned from his post, and then lost another election in 1922. He resigned from office altogether in 1929 when his party was defeated. He did not join the Cabinet for 10 years.

But he became one of Britain's greatest orators, writers and statesmen of the twentieth century, and led the country through the dark days of World War II. In 1941, he declared to students at Harrow, his old school: "Never give in, never give in, never, never, never — in nothing, great or small, large or petty — never give in except to convictions of honor and good sense!"

When Britain was surrounded by Hitler's troops, planes and ships, he issued the clarion call: "We shall fight on the beaches, we shall fight on the landing grounds, we shall fight in the fields and in the streets, we shall fight in the hills, we shall never surrender." In his final speech to the House of Commons, his concluding words were: "Meanwhile, never flinch, never weary, never despair."

This is what we must do when we are confronted by our weaknesses. We may have been derailed by them, but like all great leaders, we must pick ourselves up. We must never flinch, never despair and never surrender, but bounce back each time to fight another battle! Only then can weakness be transformed into strength.

1. Of the five steps in confronting your weaknesses, which is the most difficult for you?

2. What inspires you most about the story about my colleagues and Sir Winston Churchill's story?

Action Steps ▼

Chapter 5

DISCOVER YOUR VOICE
FINDING YOUR FIT

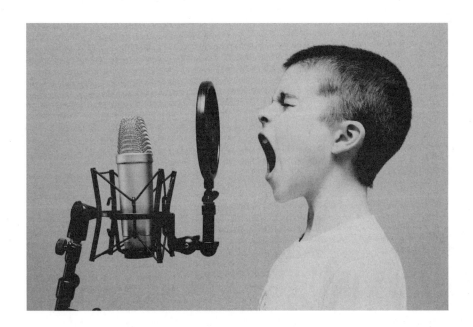

"When you find your passion, become competent in your work, and have strong values, you will be able to achieve greatness in your life and choose the organization you want to work for."

Dr. John Ng

"Music saved my life."

Shun Ng, finger-style guitarist

Job Fit
Team Fit
Boss Fit
Culture Fit
Life Style Fit
Life Stage Fit

If fit is so important to achieve greatness, how do you find your fit?

My good friend, Sam Lam, President of Linkage Asia, has worked for many years as a top-notch executive coach. He proposes a model to help you find your fit: The Can/Want/Should model.

When all these three are aligned, you find your sweet spot. Some of you may not even know what you want.

Here's an exercise to help you discover your fit:

1. WANT: Motivations, Desires, Interests, and Drives

'Want' refers to your passion that you have been endowed with, desires that you want to fulfil, your motivations that may arise from needs/concerns and drives that propel you to excel in your competence or knowledge.

Let me tell you about my son, Shun.

Like his father, he struggled with academic work from a young age. Somehow, he showed little interest in academic subjects. It was when he was 10 years old that we discovered that he had ADHD (Attention Deficit Hyperactivity Disorder) and dyslexia. He was so distracting in class as he had to walk around almost every half-hour that some his teachers made him sit in the front row for closer supervision.

We enrolled him in gymnastics classes for two reasons: First, I have always wanted to be a gymnast. Nadia Comaneci was my hero. I didn't take up gymnastics because there were no classes in school at that time. I coerced all my children to take up gymnastics. Second, I thought that would help him be more focused. He was too short for basketball and too skinny to play football. Gymnastics was a good choice for a smaller kid like him.

Shun did fairly well. He represented his school and won a number of medals. He was chosen to represent the Combined School squad. That was disaster — he could not handle the Chinese coach, who motivated the gymnasts through tortuous exercises, shouting at them for any minor mistakes and demeaning them, hoping that through negative psychology, they would be motivated to do better.

"China's gymnastic teams are known for pushing the gymnasts really hard at a very young age. I remember when I moved to the pre-national squad when I was ten years old. I had all these coaches from China who were so different, so strict. They're the kind where if you dislocated your shoulder, they would pop it back in. I hated gym," Shun recalled.

He was devastated because he already had such low self-esteem academically. He suffered. He hated gym. But I kept forcing him, encouraging him to persevere. Going to gym six times a week was a constant source of quarrel and conflict. His academic studies did not improve. He was having trouble in school.

At the age of 14, during Christmas, he asked me to buy him a guitar. I did and I taught him how to play 'Silent Night, Holy Night', playing with three-chords, one of the few songs I knew how to play.

He began to find his passion. Blues music was the first genre that he focused on when he became a student of guitar. Like most modern day blues musicians, he would turn onto a blues artist after hearing about each famous blues musician by word of mouth. First, he was blown away by the sounds of Steve Vai. Then, he heard about 'some guy' named Jimi Hendrix.

"That was when YouTube was coming out. So, I watched interviews and he'd talk about Buddy Guy and I checked out Buddy Guy. That's a whole new world in itself. Then, Muddy Waters, the Chess Records connection. Then, Howlin' Wolf and then the Texas guys, Albert Collins, Albert King, and Stevie Ray, Thunderbirds, and I was just in that world," he shared.

The rest is history.

He was so driven that he practiced for hours, sometime into the night, to the chagrin of our neighbors. His interest drove him to study harder for the IGCSE

(International General Certificate of Secondary Education) because he wanted to enroll at Singapore Polytechnic to study Music and Audio Technology.

Unfortunately, he didn't do too well at the IGCSE. He got 18 points. The cut-off for the course was 12 points. There were only 40 places for each cohort. They accepted 35 students with 12 points. The other five places were reserved for students with talent in music. Shun went for the audition and impressed the faculty.

They accepted the last five students with 15 points but Shun had 18 points and could not get in. We appealed, together with a strong recommendation from his mentor, Dr. Kelly Tang, who was a music professor at the NIE (NTU) School of Music, Singapore. They opened up a 41st place and accepted him.

Shun always says, "Music saved my life."

Even at Singapore Polytechnic, he didn't excel because most of the subjects were too academic. His dyslexia didn't help. Once, he wrote a great piece of music for a music composition class. It was so brilliant that the professor has made it a showcase piece till today. But because of the academic requirements, he had to write out how he developed the composition. He couldn't do it because music comes instinctively to him. He barely passed that course.

Although music gave him hope, the academic struggle was petrifying. Even what saved his life couldn't help him at that school. His school taught everything from studio engineering to live sound to composition and theory, which he also didn't do very well in but learnt as much as he could.

Shun shared, "Academia was always a struggle for me, especially when you combine it with music because somebody who is insecure about academia, and remember, in Singapore, that's a big deal. It's a huge deal culturally. In society, it rates pretty high."

After immersing himself in his acoustic guitar work, things started speeding up for Shun. He performed at festivals in Montreal, Osaka, and Singapore. He performed for the President's Challenge in 2013. In 2012, he released his first album, Funky Thumb Stuff. He studied an advanced training program at Berklee College of Music for two years, signed with Ralph Jaccodine Management, played with Livingston Taylor, and was briefly mentored by legendary producer Quincy Jones.

He is a three-time Boston Music Award nominee and in 2015, won International Artist of the Year. Shun was presented with Songmasters' prestigious 2016 Holly

Prize at the Songwriters Hall of Fame Induction Ceremony, a prize that was created as a tribute to the legacy of Buddy Holly.

Shun had found his passion, interest and motivation. That saved his life and he began to excel in it. You too can find your WANT. This set of questions will help you.

1. What motivates you in your work?
2. What aspect of your work interests you the most?
3. What gives you great energy?
4. What do you enjoy most in your job?

2. CAN: Competencies, Skills, Gifts and Talents

'Can' refers to a set of knowledge that you have acquired, competencies which you spend time developing, gifts and talents that you have been endowed with. They are usually recognized by people who are closer to you and whom you have the opportunities to work with and work for.

Since Shun discovered his incredible talent in music, he has put in much work, spending five to six hours a day mastering his craft. It is a truism that "If I don't practice for a day, I know it. If I don't practice for two days, my wife knows it. If I don't practice for three days, the world knows it." So said classical pianist Vladimir Horowitz.

Having a passion alone is not enough. Michael Howe, Jane Davidson, and John Sluboda's research[xx] refuted the notion that excelling is a consequence of possessing innate gifts. " Shun had to put in the hard work of making music. This is his story.

"I would learn everything from the bass line to the rhythm to the horn line to the chords and I'll see where I can go from there," he said. The guitar is merely his medium of expression as Shun is a musician in the larger sense of the word. "I love music. I'm not that into the guitar. I love music, everything from country to Hungarian dance music," he said.

At that time in his life, Shun decided to stick with the acoustic guitar. A meeting with legendary guitar maker Jeffrey Yong was the turning point. "Before that, I never really knew there was this thing called 'finger style guitar'. I wanted to do something different. I wanted to have my own voice and play the music that I love.

[xx] Howe, Michael J. A.; Davidson, Jane W. & Sloboda, John A. (1998). Innate talents: Reality or myth? *Behavioral and Brain Sciences* 21 (3):399–407.

Whenever I played blues, I felt I was leaving out a big part. When I found the acoustic guitar, it was like I could play all of it. I could play bass lines and it would still sound big. It seemed like the instrument with the most possibilities."

He is always experimenting, pushing himself to do things differently. One of these ventures is playing and singing solo, in all four parts, using only his guitar to perform the famous Queen piece, Bohemian Rhapsody. He took a few months to master the piece.

Besides, Shun can adapt his world-class fingerstyle acoustic guitar virtuosity to numerous formats. One of these outfits, known as Shun Ng And The Shunettes, features Shun performing with two female African-American gospel-style singers.

This format came together accidentally. He initially played with a group of friends from Berklee College of Music at a Christmas concert in Singapore. When Shun discovered that singer Deon Mose had arranged the music for that concert, he was blown away by what she could do with his songs.

He gave her the song *Get On With It* and she worked wonders with it. Eventually, they all returned to Singapore and Malaysia for more shows. Both the Shunettes attended Berklee College of Music in Boston. Deon Mose is from North Carolina and the second singer Angel Chisholm is from Detroit, Michigan.

Talking about the trio, Shun opined excitedly, "The interactions are so different with their vocals. The human voice is so versatile. We arrange it such that the voices can go from horns to strings to very percussive. It can create so many different elements. When there's no band, and it's just two singers and a guitarist, everything becomes more volatile. It's so minimalist. There are so few elements that every element matters so much. That's very exciting as a musician, because anything can happen."

If that combo isn't enough, Shun also keeps himself busy in a duo he has formed with harmonica man Magic Dick, of New England's legendary J. Geil's Band. "I love working with Dick. That's another thing in itself," Shun said. "The guitar-harmonica format is just something that's very exciting in the minimalist fashion too. I used to work as an arranger. A lot of this comes from my love for arranging, why we use different instruments."

As you can see, Shun never stops experimenting. He is open to fresh ideas with fresh music. He is committed to developing his competence to become the best he can be. At every concert, he gives his best.

No wonder Quincy Jones has said of him, "You won't believe your eyes nor your ears, he belies all stereotypes, all premonitions. I was simply blown away by both his soul and his science — his creativity and his uniqueness is astounding."

According to John Horn and Hiromi Masunaga, research professors and authors of the paper "A Merging Theory of Expertise and Intelligence", talent needs ten years of hard work to become great.[xxi] "The ten-year rule of hard work before becoming world class represents minimum age." Shun is always pushing himself to the next level.

To find the right fit, you have to work on your competence, improving and developing it. Work on these four questions concerning CAN:

Think about both your current work and the future.

1. What are your two most prominent competencies?
2. What do others say you are good at?
3. What knowledge and competence are you spending time developing to become better in what you do?
4. Which talents and competencies have produced most impact on people?

3. SHOULD: Values, Principles, Culture and Organization Value

To really find your fit, there's another piece of the puzzle. That is the 'Should', which refers to the values which you hold fast and believe in, even when things don't go your way and circumstances are tough. It is set of principles that push you to give your best to what you are competent to do and which you have passion for. You then create a culture based on these values and principles or you work in organizations that share the same values.

Shun believes that music can truly make a difference in people's lives and transform society. When interviewed by SP Magazine, he was asked where his inspiration comes from. His reply: "I think a lot of my inspiration comes because there're so many bad things in the world and issues I feel strongly about. It makes me want to use music to share about things like loving your family or remembering the people in your life."

[xxi] Horn, J., & Masunaga, H. (2006). A Merging Theory of Expertise and Intelligence. In K. Ericsson, N. Charness, P. Feltovich, & R. Hoffman (Eds.), *The Cambridge Handbook of Expertise and Expert Performance* (Cambridge Handbooks in Psychology, pp. 587–612). Cambridge: Cambridge University Press

From a young age, he had spent time on mission trips to Chiang Rai, spending his Christmas vacation with the tribal kids there. He would play with them, become their friend and sponsor some of the kids' school fees/hostel accommodation through his savings.

When he was serving in National Service in Singapore and could not obtain leave to visit his hostel friends in Chiang Rai, he organized a concert. The sale proceeds from the concert and sales of an album went to sponsoring one kid's entire four-year living expenses in the university.

When Shun told my wife Alison and I that he wanted to be a professional musician, we, like any other Singaporean parents, were concerned for his livelihood. Speaking to my Singaporean friends was most discouraging. There were usually three responses. First, they would say, in typical Singaporean English, "Can make money or not?" The second, in pathetic consolation, *"Sayang!"* (Malay for "What a waste!"). The third would be an exclamation of incredulous disbelief, "You must be crazy!"

Anyway, Shun was determined to fulfil his dream. He truly believes in what he wants to do. When he decided to settle in the US, we decided to release him to pursue his dreams.

His values are best summarized in a letter he wrote when he was struggling with eking out a living as a professional musician in Boston.

> *"Musicians are some of the most driven,*
> *courageous people on the face of the earth.*
> *They deal with more day-to-day rejection in one year than*
> *most people do in a lifetime.*
>
> *Every day, they face the financial challenge of living a freelance lifestyle,*
> *the disrespect of people who think they should get real jobs, and their own*
> *fear that they'll never work again.*
> *Every day, they have to ignore the possibility that the vision they have*
> *dedicated their lives to is a pipe dream.*
>
> *With every note, they stretch themselves, emotionally and physically,*
> *risking criticism and judgment.*
> *With every passing year, many of them watch as the other people their*

age achieve the predictable milestones of normal life — the car,
the family, the house, the nest egg.

Why?
Because musicians are willing to give their entire lives to a
moment — to that melody, that lyric, that chord, or that interpretation
that will stir the audience's soul.
Musicians are beings who have tasted life's nectar in that crystal
moment when they poured out their creative spirit
and touched another's heart.
In that instant, they are as close to magic, God, and
perfection as anyone could ever be.
And in their own hearts, they know that to dedicate oneself to
that moment is worth a thousand lifetimes."

That's why Shun never turned back. He described it this way, when he was asked how long he practiced each day, his reply demonstrated his passion and his values: "In some ways, it's never practice to me because it's always fun. If you love something, you just do it. If you love your girlfriend, you don't count, "I spent seven hours with you today" (laugh)."

To help you understand your values in relation to your work, these are some questions you can answer to see if your CAN/WANT/SHOULD are aligned.

1. What personal values are most important to you? Why?

2. Which corporate values in your organization are you most aligned to? Why?

3. What are the most important priorities in your work/your role?

4. What expectations do you have for your work?

I hope the story of Shun has inspired you and helped to show that when your CAN/WANT/SHOULD are aligned, you are on the path to greatness in what you want to be.

You can truly be the best that you can be. If you enjoy what you are doing, it's not work. It's a joy.

Find Your Fit by Answering these Questions

CAN: Competencies, Skills, Gifts and Talents

Think about both your current and future work.

1. What are your two most prominent competencies (leadership and professional competencies)?
2. What do others say you are good at?
3. What is unique about your talent and competence?
4. Which talents and competencies have produced the most impact on people?

WANT: Motives, Desires, Interests, and Drives

1. What motivates you in your work?
2. Which aspect of your work interests you the most?
3. What gives you great energy?
4. What do you enjoy most in your job?

SHOULD: Values, Principles, Culture and Organization Values

1. What personal values are most important to you? Why?
2. Which corporate values in your organization are you most aligned to? Why?
3. What are the most important priorities in your work/your role?
4. What expectations do you have for your work?

Action Steps ▼

Chapter 6

KEEP PURE
ADDRESSING YOUR SEXUAL TEMPTATIONS

"Given the right circumstances, the best among
us can commit the worst crimes."

Dr. John Ng

"Sexual temptation is rooted in virtue not vice. What begins as legitimate ministry — a shared project, compassionate listening, the giving of comfort — becomes an emotional bonding, which ultimately leads to an illicit affair."

Richard Exley

Keeping pure is the most difficult thing to do. The first question you need to ask yourself, "Do I want to keep pure?" If you don't, you will not get it and sexual impropriety will become a way of life.

If you want to learn, then read on. If not, you can skip this chapter. You decide.

One of the key ingredients of greatness is a healthy marriage and family life. If you subscribe to this, you should read on.

Why should we avoid sexual temptations?

Let's start with pornography. Allow me to list 10 destructive effects of pornography as described by Ann Tolley[xxii].

1. **Creates emotional bond with the artificial:** When someone views pornography, they end up creating an intimate bond with an artificial, fake world and can actually lose the ability to bond with real people.

2. **Sex without intimacy:** Because it is sex without emotional closeness, the underlying hunger remains unsatisfied.

3. **Unsatisfying:** While pornography use may result in a short term high, it eventually results in feelings of emptiness, low self-esteem and deep loneliness.

4. **Triggers addiction cycle in brain:** Because pornography use can become an actual addiction, viewers are not able to stop via their own will power.

5. **Unfulfilling:** When the rush of pleasure disappears, the feelings a user is trying to escape from reappear stronger than ever, and they are compelled to repeat the cycle.

[xxii] Ann Tolley. 10 toxic side effects of pornography use. Available at: https://familyshare.com/394/10-toxic-side-effects-of-pornography-use

6. **Great deception:** Initially, you were attracted to pornography because of the positive things it can do for you ("I love the rush I feel") . Eventually, it will do just the opposite. ("I no longer feel an emotional response to anything.")

7. **Imitation of the real thing:** Sex is no longer a wonderful source of connection between our deepest selves and a beloved partner; it becomes a commodity used to avoid intimacy and mask needs that should be met through human connections.

8. **Always hungry:** This appetite increases over time as you spend more and more time viewing pornography.

9. **Escalation:** We escalate to view things which we once would have considered as going too far or totally wrong.

10. **Blunt truth:** In the long run, pornography will not shore up a shaky ego, will not fill the emptiness left from childhood wounds or abandonment, will not save a shaky relationship or failing marriage and is not satisfying.

In terms of actual sexual abuse, sexual impropriety or sexual harassment cases, we also see the destructive consequences.

Too many careers have been derailed by sexual abuse and sexual impropriety. President Bill Clinton, CIA Director David Petraeus, Hewlett-Packard CEO Mark Hurd, and Boeing CEO Harry Stonecipher are among a cast of hundreds, who have occupied The Hall of Shame for their sexual behaviors, which did harm to important institutions.

In Singapore, we have Peter Lim, Ex-SCDF (Singapore Civil Defence Force) Chief, Ng Boon Gay, former CNB (Central Narcotics Bureau) Chief, Michael Palmer, Speaker of the Parliament, and Yaw Shin Leong, ex-Opposition MP for Hougang, who have all resigned because of alleged or proven sexual imprudence.

The China list includes Liu Zhijun, Minister for Railways, Bo Xilai, former Chongqing Party Chief, and Lei Zhengfu, former Beibei District party chief.

Too much shame and pain has been brought to families. Parents, who are involved in persistent sexual misconduct, may bring out the worst in their children. Children follow their parents' examples and parents live to regret it. I am sure if you asked all those listed above, their spouses and children would share that they faced humiliation and agony for years.

It is also too high a cost for business. In an article by the *San Diego Tribune*, "Sexual harassment: Bad for business", journalist Dan McSwain outlines the enormous cost businesses have to pay the victims of sexual harassment. In 2012, a jury awarded US$168 million — including $125 million in punitive damages — to one woman who was fired by a Sacramento hospital after filing 18 complaints to the human resources department over two years.

So, I hope I have convinced you that having a strong, healthy family is worth investing your time in. The first step is to address these sexual temptations squarely.

1. Don't play with flame before it turns into fire

> *"Sexual temptation is rooted in virtue not vice. What begins as legitimate ministry — a shared project, compassionate listening, the giving of comfort — becomes an emotional bonding, which ultimately leads to an illicit affair."*
>
> Richard Exley

Most extra-marital affairs don't strike randomly or suddenly. It has a gestation period. It is a product that starts with a series of small compromises: innocent friendship, meaningful glances, friendly smiles, inappropriate thoughts, sensual feelings, soft touches, caring hugs, brushing of flesh with tingled sensations, remembering the sensations, confiding deeply, friendship turns into something else, and then the door opens into something else....

Walter Wangerin, well-known author, writes that when a desire is born, you have a choice. When it exists in its infancy, you have a choice. When your feelings come, you have a choice as well. When you fantasize desire into existence, you feed it. Soon, you will lose your freedom. You have lost the free will to choose. The desire itself empowers you, commanding action, demanding satisfaction. He is right to conclude, "If we give it attention in our souls, soon we will be giving it our souls."

You see, as Peter Chao, my business partner for 49 years, poignantly points out, "the sin is not in the bait but in the bite."

2. Don't be overconfident — assume the worst in yourself

Given the right circumstances, the best among us can commit the worst crimes. The sooner you come to accept this painful truth, the better it is for you. Overconfidence can set you up for failure, especially in the area of sexual imprudence and moral failure. It makes you naïve and makes you take unnecessary risk.

Gordon MacDonald, the famous pastor of Grace Church in the US, was asked what his greatest temptation was. His response was, "I will never be tempted with adultery." The next moment, he had fallen right into it.

Succumbing to sexual indiscretion may be the furthest thing from your mind. You could have overworked yourself. You spend extended hours with your secretary or client for business. When the inevitable temptation comes, you get blind-sided and you fall into it.

Another factor to moral indiscretion is taking unnecessary risks. You are addicted to danger and excitement, like a moth to a flame. You think you are strong enough to handle it. You experiment with long hugs, long kisses, drunken stupors, shared rooms, various postures of undress and before you know it, you go all the way.

The fatal flaw is overconfidence.

3. Don't entertain lustful thoughts

You and I are people with feet of clay. You and I have emotional needs. You and I have raging hormones. I am not just talking about teens. You and I will be filled with lustful thoughts and fantasies. You and I will be excited by pictures and photos as well as real people, who are sexually attractive. You and I are mere mortals with real sexual needs and desire.

You cannot prevent the bird from flying over your heads but you can prevent it from building a nest on your head.

You have to set some boundaries for yourself as I do, such as:

- Try not to travel alone, whenever possible.
- Avoid places where your temptations abound.
- Turn off 'X'-rated channels in your hotel room television.

- Don't drink excessively especially with clients/colleagues of the opposite sex.

- Delete porn sites and photos whenever they appear on your phone or screens.

- Whenever you are having prolonged conversations with members of the opposite sex, do it in your office or in more public places. Better still, get another colleague to join you.

4. Watch out for tell-tale signs of trouble

Best-selling author Richard Exley reminds us of the earliest warning signals of emotional entanglement including but not limited to[xxiii]:

1. *A growing fascination with this person*, when he/she regularly intrudes upon your thoughts, even when you are with your spouse and family.

2. *A heightened sense of anticipation as his/her appointment draws near*, when you find yourself looking forward to "business" opportunities when you can legitimately be alone with the person, or when you create projects so the two of you can be together.

3. *A growing desire to confide in him/her*, when you are tempted to share the frustrations and disappointments in your marriage.

4. *An increased sense of responsibility for the person's happiness and wellbeing*, when you think more about his/her needs than the needs of your spouse and family.

5. *Emotional distancing from your spouse*, when you keep from your partner your secret thoughts and feelings for the third person.

These tell-tale signs are helpful indications that trouble is brewing. Quickly get help.

5. Have accountability partners

When you sense sexual troubles in your life, confide quickly to your spouse, close friends, your parents and your religious leader. Get it out in the light. This is

---

[xxiii] Richard Exely. "Handling Sexual Temptation." In Richard Exely, Mark Galli, John Ortberg. Dangers, Toils & Snares: Resisting the Hidden Temptations of Ministry. 1994. Multnomah Books.

especially lacking in the Asian context among Asian men. The loss of face and the shame are enormous.

In other words, we conceal our sex problems from our spouses, close friends and business associates. Dr. Barry McCarthy, a psychologist and sex therapist, says, "You have to be open to talk about what you value and your vulnerability."

No one teaches us how to do that.

Gordon MacDonald, pastor of Grace Chapel in Lexington, Massachusetts, and author of *Ordering Your Private World* and *Rebuilding Your Broken World*, speaks as a pastor who has experienced the tragic consequences of a moral failure. In an interview with *Christianity Today* following his public confession of adultery, he explained, but did not excuse, his behavior.

One of the contributing factors, he said, was a lack of accountability — friendships in which one man regularly looks another man in the eyes and asks hard questions about his moral life: his lust, his ambitions, his ego.

If a pastor can feel that, how much more lay people like you and me.

6. Enjoy sex with your spouse

> "*Sex without love is merely healthy exercise. Love without sex is sheer boredom.*"
>
> — Anonymous

Prevention is better than cure.

Marital intercourse is noble and honorable where spouses should experience pleasure and enjoyment of body and spirit.

A great sex life is the best antidote to extra-marital affairs and pornography. When we enjoy sex with our spouse, we don't need cheap substitutes. But if our sex life is boring and unsatisfying, the chances of our spouse finding surrogate sex outside marriage is so much greater.

Enjoyable and satisfying sex is important in building emotional connection with your spouse. It energizes your relationship. It makes you and your spouse feel desired and desirable and serves as a buffer against trials and difficulties. As Dr.

McCarthy adds, "When a couple avoids or is conflicted about sex, the disconnection can play an inordinately negative role. Often, if you can repair the sexual bond, the relationship improves as well."

Great sex is predicated by having a great relationship. Strengthening the emotional connections outside of sex is a strong antidote to extra-marital affairs. Unfortunately, in today's life, marital relationships have become functional. You don't emotionally connect with your spouse. What is emotional connection? This short passage will illustrate it.

<u>Before marriage....</u>

He: Yes. At last. It was so hard to wait.

She: Do you want me to leave?

He: No! Don't even think about it.

She: Do you love me?

He: Of course! Over and over!

She: Have you ever cheated on me?

He: No! Why are you even asking?

She: Will you kiss me?

He: Every chance I get.

She: Will you hit me?

He: Are you crazy!

I'm not that kind of person!

She: Can I trust you?

He: Yes.

She: Darling!

<u>After marriage....</u>

Simply read from bottom to top.

7. Understand that men and women have different expectations about sex

In having great sex, gender difference is most apparent. Dr. Clifford and Joyce Penner, two of the world's foremost experts in this field, have written numerous books on the subject of men and women's sexuality. They suggest that to have a healthy sex life, we need to understand how men are different from women.

Toyota truck versus Maserati: Men are simpler than women. Women are more complex. According to the Penners, men function on one track: the physical track. Women function on two tracks: physical and emotional. Women may be physically prepared but may not be emotionally prepared. Men just want the physical and get to sex acts quickly while women prefer to be nurtured emotionally first, before the physical sex becomes more attractive for them.

Women are like the moon. They are different and always changing. While, men are predictable like the sun, regularly rising and setting each day. In the study of the brain structures of men and women, it has been found that for women, sexual pleasure rests in the complex part of the brain. On the other hand, for men, sexual pleasure occupies the simpler part of the brain.

Hence, when it comes to sex, men are like Toyota trucks — they just drive through. But women are like Maserati — they need to be pampered, and driven more sensitively. If sex is going to last for a lifetime, it must be good for both.

Men are more goal-oriented while women more process-oriented. Men's focus in sex is sex. That's their goal. But women need to be nurtured and stroked physically. For them, the process is as important as the product. Men must remember that. They have to value the process and connect with her in the process before reaching the goal.

As such, Clifford and Joyce Penner remind men that they must make the major sacrifice, create the sexual desires in women, and give up his most profound yearning, which is to have sex as quickly as possible. In other words, husbands give up part of their maleness. Only then would women find sex satisfying.

Since the man is never truly satisfied unless the woman is, he has to shift from his goal orientation to her process orientation. He has to learn to soak in and enjoy, rather than press the right buttons and get her to respond. The Penners' advice for married couples: "Don't focus on orgasm but on pleasure."

Women lead, men follow. A woman must affirm her sexuality by learning to take her sexuality seriously. During sex, she leads by listening to her body, taking in the good feelings, and inviting him to enjoy her body as she enjoys his..

A turned-on woman is usually a turn on to a man; but a turned-on man does not mean a turned-on woman especially when he becomes demanding and pressurizes the woman to have sex.

Finally, Clifford and Joyce Penner conclude that it is the combination of men's simplicity and predictability, and women's ever-changing nature, that is the key to keeping sex alive and interesting in marriage. Sociologist Andrew Greeley rightly observes, "Sexual pleasure heals the frictions and conflicts of the common life and reinforces the bond between husband and wife." Enjoy sex and make it a great marriage.

1. Why is sexual temptation so difficult a topic to discuss today, especially in Asian cultures? How can you break this cultural malaise?

2. Have you been likewise tempted to commit sexual imprudence? What has helped? What has not?

Action Steps

Chapter 7

GIVE IT AWAY
KEEPING YOUR GREED IN CHECK

"Only when you learn to give, will you be able to stop
the tide of global greed that is innate in us, and you
will be happier, more fulfilled and more generous.
Then you know greed has slowly dissipated away."

Dr. John Ng

"Generosity is what keeps what we own from owning us."

Anonymous

Greed is in all of us. It is fueled by your desire to do better, to want more for yourself. The only guard against greed it generosity. I am not just talking about money.

1. Generosity goes Beyond Comfort Zone — Practice 'Creative Hypocrisy'

To overcome greed, you have to overcome your fears of being generous. These fears are real and include:

- Fear of being taken advantage of and exploited
- Fear of giving to the undeserving
- Fear of giving to 'organized poverty'
- Fear of feeling like a hypocrite because you don't feel like doing it

You have to get out of fear to be generous. Your actions must come before your minds. You don't have to wait for pure motives to give. You have to practice, what I call, 'creative hypocrisy' — do it even if you have mixed motivations, even if you have fears, even if you don't feel like doing it.

As the Nike slogan says, 'Just Do It'. The truth is you will feel better after that, even if you don't have the purest motives. Or you may have to 'fake-it-till-you-make-it'. Just get going.

2. Generosity goes Beyond Talking — Work on Doing and Behaviors

You must *do* generosity not just *talk* generosity. You cannot say, "I am not going to be greedy". You have to do things to get rid the grip of greed. You have to give.

As John Wesley, the Founder of Methodism, writes,

Do all the good you can

By all the means you can,

In all the ways you can,

In all the places you can,

At all the times you can,

To all the people you can,

As long as ever you can.

When you have a giving mentality, as you make time for people and as you help the poor and disadvantaged, you will experience happiness and greater sense of well-being. The best way to put it is that ultimately we have to pursue living well, and then ultimately you will be happy.

3. Generosity goes Beyond Money — Learn Hospitality and Availability

Americans who describe themselves as "very happy" volunteer an average of 5.8 hours per month. Those who are "unhappy"? Just 0.6 hours. This was a finding in *The Paradox of Generosity*, a book by sociologists Christian Smith and Hilary Davidson.

Americans who are very giving in relationships — being emotionally available and hospitable — are much more likely to be in excellent health (48 percent) than those who are not (31 percent).

There is a causal relationship: Generosity involves neurochemical changes in the brain, that gives people more pleasure chemistry in their brain, a sense of reward for having done something good[xxiv].

The more happy and healthy and directed one is in life, the more generous one is likely to be. It works as an upwards spiral where everything works together, or it works sometimes as a downward spiral if people aren't generous.

[xxiv] Jordan Michael Smith. "Want to Be Happy? Stop Being So Cheap!" The New Republic. 14 Sept 2014.

4. Generosity goes Beyond a Once-off — Make Giving a Way of Life

Generosity has to be a practice: it has to be something that you sustain over time and that you engage in regularly. One-off things or events don't affect us that much. On the other hand, repeated generosity and generosity sustained repeatedly in our bodily behaviors and in our minds, have tremendous effects on us. The empirical evidence is very clear.

5. Generosity goes Beyond Family — Share with the Disadvantaged and Strangers

The circle of generosity must grow beyond family to people beyond your most comfortable or most intimate. To get rid of greed, you can easily give to family and benefit your own kin. It must go beyond helping of "the other," and not just one's own tribe, so to speak. That's an important threshold to cross in being a generous person.

6. Generosity goes Beyond Culture — Work in Different ways for Different Cultures

Generosity in different cultures is very different. If you have ever travelled to poor countries, sometimes they can be immensely generous. They have very little but they are incredibly hospitable. When my family was in Chiang Rai, locals killed their pig and gave us a very nice dinner when they invited us as guests to their homes, and took us around their village and town hall, which was an act of honor. Similarly, there are other forms of generosity that you must not ignore.

If the poor can give, those of us from wealthier nations should do much more. I was surprised that even in Singapore, we have so many people who don't give a dollar to anything in an entire year.

Another thing that is surprising is that the percentage of people's salaries that they give is unrelated to how much they earn. That is, as people earn more and more money, they don't give relatively higher proportions of their income. Their giving remains the same. It's really not the case of being unable to afford it. It's the mind set.

Only when you learn to give will you be able to stop the tide of global greed that is innate in us and which is often driven by your self-interest. You will be happier, more fulfilled and more generous. Then you will know greed has slowly dissipated away....

1. What fears do you have of being generous? How can you overcome your fear?

2. Who can you be generous to and how can you increase your level of generosity?

Action Steps

Chapter 8

REFRAME THOUGHTS
OVERCOMING YOUR FEARS

"You fear because of an overactive imagination;
It is the IWP syndrome: 'Imagination of the Worst
Possible.'"

Dr. John Ng

"We fear things in proportion to our ignorance of them."

Christian Nestell Bovee

Fears are as real as you have them to be.

- You fear the future.
- You fear losing.
- You fear failures.
- You fear crisis.
- You fear fear.

How do you overcome fear?

1. Protect Yourself From 'Fear Conditioning'

"There is no passion so contagious as that of fear."

Michel de Montaigne

You must beware of fear conditioning — the ability of circumstances to make us afraid of things we typically should not be fearful of. This is evidenced by John B. Watson's 'Little Albert' experiment in 1920. In this study, an 11-month-old boy was conditioned to fear a white rat in the laboratory. The fear became generalized to include other white, furry objects. "We fear things in proportion to our ignorance of them," as the writer Christian Nestell Bovee has said.

As an individual emotional state, fear can affect the unconscious mind, which can be manifested in the form of nightmares. Fear may also be experienced within a larger social network. In this way, personal fears can be compounded to become mass hysteria.

You have to surround yourself with people who are realists but optimists. Pessimistic people love pessimism and love to hang around pessimistic people. Don't fall into the trap or else you may spiral into 'fear conditioning'.

2. Prevent your Fear from Escalating into Panic

Fear is not the enemy, panic is.

But sometimes, you make your fear come to pass through self-fulfilling prophecies and create more fears. Then you spiral in a cycle of panic. That is what normally happens in a financial crisis.

As people watched governments all over the world bailing out troubled countries, financial institutions and companies, and frantically trying to restore bank deposit rates, it created so much panic that consumer confidence hit an all-time low.

Panic drives the financial world into a crisis, and as a *Straits Times* article aptly headlined "Hell in Asia" put it: "Asian markets had a panic attack on fears that financial crisis was fast resembling a runaway train that no amount of intervention could stop." People were trading on panic in this massive bear market, where prices were falling out of control.

During the 2008 crisis, governments all over the world cut interest rates, some by a whopping two percent. This measure was aimed at unfreezing credit markets, where confidence has fallen so low that banks turned defensive and slowed lending to companies and one another. Former Japanese Prime Minister Taro Aso summed it up well: "The market plunge is not normal. Frankly, it is beyond our imagination. We have huge fears going ahead."

The Greece crisis in 2015 almost threatened the dissolution of the European Union and the collapse of Greece, which would lead to a contagion effect, threatening Spain, Portugal and Italy. This then spiraled downwards into irrational cost-cutting, and unrivaled panic decision-making. Greece threatened to pull out of the European Union.

European countries like Germany faced angry massive protests over bailing out Greece. Then in 2017, Greece was in trouble again. The European leaders are not sure if Greece can fulfill its financial obligations and economic target. Apparently, it has not gotten out of the woods.[xxv]

That's why it's important to prevent your fears from spiraling into a panic. It is most difficult to remain sane and rational in crises and look for short-term gains and long-term solutions.

[xxv] Tyler Durden. "Greece Is in Trouble Again: Bonds, Stocks Plunge as Bailout Talks Collapse; IMF Sees "Explosive" Debt". Available at: http://www.zerohedge.com/news/2017-01-27/greece-trouble-again-bonds-stocks-plunge-bailout-talks-collapse-imf-sees-explosive-d.

Panic makes an already bad situation even worse.

3. Produce 'Comedy Shows' instead of 'Horror Movies'

Nightmares are when your imagination plays tricks on your mind.

Fear is a mind activity that you make live in your brain. It is simply because you are not living with life, you are living in your mind. You fear what is going to happen next. It's about something that does not exist and may never happen. It exists in your mind.

Sometimes, you fear because of excessive imagination. Parents particularly have the IWP Syndrome: 'Imagination of the Worst Possible.' Fear makes you the producer of horror movies in your mind. You create imagined events and scenarios that may never happened. You fear 100 things and 99 of those things may never happen.

You deal with fear by changing the script and produce a different movie in your mind. Instead of a horror movie, you can produce a comedy show. It's in your mind.

Instead of being driven by the fear that your teenage daughter has been waylaid or sexually abused because she didn't answer your call, you can change the plot. Try thinking that your daughter has lost her phone or that her phone battery has died, and you will feel calmer and more relaxed.

Instead of imagining the worst possible scenario of business uncertainty or collapse, you can look for potential opportunities in the midst of all the chaos and fears. It means changing your script.

4. Pinpoint Your Fear and Take Action

You have to confront the situation squarely instead of moaning and groaning about it and become depressed. You relook strategies that have gone wrong, reprioritize your resources, reengage your team and re-implement new initiatives to address the challenges.

Allow me to share my own experience with one of my clients.

I was serving as consultant with Sunway Malaysia in the Sino-Singapore Tianjin Eco-City, China in late 2014. They have built 642 apartments and that year, they had only sold 67 units the whole year. They were not the only developer that suffered from the collapse of the property market. Other developers also had poor sales. In fact, two other major developers in Tianjin Eco-City pulled out completely.

In 2014, the newly appointed Deputy CEO of Sunway China, Daniel Lim, who hired us, was very realistic about the situation. The mood was very dark. The government's cooling regulations and the bank's lending policies had depressed the sales significantly. To make matters worse, the plot of land was not in the best location in the Eco-City!

Morale was down. The staff then were very pessimistic. I remember my interview with the Sales Manager during a visit. I asked him to project his sales for 2015, and this is how our conversation went:

> Sales Manager: "My boss wants us to sell 200 this year but this is totally impossible."
>
> John: "How about your own target?"
>
> Sales Manager: "100, but that's also an impossibility!"
>
> John: "Let's start from there."

Through his dynamism, optimism and visionary leadership, Daniel Lim inspired and challenged the staff to re-envision the project. He re-energised the spirit of the Sunway Tianjin team of 35 staff. His strategy was clear. He wanted to have a customer-centric focus by creating value for their targeted market, increasing awareness of the brand, and ensuring that the project is well executed.

As he says, "You can have the best strategy. But without the execution and a series of clear tactics to get both the Malaysian and Tianjin staff to implement the plan, it will not be possible to see the results."

Together, we identified the key challenges and created joint ownership of these challenges. We engaged the staff directly and transformed their 'Can-Not' mindset to a 'Can-Do' mindset. We formed S.A.L.T. (Strategic Action Learning Transformation) Teams to work out and implement an intentional, integrated customer-centric strategy, focusing on the three critical aspects:

Product: We created a new Sunway Tianjin culture and values where we focused on our niche, with refurbished show flats and lobby entrance to create higher value. The staff inspected each unit three times for defects and rectified them until they were personally satisfied before handing over to the customers. My challenge to them was, "Unless you are happy to live in the apartment, don't handover." We increase marketing efforts to raise brand awareness.

Process: We improved inter-department collaboration and coordination by having regular meetings. We implemented a new sales strategy to increase awareness and interest while other developers were pulling back on these efforts. We reworked sales incentives for leads, prospects and sales.

People: We trained every staff member in every department to be more customer-centric, and gain skills in dealing with customer complaints, and constantly engaged and empowered the staff to try new ideas.

By June 2015, we had already sold 82 units.
By end 2015, we sold 331 units in total and leased out 114 units.
By June 2016, we had sold all the launched units.
By October 2016, when they launched another block of 98 units, they were sold out in two days!

The average prices per square meter went from 8,500 RMB to 12,500 RMB! They were one of the most profitable business units as well as the unit with the highest staff engagement score within the Sunway Group.

To be fair, in 2015, the Government did relax the housing regulation and the Tianjin explosion disaster helped increase demands. But because we did not flinch from our marketing and sales effort, the products were upgraded and the team worked harder. The sales shot up. We were also top-of-mind for potential customers because of all the relentless marketing efforts that occurred during the lull period in the property market.

I shared this story to underscore that when fear and panic set in, there is a higher likelihood of becoming pessimistic and us making bad decisions. For me, it is the time to re-group, re-strategize, re-focus on the other opportunities, and re-implement fresh plans and learn to fine-tune along the way.

Similarly, in your personal life, you need to pinpoint the fear that's plaguing you the most — about your body, finances, love life, career, dreams or yourself — and hold it up to the light of your awareness.

You overcome your fear by taking one single bold step forward in the direction of your dreams, to prove to yourself that you are willing to do what it takes.

I like what life coach Elyse Santilli writes:

> Ask yourself honestly: Is this thought really true? Can I know for sure? Is there another way of looking at this? What would the highest version of me say about this?
>
> Remember, the word 'thought' is not synonymous with the word 'truth'. Your thoughts are not necessarily true or important and you don't have to take them so seriously.
>
> Think of them like passing clouds in the sky — they come and they go. Your true self is the ever-present observer who watches your fear-based thoughts as they pass by.[xxvi]

Don't cry over spilt milk. Allowing a bad situation to keep bleeding us only exacerbates the problem, so retreat if necessary and wait to fight another battle. As my good friend, motivational speaker Paul McGee, also known as The SUMO Guy, used to say, 'Shut Up and Move On!'"

5. Persuade People to be Hopeful

In your ever-changing environment and depressing world economy, you must stay hopeful and inspire hope. I believe that your life shrinks or expands in proportion to your hope, resolve and perseverance".

You can inspire hope by giving a clear vision and clearly articulating your game plan. You must have the resolve to see your plan through and make it work, learning and adapting along the way. Then, finally, you must have the perseverance to overcome the obstacles and press on to fulfill your vision and dream. You must be prepared to learn, unlearn and relearn.

You also do that by focusing on you and your team's strengths. Focus on what you have, rather than what you don't have.

[xxvi] Elyse Santilli. "7 Ways to Overcome Fear and Live Your Dreams". Huffington Post. 16 Aug 2016.

Ask yourself these questions:

—   What continues to give me hope?

—   To whom can I turn to help me get out of this rut?

—   Which areas of my strengths can help me through this?

—   Who and what are your team's bench strength?

Keeping things in perspective is important. First, keep the good years in mind and be thankful for them. Tan Sri Lee Oi Hian, Chairman, KL Kepong puts it well, "We had a few very good years of bumper crops when palm oil prices sky-rocketed. Today it has become more realistic; our earnings are down 80 percent. We had our good years. And we need to thank God for that."

Fear is real. We need patience and perseverance to overcome it.

It takes great strength and resolve to be patient and wait for the good times to return. Perseverance is a true virtue during times of crisis. It involves not running away from or suppressing fear, but confronting it. You must learn from it, yet keep fear in perspective. Take concrete steps to disarm it. Only then can fear be overcome — one step at a time.

1. What is your greatest fear? How have you dealt with your fear so far?

2. Based on this chapter, what concrete steps can you take to overcome your greatest fear?

Action Steps

Chapter 9

BE OPEN TO FEEDBACK
REDUCING TOXICITY

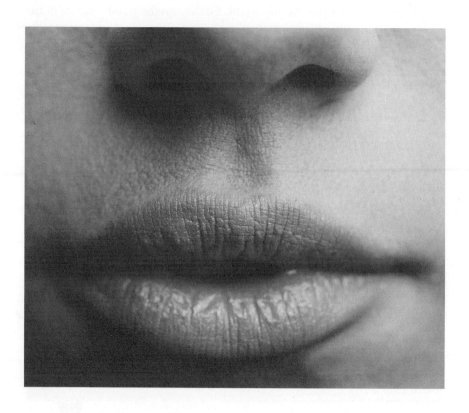

"When things taste sour, the toxic person says,
'There's nothing wrong with the milk — it's your
mouth."

Dr. John Ng

"When we are humble, we respect others.
When we lose civility and character, we lose ourselves."

Anonymous

What are the symptoms of toxicity? The best way to reducing toxicity is to check your toxicity level. Here are seven questions that can evaluate the level of leadership toxicity in your life.

1. Do your followers live in fear and guilt?

Toxic leaders lead by fear and guilt. You instill fear among your followers (staff and children) and threaten them with job loss, money freeze, uncertainty, estrangement, emotional blackmail and severe punishment. You promote "group think," stifle constructive criticism, promote mindless compliance and play to your followers' basest fears and needs.

You divide and conquer for you fear consolidation of power and influence among the rank and file. Fear in itself is not a bad motivator, but used as a primary form of motivation, it subsequently destroys trust. Used constantly, it creates unnerving uncertainty, blind loyalty and ultimate chaos.

In contrast, greatness involves creating a culture of love and learning.

2. Are your followers worse off now than before?

You tend to leave your followers worse off than when you found them. You wear people out. You create suspicions among the staff. You poison people by propagating fraudulent values. You promote incompetent loyalists and the corrupt people.

Most of all, you manufacture a culture of mistrust. You do so sometimes by eliminating, undermining, or firing. The result is that your biggest asset — people — live in perennial fear and guilt. You impair followers' capacity for truth, honesty, respect, kindness, excellence, independence and fairness.

Worse still, your followers will never blame you. When things turn sour, you and your followers will proclaim, "There's nothing wrong with the milk — it's your mouth."

In contrast, greatness involves you making time and expending resources to make your followers (including your children) better than when they first come into your life.

3. Do you subvert the structures of justice, transparency and excellence?

You treat with disdain any system and process that prevents you from consolidating your followers' power, aggrandizing themselves and accumulating their wealth. You promote incompetence and inefficiency by encouraging a patronage system. There is a growing propensity to conceal. You confide only in a trusted few.

Your greatest confidant is usually the finance person. You use money and reward to control your troops. Together, you do some creative accounting. This is where you reward those who "cooperate" with you. You also subvert the structures of fairness. Your performance management system tends to be driven by personal fancies than a transparent, equitable system.

In contrast, greatness involves you building structures and systems of transparency, good governance and fairness.

4. Do you use dishonest means to justify your ends?

In his book *The Battle for the Soul of Capitalism*, John C. Bogle, a 79-year-old Wall Street insider and Founder-CEO of The Vanguard Group, Inc., abhors the rampant cheating among his peers, and makes this astonishing remark, "I believe the barrel itself — the very structure that holds the apples — is bad."

He concludes that it is not just a handful of notorious companies like Enron and WorldCom that have overstated their profits. He notes that up to about 60 major corporations would have to restate their earnings as their stock market value equaled $3 trillion! That is "an enormous part of the giant barrel of corporate capitalism."

You become obsessed with the bottom line. You are driven primarily by economics. You will not hesitate to mislead by giving misinformation or by misdiagnosing issues and problems.

In contrast, greatness involves checking your motivations, ensuring your means are as right as your ends, and working for long-term benefits of the organization.

5. Do you treat shabbily those at the bottom of the heap?

One significant indicator of toxic leaders is how you treat those at the bottom of the totem pole in the organization. You usually see them as means to your own economic ends.

If you do treat the marginalized people 'well', is it part of a Public Relations "kiss-the-baby" type campaign to bolster your own image and strengthen your base of support? Then you have the veneer of compassion but it's all a show. In other words, you use people and press for your own selfish ends.

In contrast, greatness involves you lifting the dignity of your staff, no matter where they stand in your organization, respecting diversity and ensuring that the income gap between the highest paid individuals and the lowest paid individuals is fair and reasonable.

6. Do you only clone successors of your own kin and kind?

You seldom nurture your leaders, except your own kin or kind. You rather concentrate your resources on strengthening your base, building monuments for yourselves, and enriching yourselves rather than build up the organization through strong value-centered, competent leadership. You clone yourself.

You prefer building a totalitarian or dynastic regime. Often, you reward loyalists and hangers-on. Furthermore, the cost of overthrowing you is so much higher or more painful that it is better to keep you where you are.

In contrast, greatness involves finding the most values-based, highly competent, great team players and nurturing them to be better.

7. Do you behave 'god-like'?

You are unfortunately imbued with such powers by yourself, your followers and the system that you often think that you speak on behalf of 'god' and behave like god. Sometimes, your followers are even embarrassed because they find that you are unable to grasp the real issues, or act competently and effectively. But they seldom question you, like the emperor who wears no clothes.

The scary part is that you evoke 'divine or spiritual favor' for your inept behavior. You believe you are right. And when you are proven wrong, you blame others or the situation. You never admit your mistakes. Your enormous ego has limited your capacity for learning, except to maintain status quo.

In contrast, greatness involves staying humble, other-centered, acknowledging your humanity and developing a learning posture to make your staff and organization great.

I like the principles laid down by Mahatma Gandhi:

Let the first act of every morning be to make the following resolve for the day:

- I shall not fear anyone on Earth.
- I shall fear only God.
- I shall not bear ill will toward anyone.
- I shall not submit to injustice from anyone.
- I shall conquer untruth by truth. And in resisting untruth, I shall put up with all the suffering.

Go through this toxicity survey to measure your own toxicity and discover which areas you should improve.

How Toxic Are Your Leaders? Check if you are a toxic leader/ follower by asking yourself the following questions.	6 — Almost All the time 5 — Almost most of the time 4 — Often 3 — Only sometime 2 — Very few moments 1 — Almost not at all
1. Am I living in constant fear and guilt?	1 2 3 4 5 6
2. Am I worse off now than before?	1 2 3 4 5 6
3. Do I feel that the structures of justice, transparency and excellence are being subverted?	1 2 3 4 5 6
4. Do my leaders use dishonest and questionable means to justify their ends?	1 2 3 4 5 6
5. Do my leaders treat those at the bottom of the heap shabbily?	1 2 3 4 5 6
6. Do my leaders only nurture successors of their own kin and kind?	1 2 3 4 5 6
7. Do my leaders speak like 'gods' and behave like 'gods'?	1 2 3 4 5 6

7 — 20   Low Toxicity: You are in good stead. Correct some of your leaders' behaviors and provide feedback for change.

21 — 34   Medium Toxicity: You need to provide more checks and balances.

35 — 42   High Toxicity: You better fear for your life and for your organization.

Action Steps ▼

Chapter 10

LOVE YOUR ENEMIES
Reining in Rage

"Radical rage demands radical action.
My antidote for reining in rage is radical love:
Love your enemies."

Dr. John Ng

"The Bible tells us to love our neighbors, and also to love our enemies;
probably because generally they are the same people."

GK Chesterton

Rage is at its wildest in our world today. Every minute of every day, we hear and read of cyber bulling, domestic abuse, modern slavery, sexual exploitation, and other atrocities being committed across the globe.

How do you rein in rage that is:

- An emotional state triggered by hot buttons and uncontrollable Amygdala Hijack;
- Supplanted by suppressed bitterness, wilful revenge and unbridled hatred;
- Caused by distorted prejudices and ideologies; and
- Fueled by continual unrealized and unrealistic economic goals?

Radical rage demands radical action. My antidote for reining in rage is radical love: Love your enemies. This may sound absurd, I believe the key is LOVE. Allow me to share my vision and passion.

First, love begins with a fresh perspective of yourself

I never realized how fortunate I am to have been born in Singapore until I visited a rented dormitory in Chiang Rai, a city in Northern Thailand in 2001. It was there that I saw abject poverty, where 20 children were crammed into a small, dilapidated house. I saw the children eating plain rice and soup every day.

Because we were guests, we were invited to dinner one night and were given a plate of vegetables, which was most unappetizing to say the least. Out of politeness, we ate some. The picture of these kids sitting on the sandy floor stuck indelibly in my mind, reminding me of my own childhood days in Singapore, in a much less harsh environment, a past that I had conveniently forgotten.

The children lived there because it was the only way that they could be educated. The dormitory leader told us how he had started the dormitory.

They had come from the villages in the mountains to study at a government school built for the tribal kids in Chiang Rai, as it was difficult to get an education in the mountains. Many lived hundreds of kilometers away.

Although education at school was provided by the Thai Government, the school uniforms and shoes, and the cost for accommodation and food amounting to S$80 (US$65) per month for each child had to be catered for.

I remembered that year and for the next 10 years, my friends in the Eagles and I organized a gift collection for the home. We consolidated all the money we used to spend on one another at our annual Christmas party, to sponsor all 80 children that year.

My wife Alison has since organized trips to spend Christmas with them every year. My family sponsored five children and even helped some of them complete university education. It was a commitment we made.

What motivated me to do this?
I often imagine myself being born there.
I am always reminded that I could be one of the refugees living in Syria, or born as one of the displaced Rohingya people in Myanmar, or as a poverty-stricken child sold by their parents in Thailand, or a homeless flood victim in the Philippines or a poor farmer's boy eking out a living on the streets of Calcutta.

This perspective has made me see each individual in each ethnic tribe or class differently. It gives me a fresh perspective of myself. It helps me to love again. It moves me from being angry for what I do not have to taking concrete actions to make a difference in the lives of the less fortunate.

Second, love focuses on the half-full rather than the half-empty

Love has a grateful heart. In the past, I used to be a chronic complainer. I fell into a trap of being a whiner.

If I do not maintain a deep sense of gratitude, it is very easy to gripe and groan. I find that when I am grateful, I become less angry and it helps me to stop the rage in me.

I like the Chinese character 感 (*gan*), which means gratitude. Within the character are embedded the symbol of feeling, that of the heart (心, *xin*) and speech (口, *kou*). From the heart, I express my feelings. I learn not to take things for granted.

Truly, I find that life is best for those who are grateful and enjoying it, and difficult for those who constantly compare their lives to others. It is worst for those who are criticizing and cynical about it. Your own attitude defines your life.

So I have learnt to be grateful and to enjoy the little moments in life.

I am reminded of my 'haves' instead of focusing on my 'have-nots'. I am always challenged by the words of this poem.

Gratitude

Even though I clutch my blanket and growl when the alarm rings,
Thank you, God that I can hear.
There are many who are deaf.

Even though I keep my eyes closed against the morning light
as long as possible,
Thank you, God that I can see.
Many are blind.

Even though I huddle in my bed and put off rising,
Thank you, God that I have the strength to rise.
There are many who are bedridden.

Even though the first hour of my day is hectic,
When socks are lost,
Toast is burned and tempers are short,
My children are so loud,
Thank you, God, for my family.
There are many who are lonely.

Even though our breakfast table
Never looks like the pictures in magazines and
The menu is at times unbalanced,

Thank you, God, for the food we have.
There are many who are hungry.

Even though the routine of my job often is monotonous,
Thank you, God, for the opportunity to work.
There are many who have no job.

Even though I grumble and bemoan my fate from
day to day and wish my circumstances were not so modest,
Thank you, God, for life!

Third, love seeks to uplift the marginalized

I am committed to the poor. I encourage all my family and friends to embody a heart of gold, to learn to care for the less fortunate.

We make trips each year to the tribal region in Northern Thailand.
I have already shared what my oldest daughter, Meixi is doing to educate the poor in Thailand. My son Shun's heart or passion in music is to reach out to the educationally handicapped as he shares his own struggles with dyslexia and ADHD. My youngest daughter has developed the habit of thanking every member of the tech crew, the ushers, and the administrative personnel after each project she manages.

I try to live my life by treating each person with dignity. I have also made it a habit to greet and thank those around, whether a maid, a road sweeper, or an older lady cleaning the plates at our hawker store.

This poem by Emily Dickinson has been my mantra.

If I can stop one heart from breaking.
I shall not live in vain.
If I can ease one life the aching.
Or cool one pain,
Or help one fainting robin
Unto his nest again
I shall not live in vain.

I am also interested in changing perspectives at the macro level, in organizations and governments. My consulting work allows me to be in touch with the commercial realities and economic challenges facing businesses and organizations.

It is heartening for me to see real transformative work in so many organizations and sectors over these past years (www.meta.com.sg). I believe this can be done. And change has happened.

But, first, we must engage our clients in love, by building trust through believing in the potential of each person. We do this by engaging their hearts, by giving workers a voice, by inculcating disciplines of hard work and by encouraging them to find solutions to their problems in creative and practical ways.

In this way, we can help reduce rage in ourselves, in families, in companies and in our society.

Fourth, love means being willing to listen to and learn from different and opposing viewpoints

I know I am prejudiced. I have my own political inclinations. By now you will begin to see I do hold some strong convictions. I have my points of view, which I believe strongly in.

As I grow older, I struggle:

— Between compassion and conviction: How do I hold on to my convictions and be compassionate towards those who disagree with me?

— Between comfort and courage: How do I comfort those who have disappointed me and yet have the courage to confront their wrongdoings?

— Between discourse and directive communication: How do I allow discourse over issues and yet become directive when actions need to be taken?

— Between objectivity and subjectivity: How can I learn to be objective about issues with those whom I am subjectively biased towards?

So, for my own growth, I need to learn to be more open and less judgemental. I want to be exposed to different points of view.

In the past, I used to get my news from watching CNN. Then I also started to watch Fox News, which carries the same news but with a totally different perspective. Many times, I am left to wonder who is telling the truth.

Being aware of my own political inclinations and economic persuasions, I now tune into several other news channels like BBC, Singapore's Channel NewsAsia, and news channels from China and Russia to give me fresh, diverse perspectives on the same issues.

I also read a variety of online news from Singapore's The Straits Times, Malaysiakini, Asian Wall Street Journal, and International Herald Tribune. Whenever I travel to different cities, I catch up with different points of view by perusing their local newspapers.

I am an avid learner. Reading widely on different disciplines from medicine, arts, entertainment, sports, technology, politics, finance and business gives me a broader perspective on life. I enjoy watching well-researched documentaries of various subjects to help me better understand life. Recently, because of my consulting assignments in China, I have taken an interest in China's history, politics, culture, cities, etc., and watch documentaries on these subjects.

Finally, I am very inquisitive. I ask lots of questions. I love to interactive with different people from different strata of society, different age groups, different educational backgrounds, different cultures and ethnicities. In particular, I love to listen to the younger generations. They have much to share and I enjoy learning from them and hearing their many fresh and new ideas. You will be surprised how much they can tell you and how much you can learn from them!

Tuning into different perspectives and news sources has given me a deeper understanding of issues and helped me make better judgements.

Fifth, love means being able to address evil and stand up for good

This is for me one of the most difficult parts of love.

Love is not some wishy-washy, mushy feeling that is all about being kind and nice. The truth is that if good people don't deal with evil, evil will spread and dominate.

I want to challenge the distortions or the extremes. But I don't want to do so in an aggressive and confrontational manner. Instead, I seek to win the hearts of the people, to create dialogue and to sensitively address issues. I use David's Ausberger's carefronting method: Caring for the person but Confronting the issue.

I am always saddened and angry when I hear of atrocities around the world (whether they are in the US or in Syria), the ethnic-conflicts (whether they are in Myanmar or Ukraine), the abuses (whether they are in Mexico or Botswana), the killings (whether they are drone attacks or suicide bombers), or the human exploitations (whether they are sex slaves or work slaves).

I realize I can't save everybody and I can't do everything. So, I focus on what I can do well and do best. One of my strengths is in creating and connecting networks. I helped started and have dedicated myself as honorary Chair to the Eagles Leadership Institute, bringing the best speakers to continually motivate leaders to be better leaders, encouraging them to be value-based leaders, nurturing them with skills to strive to do their best and challenge conventional practices to impact businesses, communities, and governments.

Another key concern that I have is for marriages and families, as I have tried to articulate earlier in this book on what it means to be great. When I returned from my Ph.D. studies at Northwestern University in 1994, I launched EMCC (the Eagles Mediation and Counseling Centre) with a focus on providing holistic therapy and mediation services to individuals, couples and families. I had the distinct honor of being the Founder-Chairman of EMCC for 10 years. Two years ago, I stepped down and helped to develop a new set of Board members. Today, it is heartening to see that EMCC is a full-fledged, well-funded non-profit organization, providing niche services to our communities.

I also helped pioneer the mediation movement in Singapore because I have a strong belief in peace-making. Today, mediation has moved from ADR — Alternative Dispute Resolution, to a Primary Dispute Resolution (PDR) forum. Mediation has made inroads into almost every industry.

Sixth, love is learning the art of radically loving your enemies

I am reminded of the words of Mahatma Gandhi, whose instructions I admire but seldom practice: "It is easy enough to be friendly to one's friends. But to befriend the one who regards himself as your enemy is the quintessence of true religion. The other is mere business."

I aspire to the quintessence of my faith, and not merely seek mutually beneficial relationships. I am always chided by Jesus' saying: "If you love those who love you, what reward will you get? Are not the tax collectors doing that? And if you greet only your own people, what are you doing more than others?" I want to learn how to supplant insane rage with radical love for my enemies.

So, I want to learn to do the hardest thing in love: Love my enemies. I am haunted by the words of the great Martin Luther King, Jr. He has said it so brilliantly:

> Now there is a final reason I think that Jesus says, "Love your enemies." It is this: that love has within it a redemptive power. And there is a power there that eventually transforms individuals.
>
> Just keep being friendly to that person.
>
> Just keep loving them, and they can't stand it too long.
>
> Oh, they react in many ways in the beginning.
> They react with guilt feelings, and sometimes they'll hate you a little more at that transition period, but just keep loving them. And by the power of your love they will break down under the load.
>
> That's love, you see. It is redemptive, and this is why Jesus says love.
>
> There's something about love that builds up and is creative. There is something about hate that tears down and is destructive. So love your enemies.
>
> *Martin Luther King, "Loving Your Enemies", from A Knock at Midnight*

GK Chesterton's insight is profound: "The Bible tells us to love our neighbors, and also to love our enemies; probably because generally they are the same people." I can be a neighbor to some and an enemy to others. It is also true that I can be both a neighbor and an enemy at the same time. Sometime, I behave like an angel to my wife and children and yet at other times, I behave like a devil to them.

Let me relate a story how this is true and how we can learn to love.

In June 2017, my wife and I were vacationing in Chengdu, China with my youngest daughter, Meizhi, who had just graduated from NYU-Shanghai. We were staying in a hotel.

One late night, back at the hotel after a very exhausting day, we decided to order some drinks. Meizhi loves to order through delivery apps which will mean having food delivered from outside into the hotel. It was quite a common practice in China. My wife wanted a coffee and so my daughter ordered hot drinks for all of us.

She ordered some drinks from a particular vendor who promised the delivery to our hotel by 12.01am, but at 12.25am, the drink costing RMB35 (US$5) still had not arrived.

Being exhausted and wanting to retire for the night, she decided to cancel the order and get a refund. She called up the delivery guy, who refused because the drinks were already on the way and he did not have the authority to fulfill such a request. And she found out that he was going to need an additional 15 minutes to arrive, which would be 12.45 am! What use would those drinks be then? Finding the customer service hotline offline made Meizhi even more frustrated and angry.

Next, she called the coffee shop vendor to request for a refund instead.

After some time, the vendor explained: "I am just a small shop owner. To refund an order would have a large impact on my business and its delivery practices. I am sorry for what happened. I just called up the delivery guy and it is a young person. He will be there as soon as he can. In the meantime, instead of a full refund, let me compensate you RMB10 (US$1.45)."

Upon hearing that, Meizhi immediately felt bad for him as she was haggling over a small sum. When she refused the compensation, the vendor offered a full refund of RMB35, which made her feel even worse because it was only SGD7.

Not only that, the vendor and delivery person were not malicious but sincerely trying to make the best of the situation. The further irony of staying in a 5-star hotel and still making such a big fuss over RMB35 made her realize her unreasonable and obnoxious behavior. For a young kid to be delivering food at such an hour, surely it must represent a real need he had. Seen from that perspective, how could her own anger be justified?

Then the delivery person called. She picked up the drinks from the sullen-looking boy, who had probably been severely reprimanded by the vendor.

Over SMS, the vendor texted, "I am sorry for all the inconvenience. I am very grateful. I hope you will enjoy Chengdu. If you need any advice, I can recommend some places to visit. Once again, let me just reiterate how thankful I am for your empathy and tolerance."

Meizhi then texted the delivery person as well, "I am so sorry for what I said over the phone." The delivery person texted back, "No problem. Thank you for understanding my position."

From being enemies, they became neighbors again.

It is such a simple story. My daughter was first a neighbor to the vendor, whom she wanted to patronize to fulfill her needs but became his enemy because of poor service and mismatched expectations.

Neighbors became enemies.

The vendor, who started off as her neighbor by serving her gastronomical needs, became her enemy. But through apology and kindness, the rage and animosity turned into kindness and love. Enemies became neighbors again.

Therein lies the hope that I have for humanity. Just like Mezhi, if you and I can start recognizing that sometimes, our behaviors can be obnoxious and if we are willing to apologize for our reactions, doing one small act of careful listening to the other's points of view, one sincere apology, and one simple gesture of kindness, we can turn our enemies into neighbors again.

On the other hand, if we insist on being right, refuse to understand and feel the pain of the other person, spew out words of anger and act rashly in rage, we can turn our neighbors into enemies.

Seventh, love is being committed to peace making

I am convinced that unless you see yourself as both a neighbor and an enemy, you cannot be an effective peacemaker. Until we learn to see our enemy as our neighbor, it is very difficult to manage conflict and bring peace to our world.

This perspective has changed my life. It is to this end that I am dedicating the last phase of my life: Transformational Peace-Making.

Some years ago, I learnt about "Barefoot Doctors" in China (赤脚医生, *chijiao yisheng*) who worked in rural villages. They were farmers who had received minimal basic medical and paramedical training and promoted basic hygiene, preventive health care and family planning, and treated common illnesses.[xxvii] The name comes from southern farmers, who would often work barefoot in the rice paddies.

Their purpose was to bring primary health care services to rural areas and grass-root levels, where urban-trained doctors would not settle. They were given Chinese and Western medicine that they would dispense. They focused mainly on prevention rather than treatment. Often, they grew their own herbs in their own backyards, integrating both Western and Chinese medicine like acupuncture and moxibustion.

An important feature was that they were still involved in farm work, often spending as much as 50 percent of their time on this — which meant that the rural farmers perceived them as peers and respected their advice more. They were integrated into a system where they could refer seriously ill people to township and county hospitals.

The work of the barefoot doctors effectively reduced health care costs in China, and provided primary care treatment to the rural farming population. The World Health Organization regarded this as a "successful example of solving shortages or medical services in rural areas." Two-thirds of the village doctors currently practicing in rural China began their training as barefoot doctors.

[xxvii] Barefoot Doctors. Available at: https://en.wikipedia.org/wiki/Barefoot_doctor

I find this concept very fascinating and wonder if we can incorporate this model into peace-making. Although the barefoot doctor system was abolished in 1981 with the end of commune system of agricultural cooperatives, there's much we can learn from this.

I was trained as a mediator and I trained mediators. However, after many years of trying to promote this field to help resolve conflict, the result has not been very encouraging: Conflicts do not seem to have subsided, examples being that divorce rates and family disputes are still on the rise.

By the time many choose to go for mediation, they are reluctant to settle their conflicts amicably as is almost a lost cause. Relationships would have already soured severely. At most, mediation would seek to resolve issues but may still leave a bad taste in relational conciliation.

In Singapore, while there are more mediated cases, the result is still unsatisfactory despite the immense publicity, high investment in infrastructure such as the setting up of community mediation centers and the relatively lower cost involved compared to litigation or arbitration.

Conflicts rage at every level in the family and at work. It is my hope that more people can be trained in the art of conflict management so that the world will be a more peaceful place and that people will be less angry.

I want to take conflict management upstream and raise an army of Peace Making Conciliators, likened to the Barefoot Doctors, who are armed with the skills to manage conflict better and become a conflict conciliator in the family and workplace. My desire is to:

1. Provide grass roots training in basic conflict management skills.
2. Integrate both Western and Asian perspectives and approaches in conflict management.
3. Provide training on deescalating conflicts.
4. Diagnose conflict symptoms and refer more serious cases to specialist counselors, therapists, and mediators when needed.
5. Reduce the emotional pain, psychological trauma, and economical cost of marital breakdowns, family disputes and business conflicts.

6. Use Tutorial Relationship (see the table at the end of this chapter) as a pedagogical tool to create communities of conflict conciliators.

7. Nurture a community of grassroots people to become practitioners in effective conflict management and peacemaking in all areas of life.

This is my vision.

PEACE PACT Vision
Restoring Relationships

PEACE PACT Mission
Nurturing a practicing community of Peace Conciliators to manage conflict at grassroots levels.

PEACE PACT Values
Person-Orientation: Be other-centered and place value in the dignity of persons.

Example-Setting: Be honest about our own struggles and yet practice peace-loving behaviors.

Active-Listening: Learn to be impartial and appropriately employ paraphrasing, listening to positive voice, and summarizing skills.

Care-Fronting: Care for the person and confront the issues.

Encourage hope: Stay hopeful and help parties to recover from conflicts.

My daughter Meixi's Tutorial Relationship pedagogy has already been proven successful in Mexico and Thailand, and I want that to spread that conflict management movement and nurture a pool of peace conciliators. I have experimented on this in a few organizations using her pedagogy, to great success with positive results.

I hope you can pray for and support this effort to reduce rage and promote peace.

Finally, it is my desire that you join me to make love your way of life so that rage can be reduced and relationships can be restored again!

Mother Teresa is said to have had this poem hanging in her room. This has guided the way she lived. It is worth sharing with you. It has inspired and challenged me. I trust it will do the same for you.

Mother Teresa's 'Anyway' Poem

People are often unreasonable, illogical and self-centered. Forgive them anyway.

If you are kind, people may accuse you of selfish, ulterior motives. Be kind anyway.

If you are successful, you will win some false friends and some true enemies. Succeed anyway.

If you are honest and frank, people may cheat you. Be honest and frank anyway.

What you spend years building, someone could destroy overnight. Build anyway.

If you find serenity and happiness, they may be jealous. Be happy anyway.

The good you do today, people will often forget tomorrow. Do good anyway.

Give the world the best you have, and it may never be enough. Give the world the best you've got anyway.

You see, in the final analysis, it is between you and your God;

It was never between you and them anyway.

1. Why is it difficult for you to love your enemies? What is one step you can take to do that?

2. How much do you agree with G.K. Chesterton's statement, "The Bible tells us to love our neighbors, and also to love our enemies; probably because generally they are the same people"? How will this perspective change the way you treat people?

Action Steps

Tutorial Relationship

Interest *Broad area of interest [e.g. Conflict Management (Genre), Types of Conflict (Topic), Identifying Personal COSPI (Skill)]*
Objective: Tema Learning Target/s (Tema is a Spanish word, meaning theme or topic.) *Be as clear and specific as possible*
Launch: Choosing the Temas *Build personal relationships, introduce the Tema(s), guide learner to choose a Tema*
Experience: The Learning Experience for Mastery *Tutor: Determine own mastery* *Learner: Journey to demonstrate mastery* *This could include:* ■ *Questions to open deep dialogue: Have a toolbox of questions and activities to personalize learning, make connections to life, culture & family* ■ *Anticipate challenges to reach learning goals* ■ *Identify key areas for research and use of other expertise* ■ *Identify resources to be used (Collect materials or create bibliography of resources)*
Summary: Final product or outcome (Success Criteria) ■ *What are some of your big takeaways in one sentence/ paragraph? (E.g. understand the use of metaphors in a poem, creation of own poem to express emotion)* ■ *What are some areas you can identify for further research (or a spin-off Tema?)* ■ *How will I, and my tutee, know that they have met the learning target?* ■ *Think about what the learner could say, do and or write to meet the learning target.*

Reflection: Writing the Registry

Recording the learning process & the future tutoring process for both learner and tutor. Be as specific as possible.

Demonstration: Sharing the learning process with the community

Resource Used: Ng, John. *Smiling Tiger, Hidden Dragon: Managing Conflict @ Work and Home,* Armour Publishing Pte Ltd, 2012.

Part 4

HOW TO SUSTAIN YOUR GREATNESS
The Power of Self-Leadership
(What you must practice)

Chapter 1

WHY SELF-LEADERSHIP?
THE POWER OF PURPOSE

"Continual self-leadership is a mark of your maturation. Self-leadership is a never-ending work in progress that draws on continually maturing self-understanding."

Dr. John Ng

"Exceptional leaders distinguish themselves because of superior self-leadership."

Daniel Goleman

After reading all the factors that can derail greatness, you must be wondering, "Can I still achieve greatness?"

Yes, you can. But to achieve greatness, it must begin with YOU.

Greatness is a cultivated art. It begins with self-leadership. Because at the center of greatness, it is YOU who makes all the difference. Greatness begins with self-leadership.

Bill Hybels, a noted leader of one of the largest non-profit organizations in the world, points out, "The toughest management challenge is always yourself." Dee Hock, founder and CEO Emeritus of VISA, who has written about leadership for over 20 years and is a laureate in the US Business Hall of Fame, shares this wisdom, "We should invest 50 percent of our leadership amperage in self-leadership and the remaining 50 percent should be divided into leading down, leading up and leading laterally."

Chris Lowney, in his book *Heroic Leadership*, writes, "If you want your team to perform heroically, be a hero yourself."

Why Self-Leadership?

1. You are the Toughest Person to Lead

You are the only person you can manage. You choose the life you want to live. That's why you are the toughest person to lead. Your parents can guide you but you must want to be guided. Your teacher can teach but you must want to learn. Your managers can advise but you must be willing to accept their advice. Your friend can offer friendship but you must be willing to reciprocate. You choose what you say, feel, and do. Nobody can live your life.

2. You Prevent Derailment when you Develop Self-Awareness

Many hotshot rising stars self-destruct and never achieve their early potential because of the lack of self-leadership. Daniel Goleman, in his extensive study on leadership derailment, points out: "When I compared star performers with average ones in senior leadership positions, nearly 90 percent of the difference in their profiles was attributable to emotional intelligence factors rather than cognitive abilities."

In other words, they are derailed because they are not self-aware and do not practice self-care. They suffer from 'brownout' (feeling demotivated), burn out, and finally give up.

3. You Have Blind Spots

All of us have blind spots. To be great is to be constantly aware of our blind spots and derailment factors. You must be humble enough to admit your weaknesses and willing to receive feedback about your shortcomings. "Leaders thrive by understanding who they are and what they value, by becoming aware of unhealthy blind spots or weaknesses that can derail them, and by cultivating the habit of continuous self-reflection and learning," shares Chris Lowney, author of *Heroic Leadership*.

4. You Need to Cultivate Self-Care and Self-Reflection

Self-leadership involves self-care. You can be so driven and ambitious that you forget to rest, reflect and recharge. Like an over-stretched rubber band, you can suffer from health issues, become over-stressed, exhausted and experience burn-out. Self-leadership is an ongoing process of self-reflection.

As Lowney writes, "Self-awareness is not a one-time project. No less essential than the initial assessment of one's strengths, weaknesses, values, and world view is the ongoing, everyday habit of self-reflection, the examen. It's an opportunity to measure life — a little bit at a time — against principles and goals."

Taking strategic pauses and rest is part of self-care.

5. You Learn to Harness Your Disruptive Impulses

You and I have disruptive emotional impulses and character flaws. You need to work on discipline and habits to harness these negative forces and behaviors. It is easier said than done. Self-leadership is about working through the disciplines of reading, reflecting, recycling and recovery. These then become daily habits.

6. You Learn to Appreciate Others

When you truly know yourself, your strengths and weaknesses, you will appreciate others. Lowney points out that because leaders are anchored by an appreciation of their own dignity, they develop an appreciation of the aspirations, potential and dignity of others. This is the way they transform the way they look at others. If you cannot lead yourself, you cannot lead others.

7. You Focus on Being Great for the Long Haul

To achieve greatness, you have to take a long-term perspective for life and success. You are not here for the short-term but for the long haul. Only when you practice consistent self-leadership can you ensure long-term success. The temptation to push for immediate gains and short-term successes at all costs can derail you. Unless you have a keen eye on self-leadership, you cannot stay focused on that which defines greatness.

Recall the 10 aspects of greatness:

1. Greatness is Nurturing Character
2. Greatness is Enjoying Healthier Family Life
3. Greatness is Becoming Your Best Through Values and Results
4. Greatness is Developing People
5. Greatness is Developing Successors and Successful Systems
6. Greatness is Recovering from Failures
7. Greatness is Being Humble
8. Greatness is Nurturing Friendships
9. Greatness is Leaving a Legacy of Great Values
10. Greatness is Caring for the Community and the Environment

Finally, continual self-leadership is a mark of your maturation. Self-leadership is a never-ending work in progress that draws on continually maturing self-understanding. Some people never mature — they remain insecure, self-defeating, juvenile or worse still, delinquent in their emotional development.

All leaders leave legacies, whether good or bad. You decide now what imprint you want to leave behind for your family, children and the organization. Hence, effective self-leadership is essentially about leaving a great legacy for the people we are leading.

Self-leadership is imperative if you want to be a great leader.

1. What other reasons can you give to underscore the importance of self-leadership?

2. Why do you think most people lack self-leadership?

Action Steps

Chapter 2

WHAT IS SELF-LEADERSHIP?
THE POWER OF SELF-AWARENESS

"Everyone has a dark side: PFT. Potential Failure
Tendency."

Dr. John Ng

"People can only perform from strength.
One cannot build performance on weakness,
let alone on something one cannot do at all."

Peter Drucker

There are four aspects to self-leadership.

1. Self-awareness: The ability to acknowledge, understand and be conscious of one's own values, perspectives, strengths, weaknesses, leadership propensity and emotional needs.

2. Self-management: The ability to nurture and harness one's own passion, abilities, emotions and leadership capacity in decision-making.

3. Other-awareness: The ability to acknowledge and recognize the passion, gifting, strengths, weaknesses, potential and needs of others.

4. Other-management: The ability to grow and motivate other people to develop their potential and/or fulfill the organization's objectives.

Great leaders begin with self-awareness and move to self-management, then proceed to other-awareness culminating in other-management. It is not a linear but an interactive effect among all four factors.

Some leaders are conscious of themselves, their personalities, idiosyncrasies, motivations, and competencies, but they cannot manage themselves, especially their emotions and weaknesses. They lack self-control, lose their cool, become unusually critical, behave inappropriately, want to do everything, and are unable to keep their pride in check.

Let's begin with self-awareness.

Self-leadership involves self-awareness, self-management, other-awareness and other-management. The first step in self-leadership is self-awareness. What are the areas in your life you must be aware of?

1. Awareness of Your World Views and Values

The following are fundamental questions that you need to ask yourself because everyone operates from a particular world view that directs his/her way of thoughts, feelings and behaviors.

- What is your perspective of life?
- From where do you get your frame of reference in decision-making?
- How do you view the world and its people?
- What do you count as important?
- Why are some values more important than others?

If you have a mechanistic view of the world, you will perceive and relate to people functionally. They then become objects to be used to achieve your end. Just as one asks for permission to sit on a chair, you will treat them as objects to do what they are told. You will discard them when they outlive their usefulness.

On the other hand, if you have a more organic perspective of life, then you will relate to people as living human beings, with feelings, pains and dreams. You care for them as people. You respect them as fellow human beings.

2. Awareness of Your Strengths and Weaknesses

Strengths are your assets. Underdeveloped strengths are a huge potential loss, something a company can ill-afford. Peter Drucker opines, "We will have to learn to develop ourselves. We will have to place ourselves where we can make the greatest contribution. Most people think they know what they are good at. They are usually wrong. More often, people know what they are not good at. People can only perform from strength. One cannot build performance on weakness, let alone on something one cannot do at all."

You need to know what are your strengths and what are your weaknesses, what you can do and what you are not so good at doing. You spend time building on your strengths and managing around your weaknesses, and identifying people to compensate for your weaknesses.

I cannot agree with Peter Drucker more when he writes: "Discover where your intellectual arrogance is causing disabling ignorance and overcome it. First-rate engineers pride themselves in not knowing anything about people. Taking pride in such ignorance is self- defeating."

Only people who know their weaknesses can prevent themselves from being derailed. "Only those who know their weaknesses can deal with them or even hope to conquer them. Executives with careers stalled by poor self-confidence can resume an upward trajectory only by identifying and attacking their weaknesses," adds Drucker.

Chris Lowney puts it this way: "To order oneself is to take stock of one's weakness ("disordered affections"). Sometimes it involves the painful process of dragging one's weakness into the full light of day...Understanding them is the first empowering strike toward conquering them. Alcoholics Anonymous calls this, 'fearless moral inventory.'"

The problem with some leaders is that we neglect our weaknesses, and allow them to grow and destroy our lives. If we fail here, it is likely that we may be derailed.

3. Awareness of Your Potential Failure Tendency

Everyone has a dark side, Potential Failure Tendency (PFT). Left unchecked, this will become our undoing. Some of us have egos that are easily inflated, leading to pride and vanity. Others struggle with money and materialism: these have a stranglehold over their lives and they will do anything to strive after them.

Yet some others are corrupted by power and position: they relish their power, they guard against losing power and they abuse their power for self- gain. Still others struggle with deep sexual desires and fall into temptation easily. Every human being is like the moon; there is a dark side.

4. Awareness of Your Emotional Make-Up and Emotional Needs

Emotion seems to be a taboo word for some people. You don't want to be too emotional. You suppress your own emotions. But the reality is that you and I are emotional beings and have emotional needs. You feel pain. You can be lonely. You can become jealous. You feel anger. How well do you know your emotional make-up?

— Are you easily offended?

— Do you feel jealous easily?

— Are you a caring person?

— Do you feel compassion for the poor and disenfranchised?

— Do you lose your cool and get angry easily?

— Do you yearn for affirmation?

You also need affirmation and yearn for companionship. You tend to live as though you are functional professionals and put up fronts of "invulnerability". You tend to ignore your emotional insecurities and are not willing to acknowledge your own vulnerabilities.

5. Awareness of Your Personality Traits, Leadership Styles and Communication Habits

Finally, we need to know our personality types. A good place to start is the Myers-Briggs Type Indicator (MBTI). It tells you what energizes you and how you make decisions.

You need to be conscious of your own leadership styles: Authoritative, Coercive, Democratic, Affiliative, Pace-setting or Coaching. There is no perfect style. You have to adapt your styles when working with different people in different situations. Your children will need to be parented by different styles when they grow from children to teenagers to adults.

You must also know your communication styles. Some of us are too direct, others take a more indirect approach. Some of us don't listen very well or jump to conclusions quickly.

How well you know your personality type, leadership and communication style is an important factor in achieving greatness.

6. Awareness of Your Good and Bad Habits

You have good and bad habits. Some of the good habits you may have:

— You are generous and hospitable.

— You are thankful and grateful.

— You are compassionate and caring.

— You are helpful and kind.

You may have bad habits, like:

— You borrow and seldom return.

— You expect others to pay for your meals.

— You change your mind frequently, without any explanation, and expect others to follow your bidding.

— You are very direct and offend others with curt words and actions.

Self-awareness is the first essential step in self-leadership. If we do this well, then we can talk about self-management.

Do this survey to discover how self-aware you are.

Self-Awareness Reflection: How self-aware are you? Work on the areas that you are not as self-aware in.

On a scale of 1 to 6, rate how you fare on each item.

1 – Almost always not aware.
2 – Usually not so aware
3 – Somewhat not aware
4 – Somewhat aware
5 – Usually aware
6 – Almost always aware

1. Awareness of your world views & values	1 2 3 4 5 6
2. Awareness of your strengths and weaknesses	1 2 3 4 5 6
3. Awareness of your personal failure tendency	1 2 3 4 5 6
4. Awareness of your emotional make up and emotional needs	1 2 3 4 5 6
5. Awareness of your personality traits	1 2 3 4 5 6
6. Awareness of your leadership styles	1 2 3 4 5 6
7. Awareness of your communication styles	1 2 3 4 5 6
8. Awareness of your good habits	1 2 3 4 5 6
9. Awareness of your bad habits	1 2 3 4 5 6

Action Steps ▼

Chapter 3

HOW TO MANAGE YOURSELF?
The Power of Self-Management

"You have to make 'No' choices – choosing carefully
what you do and having the courage and humility to
say "no" graciously."

Dr. John Ng

*"Only those with a deeply ingrained capacity for continuous learning
and self-reflection stand a chance of surfing the waves of change successfully."*

Chris Lowney

Self-management is our ability to nurture and harness our own passion, abilities, emotions and leadership capacity in decision-making. Author and psychologist Daniel Goleman describes it as self-regulation: "the ability to control or redirect disruptive impulses and moods; the propensity to suspend judgment — to think before acting."

It is not enough to know yourself. The next aspect of self-leadership is self-management. What are the areas you need to self-manage? Here are my 10 suggestions.

1. Managing your "over-stressed" level — this will keep you from burning out

Leaders have different over-stressed levels. It is not enough to recognize the signs of over-stress or negative stress (e.g., forgetfulness, chronic fatigue, napping intermittently at meetings, tension headaches, withdrawal from relationships or increased mood swings). You have to manage the stress. Failure to manage stress levels will result in our inability to last the long haul, resulting in burnout and depression. Effective self-care is part of self-leadership.

2. Managing your "hot buttons" — this will keep you from overreacting

Everyone has "hot buttons" – words, issues and situations that irritate you irascibly. One of my hot buttons is when I am in a conflict with my kids and they sarcastically remark: "John… You call yourself a conflict expert!" That would make me hot under the collar. You need to know what makes you mad. Understanding and managing these "hot buttons" will prepare you to avoid overreacting and allow you to confront your "hot buttons" appropriately.

3. Managing your addictions — this will keep you from derailment

Richard Leider, an international speaker, writes: "We must recognize our addictions to discover if we are being true to our essence or living in a self-imposed prison, driven by others' or our organization's expectations. Leaders who feel like victims are often perfectionists, idealists or workaholics who can never truly please themselves." How true!

Unmanaged addictions (brandaholics – addiction to brand-names, workaholics – addiction to work, sexaholics – addiction to anything sexy, or alcoholics – addiction to alcohol) can eventually derail you.

4. Managing your talents and competencies — this will keep you effective

Great people take time to reinvent themselves. You need to take inventory of your talents and competencies to see if you are growing. You have to keep learning and growing. You have to deliberately practice and develop your talent.

A good question to ask yourself is: "How much time do I spend doing what I naturally love?" Sometimes, you need to reinvent yourself by challenging yourself to take risks, experiment with new challenges and get out of your comfort zone.

5. Managing your compassion — this will keep you grounded

One of the best learning experiences for me is to get involved in community work. It has a way of reminding me of life's cruel realities and people who are disenfranchised. It helps me to reexamine my values, what's important, what I often take for granted, and what it means to be human. It makes me more compassionate and generous as a leader.

6. Managing your leadership community — this will ensure you're kept accountable

You must make yourself accountable to a personal board of leaders. It is very easy to get sidetracked, become disillusioned and yield to tempting unethical offers, unless you have a solid support system that will carry you through the vagaries of change. Find a group of people whose wisdom and personal counsel you value to help you through your personal life, work and leadership. Build a relationship with them. Consult them regularly.

7. Managing your commitments — this will keep you focused

One of the biggest challenges I face is over-commitment. Learning to say "no" is often difficult, especially in our Asian culture. You feel obligated, you want to "give face" to people. You have to make "No" choices – choosing carefully what you do and having the courage and humility to say "no" graciously.

Someone once said, "Beware of a full diary, but an empty soul."

8. Managing your intentions and motives — this will keep you honest

Why do we do what we do? It is often unclear. We do have mixed motives. But usually, there is a dominant intention. We have to be honest with ourselves as we examine our intentions. As Richard Leider, author of the *Power of Purpose* writes, "We must live with clear intention and make consistent contact with a higher power greater than ourselves."

Remember, motives and intentions are hidden and can be deceiving. This cuts deep into our integrity — it means doing the right things for the right reasons. Leadership integrity is built or destroyed by those little day-to-day decisions and actions. How and why we decide and act reveal who we are.

9. Managing your weaknesses — this will keep you humble

An over-utilized strength will become a weakness. Chris Lowney writes poignantly: "Executives with careers stalled by poor self- confidence can resume an upward trajectory only by identifying and attacking their weaknesses... Their careers are often derailed because they never understand and therefore can never address their weaknesses."

10. Managing your future — this will help you leave a legacy of greatness

Not only do we need to figure what we do, we must figure out first what we want to be. Leider writes again, "Working from a clear sense of personal purpose creates success with fulfillment."

Another important question to constantly ask yourself is "What do I want my family, employees and friends to remember me by?" This legacy will help you figure out what you should do now that will contribute to building a lasting legacy.

Self-Management Assessment

Please rate yourself honestly. On a scale of 1 — 6, (1 — Almost Never Able, 2 — Mostly Never Able, 3 — Sometimes Not Able, 4 — Sometime Able, 5 — Able Most of the Time and 6 — Able Almost All the Time)

How well do I manage myself?	How often?
I am able to manage my stress level well to keep myself from burning out.	1 2 3 4 5 6
I am able to manage my "hot buttons" to keep myself from over-reacting.	1 2 3 4 5 6
I am able to manage my personal indulgences to keep me from derailment.	1 2 3 4 5 6
I am able to develop my talents and competencies to be more effective.	1 2 3 4 5 6
I am able to manage my compassion to keep me grounded.	1 2 3 4 5 6
I am able to nurture my leadership community to keep me accountable.	1 2 3 4 5 6
I am able to manage my commitments to stay focused.	1 2 3 4 5 6
I am able to manage my intentions and motives to stay honest.	1 2 3 4 5 6
I am able to manage my personal strengths and weaknesses to stay humble.	1 2 3 4 5 6
I am able to focus on my future to leave a legacy of greatness	1 2 3 4 5 6

Action Steps ▼

Chapter 4

HOW TO HARNESS
YOUR ENERGY
THE POWER OF FLOW

"You must take personal charge of your Flow by
managing your energy sources. It comes down to
personal self-leadership, attitude and responsibility."

Dr. John Ng

"It is energy management, not time management that we need."

Tony Schwartz

Ask any Singaporean how he/she is and inevitably, the response would be "Very busy!" They might add, "Very tired!" Sounds familiar? This is true among urban workers around the world.

The new mantra of many high-achieving organizations is CBF (Cheaper, Better, Faster), which has added to the stress of today's workers. This is because organizations are looking for ways to increase productivity as well as cut costs and reduce headcount.

Professors Tony Schwartz and Catherine McCarthy at Harvard University conclude:

> Organizations are demanding ever-higher performance from their workforces. People are trying to comply, but the usual method — putting in longer hours — has backfired. They're getting exhausted, disengaged and sick.

I used to think that the key to effectiveness is time management. But I have come to conclude that the key is truly *energy* management. How should you manage yourself in such way that you will not burn out?

If you do not manage your energy well, you will face declining levels of engagement in whatever you do. You will get easily exhausted, you will have difficulty relating to people and soon, you will lose the passion to become great.

What is Energy Management?

Schwartz and McCarthy suggest that there are four types of energy that have to be managed: physical, emotional, mental and spiritual energy. They postulate that time is a finite resource, but energy comes from these four main wellsprings in human beings: the body, the emotions, the mind and the spirit. I have added a fifth type, social energy. Energy, unlike time, is renewable, controllable and expandable.

1. **Physical energy** is your ability to get sufficient sleep, good nutrition, proper exercise and enough rest. Not getting enough of these is associated with poor health and physical fatigue. This is the most

fundamental of all. It has a direct effect on our ability to perceive our surroundings, manage our emotions, relate better with people and make sound decisions.

2. **Emotional energy** is your ability to manage your emotional responses appropriately in troubling situations and with difficult people. The key is appreciating your emotional source based on your personality type, and to understand the functions of your brain.

3. **Mental energy** is your ability to focus and not be distracted, to consider options carefully, be creative and make good decisions consistently. A mentally strong person can perform well even under highly stressful situations.

4. **Social energy** is your ability to relate to and work alongside other people, and how you manage interpersonal relationships. Inability to manage relationship conflicts can deplete our social energy.

5. **Spiritual energy** is your ability to discover meaning and purpose in what you do. This can be derived from meaningful engagement with community outside your normal work routine as well as seeking ways to connect with the Divine through solitude, reflection, religious activities and meditation.

MANAGING ENERGY

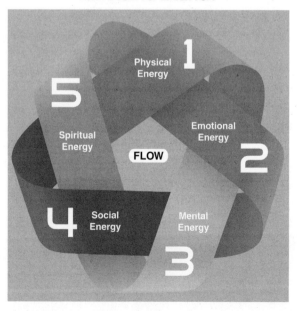

Put simply, you need to focus on investing more in sources of energy so you are energized and motivated. When you are self- energized, you bring more of yourselves to work and to family every day, and are more able and willing to put in all the required effort at work.

FLOW: The Goal of Energy Management

I postulate that the goal of energy management is what psychologist Mihaly Csikszentmihalyi (pronounced 'chick-sent-me-high', as he likes to tell his audience) calls *Flow*. To him, *Flow* is the feeling of optimal experience. It is the feeling that comes when researchers experience a breakthrough in their experiments, when engineers find the solution to a protracted problem, when speakers sense the energy of the crowd during a climax or when leaders evoke enthusiastic responses from their staff at their annual conference. A violinist might feel it while mastering an intricate piece, or a social worker when counseling individuals with personal or relational difficulties.

But *Flow* does not happen only in favorable outcomes. It is also seen in some cancer patients, who experience a deep sense of peace as they recognize that they are going to a far better place. It can come from engaging in simple events such as hearing the song of a bird in the forest.

As Csikszentmihalyi writes:

> For each person, there are thousands of opportunities, challenges to expand ourselves ... the best moments usually occur when a person's body or mind is stretched to its limits in a voluntary effort to accomplish something difficult and worthwhile.

I believe *Flow* is not only the source of fresh, renewed energy and creativity, but also the result of energy well-managed. This concept is not merely theoretical because over the years, *Flow* has been used in practical situations including therapy, rehabilitation and museum exhibit design.

In summary, *Flow* is indeed possible in everyday life. You can experience it in diverse situations — in triumphs, breakthroughs, serenity, ordinariness and even simple delight in the mundane and routine.

Flow is something you can create for yourselves, as the guru Csikszentmihalyi has written. You must take personal charge of your *Flow* by managing your energy sources. It comes down to personal self-leadership, attitude and responsibility.

Flow is the result of different aspects of life working together to manage energy. To find *Flow* more consistently and use it to your advantage, you have to manage your energy well. As Csikszentmihalyi says, "Optimal experience is something that we make happen."

You can make it happen by managing your energy.

1. Why do you think energy management is more important than time management? How have you experienced this to be true?

2. Can you recall a time when you have found *Flow* in your life? When was it and how does it make you feel?

Action Steps

Chapter 4a

HOW DO YOU HARNESS YOUR PHYSICAL ENERGY?
THE POWER OF SLEEP

"If you do not harness your sleep well, the other sources of energy simply fall apart."

Dr. John Ng

"Sleep is the chain that ties health and our bodies together."

Griff Niblack

The first and most fundamental energy source is our physical energy. Physical energy is derived from sleep, nutrition, exercise and rest. Without managing this well, all other sources of energy don't work. Over the years, I have encouraged many of my audience members and readers to focus on maintaining good physical energy. The most important aspect is sleep. This is the area I would like to focus on in this section.

Ample research from notable institutions like Harvard University has shown that most adults need seven to nine hours of sleep per night to function optimally. But, unfortunately, working adults between 30 and 64 years old received less than six hours of sleep on average within a 24-hour period! If you have less than seven hours, you may behave like and have the mental capacity of a drunk driver.

Some interesting statistics: Singapore is among the cities in the world with the least hours of sleep, clocking an average of 6 hours and 32 minutes a day. At the bottom of the list is Tokyo, where people sleep for just 5 hours and 46 minutes per night on average. South Korea comes close at 5 hours and 55 minutes.

Who sleeps the most? People in Melbourne, with an average of 7 hours and 5 minutes per night, followed by London at 7 hours and 2 minutes. These are the findings from Jawbone, the maker of UP, a digitized wristband that tracks how its users move and sleep[1].

Insufficient sleep and rest deplete your energy, so it is important that you learn to sleep well. Some people do well with 'power naps' — short periods of sleep lasting about 15 to 25 minutes at certain points in the work day. "There is more refreshment and stimulation in a nap, even of the briefest, than in all the alcohol ever distilled." says journalist Edward Lucas.

Modern research (collated at www.WebMD.com) has shown that lack of sleep can:

- **Cause accidents.** Sleep apnea and fatigue contribute to more than 100,000 police-reported highway crashes, causing 71,000 injuries and

1,500 deaths in the US alone. The problem is greatest among those who are 25 years and younger. Accidents and injuries on the job also become more frequent.

- **Dumb you down.** It impairs alertness, concentration, reasoning, learning and problem-solving. Memory also suffers due to the lack of deep sleep. Brain events called 'sharp wave ripples' are responsible for consolidating memory by transferring learnt information from the hippocampus to the neocortex of the brain, where long-term memories are stored. Sharp wave ripples occur mostly during the deepest levels of sleep.

- **Lead to serious health problems.** Sleep disorders and chronic sleep loss can put you at risk of heart attacks, heart failures and general problems, like high blood pressure, strokes and diabetes.

- **Kill sex drive.** Sleep deprived men and women have reported lower libidos and less interest in sex. This results in depleted energy, sleepiness and increased tension, which seem to cause the lack in sex drive.

- **Contribute to depression.** In a 2005 *Sleep in America* poll, depressed or anxious people are more likely to sleep less than six hours a night. Insomnia has the strongest link to depression. Sleep loss aggravates symptoms of depression, and depression can make it more difficult to fall asleep. On the positive side, treating sleep problems can help depression and its symptoms, and vice versa.

- **Age the skin.** Most people experience sallow skin and puffy eyes after a few nights of missed sleep. Chronic sleep loss leads to lackluster skin, fine lines and dark circles under the eyes.

- **Cause you to gain weight.** Lack of sleep is related to an increase in hunger and appetite, and possibly to obesity. People with less than six hours' sleep a day are 30 percent more likely to become obese than those who sleep seven to nine hours.

- **Increase risk of death at a younger age.** In the Whitehall II Study, British researchers analyzed how sleep patterns affected the mortality of more than 10,000 British civil servants over two decades. The results showed that those who cut their sleep from seven to five hours or less a night doubled their risk of death from all causes, particularly cardiovascular disease.

Sadly, sleep-deprived people are more prone to poor judgment when assessing what lack of sleep is doing to them. To some people, functioning on less sleep has become a kind of badge of honor! If you think you can do fine on only a little sleep, you are probably wrong.

I have spent much time and space discussing this aspect because managing your lifestyle goes a long way in managing your energy. If you do not harness this well, the other sources of energy simply fall apart.

Some final tips, which I have practiced and which will help you manage your physical energy better are as follows:

1. **Have at least seven hours of sleep.** You will begin to feel the difference in your mood, your energy levels and passion when you have enough sleep. Over the past three years, my average sleep time has been 7 hours and 30 minutes. When there are periods where I have less sleep, I catch up within the next two weeks. If not, our cells die and are not replenished. Deep sleep is the period when your cells are replenished.

2. **Sleep in complete darkness.** Darkness causes the body to produce more melatonin. This is why most hotels today have 'black-out' curtains to help you sleep better. Melatonin is a naturally occurring hormone mainly produced in your brain. After it is produced, it is released into your blood stream and it causes you to feel drowsy and lowers your body temperature.

   Melatonin is produced to regulate your sleep and wake cycles. That's why some people buy melatonin when traveling across time zones to help them sleep. But you don't have to do that if you can sleep in complete darkness.

   Over the years, I have learnt to carry eye-shades with me wherever I travel. Putting on the eye-shade helps me sleep faster and better.

3. **Wake up at the right time.** Over the last four years, I have invested in a smartphone application (app), 'Sleep Cycle', which wakes me up at the right time. (There are many similar apps you can download).

The right time means when you are REM (Rapid Eye Motion or Dream State, where you toss and turn) or when you are awake. To wake you up at the wrong time is when you are in deep sleep. You will feel more tired if you wake up at the wrong time. An alarm clock wakes you up at exactly the time you want (which maybe when you are in your deep sleep), while apps like 'Sleep Cycle' wake you at the REM state, making you feel more refreshed.

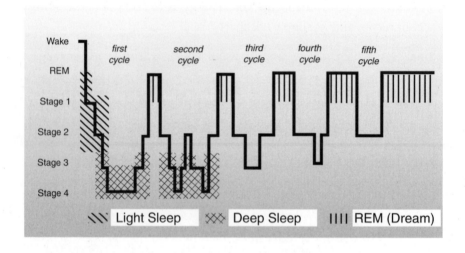

4. **Sleep First, Work Later.** This has been very good for me. Tired minds don't plan well. Sleeping first and planning later helps you become more productive. I wish I had known this earlier on in my life. I used to push myself unnecessarily hard to plan or get a report done, when I would be so tired. Usually, I missed out important considerations or was not sharp in my analysis. Journalist Camille Peri is right in saying that "Lack of sleep ... impairs attention, alertness, concentration, reasoning, and problem solving."

Now, I sleep first and wait up refreshed. My thoughts flow better and my ideas come quicker. My analysis is sharper and my quality of work improves greatly. All because of a good sleep and waking up at the right time. What used to take me three hours to complete now only takes me 30 minutes. What a time saver! John Steinbeck, an American author, correctly observed that "It is a common experience that a problem difficult at night is resolved in the morning after the committee of sleep has worked on it."

Other good practices like good nutrition and adequate exercise also help to sustain your physical energy. I am sure you can find many books and write-ups on the internet to help you. I have spent considerable time talking about sleep because it is so fundamental but is most often neglected.

Good sleep is a gift. Treasure it and be renewed by it. Remember, as Dr. Rafael Pelayo, a sleep specialist at the Stanford Center for Sleep Sciences and Medicine, writes, "Your life is a reflection of how you sleep, and how you sleep is a reflection of your life."

I agree with Kevin Cashman, global thought leader and CEO coach, that "Sleep is an amazing, natural capability for transformation, if we want to reach peak levels of performance. We abused this inherent gift with overwork, increased stress and too much stimulation."

Sufficient sleep and peaceful rest can help you achieve greatness and peak performance.

1. How much sleep do you get on the average? How has sufficient sleep helped you manage your physical energy better?

2. Which of the four tips mentioned have been the most helpful to you? Why?

Action Steps

Chapter 4b

HOW DO YOU HARNESS
YOUR EMOTIONAL ENERGY?
THE POWER OF CONTROL

"When you feel the loss of passion and motivation,
find your energy-energizers and you will feel
rejuvenated, refreshed and recharged."

Dr. John Ng

"You don't have too much emotional energy each day.
Don't fight battles that don't matter."

Joel Oesteen

Emotional energy is our ability to manage our responses appropriately in troubling situations and with difficult people. The three main approaches to managing your emotional energy are understanding your personality type, recognizing what your energy energizers are and appreciating the functions of your brain.

1. Understand your Personality Type — Recognize your Energy Source

How can emotional energy be maintained? It helps to know where that energy comes from, and the best place to begin is to *know your personality type.*

Different personalities have different energy sources. I am an extrovert. My focus is on the outer world rather than my own inner world. I get my energy from people and external situations. Sometimes, my colleagues cannot understand why even after a long meeting, I like to go out and meet up with my friends. They are already exhausted after a full day of meetings.

"Aren't you tired?" they ask. Spending time and going out with my friends energizes me! Furthermore, I enjoy the interactions and get many of my ideas by discussing and brainstorming with other people.

On the other hand, introverts get energy from their inner world. After a long, exhausting day, an introverted person would prefer to go home and spend time alone, perhaps watching television, or reading a book or newspaper. I like to say, "The computer is the introvert's best friend."

My wife, Alison, is an introvert. To recharge her emotional energy, she needs time out to be alone or with a few close friends. She also gets much of her ideas and energy by focusing on her inner world, and needs more time to process her thoughts before communicating publicly.

It is important to know your personality type and what energizes you, and that is a key part of energy management.

2. Find your Energy-energizers — Recharge your Passion

You must know what energizes you emotionally. It could be gardening, watching a good movie, reading a book, meditation, yoga, or discussing new ideas with close friends. For others, it may involve shopping, or having high tea with some friends. Whatever it is, know your energy-energizers. When you feel the loss of passion and motivation, find your energy-energizers and you will feel rejuvenated, refreshed and recharged.

For me, watching a good soccer match involving Manchester United energizes me, especially when they win. I also enjoy reading as it helps me reenergize myself.

3. Change your Attitude — Reframe Life's Successes and Failures

Having the right attitude to life is important. It is not success or failure that will deplete your energy; it is your response to them. If success makes you arrogant, it will sour the interaction and the relationship.

However, if you begin to attribute success to others as well as yourselves, you learn to honor others and become more grateful. People in turn will appreciate you more. This can become a great emotional energy-energizer.

Similarly, how you deal with failures is important. If failure demoralizes you and destroys your self-esteem and you do not recover, then it will deplete your emotional energy. But if you can learn from your failures, recover from them and move on, you become more effective. A positive attitude to life is critical to maintaining emotional energy.

4. Manage the Amygdala Hijack — Recalibrate your Anger and Fear

One of the most important findings about your brain is the Amygdala Hijack. The Amygdala is an almond-shaped mass of gray matter inside each cerebral hemisphere, and is involved with the experiencing of emotions.

It is also the most primitive part of the brain, which triggers the 'Flight/Fight/ Freeze /Faint' reactions when confronted with a threat, whether mental or physical. For example, when you are being surrounded by a hive of bees, your immediate reaction may be to fight. When a fire breaks out, you flee. Or when you come face to face with a robber, you might freeze or faint. This is called the Amygdala Hijack.

What is important to know in these encounters, is that you react in nano-seconds and the Amygdala hijacks the normal pre-frontal context functions of planning, prioritizing, impulse control and awareness of the consequences of our actions.

So, in human interactions, when you are angry or frightened (like when a teenager is reprimanded incessantly by the angry parent), both parties lose control and words/actions become irrational, resulting in completely 'fight' or 'fight' reactions.

Also, you must choose your battle. Don't sweat the small stuff because you must remember, as Joel Oesteen, pastor and author, writes, that "You don't have too much emotional energy each day. Don't fight battles that don't matter."

That's where we lose our emotional control.

It has been found that when our heartbeat goes beyond 100, Amygdala Hijack takes place. As such, I have proposed the G.R.O.W. model to deal with such situations.

G.R.O.W: Turn Conflict into Opportunity

Step One — Go to the balcony. When you are caught in such situations, your heart rate rises beyond 100. You can even feel heat going through your body. Your blood pressure rises. You have to get out of the situation, mentally or physically if you can. That's where you can practice your slow breathing technique to bring down your heart rate. You have to do it for 20 minutes.

Step Two — Reframe your self-talk. The second step you can take is to reframe your self-talk. You can't do that unless you have slowed down your heart beat. This rationalizing self-talk can only take place when you have cooled down. Then, ask yourselves these three questions.

a.   What am I really fighting about? In our anger, we lose control, becoming so emotional that we forget what the issues are.

b. Why am I so angry? Usually, we are angry when we feel disrespected, distant, or disadvantaged. That's why you need to understand why you are so angry.

c. What is one thing I can do to respond differently? To turn the situation around, you have to respond differently. You have to de-escalate the conflict.

Step 3 — Own the problem and get help. It takes two hands to clap. The conflict will not escalate if one party refuses to contribute to it or add fire to the fuel. Taking ownership of your action and reaction is a good way to diffuse the situation. If you can't do it, get help from your spouse, your children or your colleagues.

Step 4 — Wait for a better time. Timing is very important. If you fight when you are tired, in an emotional rage, or when you are exhausted, it is not a good time. You have to choose a time when there are two cool heads to discuss the issues rationally.

All these four steps take time to practice. They do not come naturally. These skills have to be honed.

When you are able to control your energy source by recognizing your personality, knowing your energy-energizers, changing your attitude towards life and recognizing the Amygdala Hijack, you are on the way to greatness through managing your emotional energy.

1. Which aspect of emotional energy resonates with you the most? Why?

2. How can you practice the G.R.O.W. model in managing your Amygdala Hijack?

Action Steps

Chapter 4c

HOW DO YOU HARNESS
YOUR MENTAL ENERGY?
THE POWER OF DISCIPLINE

"You have to create rituals to ensure focused attention
on problem-solving."

Dr. John Ng

*"Not just free-kicks; he practises dribbling, crossing, shooting, everything.
If you work as hard as he does, you get your rewards."*

**Nemanja Vidic, commenting on Christiano Ronaldo,
three-time World Footballer of the Year**

Most of us are easily distracted. In an age of interruptions, you are distracted by emails, text messages, and phone calls. In our world of multi-roles, multi-tasking and multi-jobbing, where organizations require more for less, you have to manage many tasks and activities all at once. You always have to juggle between roles as a boss, colleague, friend, spouse, and parent as they are all clamoring for your attention. Distractions are costly.

The Harvard Energy Project has found that: "A temporary shift in attention from one task to another — stopping to answer an e-mail or take a phone call, for instance — increases the amount of time necessary to finish the primary task by as much as 25%, a phenomenon known as 'switching time.' It's far more efficient to fully focus for 90 to 120 minutes, take a true break, and then fully focus on the next activity. We refer to these work periods as "ultradian sprints.""

Mental energy management is your ability to focus and not be distracted, to consider options carefully, be creative and make good decisions consistently. A mentally strong person can do so even under highly stressful situations.

Here are some suggestions on how we can manage our mental energy.

1. Focus on Your Assignment: Power of the Hour

This is true especially when you are doing complex assignments, it is important that you spend a good amount of disciplined time to work on it. We call this: Power of the Hour.

In my own consulting work, I have seen how this works. A team gets together to diagnose carefully the root causes of a major challenge, e.g., decline in sales. Instead of having knee-jerk reactions to the problem, we challenge the group to find out the contributing factors, provide evidence-based analysis, bring in expert resources if necessary and look at it from an inter-disciplinary perspective. No one comes in late and leaves the room half-way. Everyone is expected to give their perspectives and input. It often surprises them to see how productive that focused one hour can be. Some ground rules we instil at meeting include:

- Clear goal and agenda
- Fixed time: No one comes late or leaves early
- No texting or answering calls: All handphones on the table
- Good time-keeping to avoid distractions
- Evidence-based preparation on root-causes, contributing factors
- Develop practical creative solutions
- Chairperson makes final decision after in-depth discussion
- Follow through and reporting on progress is expected at the next meeting

You have to create rituals to ensure focused attention on problem-solving.

2. Retool your Competence — Take Ownership of your Development

You must take charge of your own development. Nothing is more frustrating than doing work that you are not competent in or for which you lack the necessary knowledge and skills to deliver performance. Hence, being competent in your job is very important.

How can you make a plan to become more competent?

Create a learning community. Today there is an abundance of resources. It is easy for you to encourage your family and your team to learn and more importantly, share the learning.

Being curious and willing to learn is an important mind-energizer. Keep learning, no matter how old or how experienced you are. Learn from the young and old alike, and constantly upgrade your skills and knowledge. Knowledge changes very fast, as newer and better products and methods are introduced regularly.

I am blessed to have children who keep feeding me with useful YouTube videos, articles, and blogs. I find that I have so much to learn from my younger staff, especially in the field of technology and the digital world. We learn from each other.

Create an asking culture. In our Asian culture, sometimes you fear 'losing face', which prevents you from asking questions. Some people don't know and don't ask, or even feign competence, which they don't have. Worse still, some often don't even want to learn new things.

I am sure you have heard of this injunction: "Don't come to me with your problems. Come to me with your solutions." This has prevented people from asking questions about problems they cannot find solutions to. Since they don't have solutions, they don't ask. Often, problems are swept under the carpet and eventually become a crisis. When that happens, your superiors may scream, "Why didn't you tell me the problem?" What an irony!

So, now I encourage people to ask. I urge them to ask. If not, I will coach them by asking more questions. Then, we will find the solutions together.

3. Making Time for Deliberate Practice: Sharpening your Skills

The great pianist Vladimir Horowitz used to say, "If I don't practice for a day, I know it. If I don't practice for two days, my wife knows it. If I don't practice for three days, the world knows it."

Many of us don't practice our craft. You take your God-given talent and skill for granted. You allow your skills to deteriorate. But practice is not enough. You need deliberate practice.

Malcolm Gladwell has said, "Success has to do with deliberate practice. Practice must be focused, determined and in an environment where there's feedback." In other words, hard work is not enough. You can work hard at practice but will still not improve. There are several elements to this. Take Cristiano Ronaldo, the Portuguese and Real Madrid soccer player, who is FIFA three-time Player of the Year.

a.   **Have a Holy Discontent**

At Manchester United, Ronaldo had a body transformation from a 17-year-old skinny boy to a well-chiseled, muscled man. His philosophy of 'No pain, no gain' carries him through till today. There is a holy discontent about his own ability. Discontent is the first necessity for progress.

b.   **Work out clear goals in practice**

As a professional athlete, Ronaldo is surrounded by professional fitness coaches and dieticians to help him gain the right body mass and nutritional diet to keep in shape. He is fixated about his goals in practice. This is his daily workout routine:

- 3-4 hours of daily practice that assure a very low body fat percentage (< 10 percent)
- Several periods of running for state cardio (25-30 mins)
- High intensity and 'explosive' sprinting drills (short-period exercises)
- Technical drills to enhance skills and ball control
- Football tactical exercises to improve understanding with teammates
- Gym exercises to develop specific muscles and his total body strength
- An hour a day toning his abs, sometimes while watching TV, as well as 3,000 sit-ups a day
- Good diet plan. Eating 4-6 times a day comprising small meals in a distributed manner

You have to be clear about what you want and then put this into practice.

c.   **Carve out time for micro-skill practice**

Ronaldo's free kicks are world class. He is one of the best and he does it consistently well, more so than most footballers.

Sir Alex Ferguson, the legendary Manchester United manager raved: "I've seen a lot of stuff written about how Cristiano's free-kicks are all to do with the way he places the ball or strikes it on the valve, but the bottom line is the boy practises and practises. He's always out there at the end of training, banging balls in after the session has ended."

The free-kick routine involves several micro-skills. Each is important in building the free kick. Ronaldo dedicates himself to perfecting his craft in all these areas, which include:

- Strengthening of leg muscles
- Kicking rightly: which side of the foot
- Body muscles and movement
- Size of man-wall
- Types of free kicks
- Mental training

Former United defender Nemanja Vidic also reckons Ronaldo's dedication is the reason for his spectacular strikes and remarkable goal-haul.

Ronaldo practises free-kicks all the time in training and stays behind when everyone else has gone. Vidic elaborates: "Not just free-kicks, he practises dribbling, crossing, shooting, everything. If you work as hard as he does, you get your rewards."[3]

d.   Let it flow in execution

When asked what his free-kick secrets were, Ronaldo replied, *"The success or failure at the moment of taking the free-kick is directly related to the position of the body, the way one runs towards the ball and the way one positions one's feet. At that moment, I think only about which side of the net I'm going to aim for."*

When you watch Ronaldo (CR7, as he is affectionately named), you see his instinctive execution. His dazzling dribbles, one-touch passing and championship scoring goals are precisely executed. He doesn't think too much, but does it intuitively. That's because he spends a lot of time on deliberate practice. That's what makes him such a delight to watch.

e.   Be ruthless in evaluation

Ronaldo himself is his greatest critique. He listens to people who know him and trusts them to give him good advice and suggestions.

Nothing is taken for granted. If you want to achieve greatness in your mental energy, there are mental disciplines involved:

- Focus on the assignments by having routines that clear out distractions,

- Retool your competence by taking ownership of your own development and

- Make time for deliberate practice to sharpen your skills.

1. What is lacking in your mental energy?

2. What skill do you want to sharpen and what deliberate practice must you put in?

Action Steps ▼

Chapter 4d

HOW DO YOU HARNESS
YOUR SOCIAL ENERGY?
THE POWER OF RELATIONSHIPS

"You and I don't live life in a vacuum."

Dr. John Ng

"Relationships include: Fights, Jealousy, Arguments, Faith, Tears, Disagreements, but a real relationship fights through all that with love."

Kushanowi Zoom

You and I don't live life in a vacuum.

I had the privilege of meeting Tan Teck Hock, Principal of the Singapore Sports School. I was curious to find out how he nurtures champions with values.

"In all sports, there is only one winner. How do you help your students appreciate those who are not winners?" I asked.

His immediate response hit me between the eyes, "Champions are not nurtured in a vacuum. They need parents to support them. They need coaches to guide them. And most of all, they need fellow athletes to challenge them. I help my students recognize and appreciate these people who help them become champions."

What wisdom!

Harnessing your social energy is an important element.

Social energy is your ability to relate to and work alongside other people. It is helping them to get along well in interpersonal relationships. The inability to relate with people and manage conflicts can deplete your social energy.

Experts tell us that communication is composed of two parts: *content* (what is said) and *cues* (non-verbal signals such as tone of voice and body language). Interpersonal communication scholars have found that when verbal and non-verbal communication cues clash, adults will pick up the non-verbal cues first.

Suppose I told my wife I love her. But if I delivered it gruffly and without looking at her, she would perceive it as insincere and unloving. In any mismatch between what you say and how you say it, the recipient always gets the cue from how you speak.

Note that this also depends on the quality of your relationship. If two colleagues, Michael and Peter, aren't on talking terms, what would it be like if Peter suddenly complimented Michael very nicely? It would still not work because the relationship was awry in the first place.

That's why I believe communication has a third factor — *relationship*. A lot also depends on who is speaking to you!

Communication can be expressed as an 'equation':

Communication	=	Content	+	Cues	+	Relationship
		What is said		How it is said		Who says it
		Verbal		Non-Verbal		Affinity / Respect
		Facts		Feelings		
		20% of the message		80% of the message		

Relationship is paramount in most interactions. When you have emotionally engaged relationships with others, you can navigate through the toughest of conflicts. But if a relationship is fragile, even your good intentions and beautifully constructed words of praise will be misconstrued.

There are two pillars of a strong relationship — Affinity and Respect.

Affinity and Respect

While the two may seem similar, there are not the same thing. Affinity is the degree to which we *like* each other; respect is the degree to which we *attribute worth* to one another.

You can like someone you do not respect — for instance, you may like colleagues who are outgoing and fun-loving, but if they are dishonest or unfaithful to their spouses, you will lose your respect for them because of these immoral values.

You can also respect someone you do not like, such as your bosses — they might deserve respect for their position and competence, but you will probably not like them if they are unfriendly and unapproachable.

In much of my own consulting with different organizations and family groups, I have come to discover that different relational factors that strengthen affinity and respect. These are the building blocks in nurturing relationships.

Here's what I've found from my experience:

Affinity is strengthened by these different factors:

Factor	Description
Friendly	Nice and easy-going
Courteous	Polite and well-mannered
Understanding & Considerate	Aware of and appreciating the needs of staff and others
Cheerful	Happy and pleasant-natured
Caring & Compassionate	Sympathetic and shows concern
Willing to Listen	Willing to make the time to hear others out and understand them
Humorous	Able to laugh with others and self
Eloquent	Can speak well and convincingly
Approachable	Able to relate well to all level of staff
Confident	Self-assured and self-reliant
Helpful & Kind	Willing to assist and shows spontaneous acts of kindness
Presentable	Having a neat physical appearance, and dressing well

Respect is heightened by these different factors:

Factor	Description
Responsible	Dependable and accountable for own actions
Morally upright	Righteous and virtuous
Professionally competent	Capable and qualified in professional skills
Wise & Knowledgeable	Mature, sensible and with good general knowledge
Charismatic	Able to inspire enthusiasm
Decisive	Able to decide quickly and conclusively
Willing to admit mistakes	Admits when one is wrong, and does not apportion blame to others
Humble	Not boastful
Courageous	Willing to take chances, not afraid of setbacks
Wealthy	Having a lot of cash and assets
Trustworthy	Being honest and reliable, and keeping promises
Achievement-oriented	Lots of drive to do better
A strategic thinker	Visionary: able to see the big picture and having plans to achieve goals
Fair	Treats staff with equity and without undue favor
A team leader	Able to motivate and work with people in a group
Generous	Willing to share or give to disadvantaged staff

Are some factors more important than others? My research suggests that the top five for each pillar (in no particular order) are:

Affinity

- Understanding and consideration
- Care and compassion
- Helpfulness and kindness
- Willingness to listen; and
- Approachability

Respect

- Competence
- Responsibility
- Trustworthiness
- Willingness to admit mistakes; and
- Humility

In summary, to harness your social energy, you need to build both affinity and respect with the people you work with. If you don't have either, not only will your social energy be depleted but your relationship will also dissipate. And it's harder to rebuild trust again.

If you have one without the other, you are not going to get the kind of traction in your relationship with the other party. For example, Asian parents are sometimes respected but not well-liked. That's why they may only create a culture of fear and cordiality and not love and warmth.

- The 'relationship' is more important than the 'what' and the 'cue'. Hence, good communication depends on a trusting relationship before anything else. As a parent or supervisor, if you are both liked and respected, you will earn more trust and communicate more effectively than if you have only one or neither of these factors.

- Both affinity and respect are important. Good social energy comes when you are both well-liked and well-respected.

- The more building blocks of affinity and respect there are, the stronger the relationship. You have to focus on those crucial aspects of affinity (understanding, caring, helpfulness, willingness to listen, and approachability) as well as the respect factors (competence, responsibility, trustworthiness, humility and willingness to admit mistakes). Communication depends on affinity and respect being there in the first place — before it depends on how the parties speak or act.

To have strong social energy, you have to begin to build good relationships through affinity and respect in your home as well as work.

Unfortunately, social energy can be depleted at home because of broken marriages and neglect of family relationships. I have seen too many people who cannot cope with their work and become emotionally stressed. Some even fall into depression because of serious marital and family conflicts that cannot be resolved. Worry, anxiety and being emotionally drained are all the results of a stressful family life.

On the other hand, nothing is more energizing for you than having a supportive, loving spouse, or when your children relate well with you. Imagine having your spouse and children share your joys and sorrows, appreciate your successes and comfort you in your failures. Strong families make life more wonderful and meaningful.

Giving the highest priority to your family life is indeed a very important aspect of energy management. Time must therefore be given to building a strong marriage and family. I once read an anonymous quote: *"Relationships include: Fights, Jealousy, Arguments, Faith, Tears, Disagreements, but a real relationship fights through all that with love."* A healthy relationship allows conflicts to be managed better.

You live and lead out your marriage life. After all, don't we all believe that 'family is the basic unit of society'!

1. Look at the five critical Affinity factors (understanding and consideration, care and compassion, helpfulness and kindness, willingness to listen; and approachability). Which factor do you need to strengthen in your relationships at home and at work?

2. Look at the five critical Respect factors (competence, responsibility, trustworthiness, willingness to admit mistakes; and humility). Which factor do you need to strengthen in your relationships at home and at work?

Action Steps ▼

Chapter 4e

HOW DO YOU HARNESS
YOUR SPIRITUAL ENERGY?
THE POWER OF MEANING

"Don't just stay in a rut; push yourself forward. Those who stay in one place lose energy in what they do."

Dr. John Ng

"Our scientific power has outrun our spiritual power.
We have guided missiles and misguided men."

Martin Luther King, Jr.

In a world of rush and furry, you need to find your True North.

Bishop John Reed from Australia tells the story of a group of sailors who visited London. Just as luck would have it, they were met by the infamous London fog. They could hardly see anything beyond a metre away.

To their horror, they realized that they were lost. Then they saw a pub and started wandering towards it. As they approached the pub, they met a man. Unknown to them, this gentleman was a very distinguished general. So, one of them, a burly Australian asked him, "Hey, bloke, do you know where we are?" In disgust, this distinguished general replied, "Do you know who I am?"

Then the Australian turned around to his mates and said, "We are really in trouble. We don't where we are and this chap doesn't know who he is!" This aptly describes the condition of humankind. We are all living at such a hurried and frenzied pace that we have lost touch with where we are and who we are.

Hence, we need spiritual energy to help us find meaning and fulfilment in life. Spiritual energy is your ability to discover meaning and purpose in what you do. This can be derived from meaningful engagement with community outside your normal work routine as well as seeking ways to connect with the Divine through solitude, reflection, religious activities and meditation.

1. Look for Fresh and New Challenges

There must be a hunger in you to push yourself. It is important that you set standards for yourself: You must look for greater opportunities, ways to learn and explore where to take on greater responsibilities. Don't just stay in a rut; push yourself forward. Those who stay in one place lose energy in what they do.

In working with many 'Generation Y' people, I find that they love new challenges. They thrive on new learning opportunities and become easily bored if their jobs become mundane. They want to set new standards. You need to stay fresh and passionate in what you do.

2. Be Involved in Regular Non-Profit Work

Another key aspect of spiritual energy management is learning to find meaning in a worthy social cause or mission. Don't just give money or do it periodically. Be a regular at an old folks' home, mentor a delinquent person, employ less fortunate people, help raise funds for worthy charity causes, serve in community work or teach a Sunday School Class.

Find what you enjoy doing, be it administrative, management or relating to people; use your passion for a greater cause. Being involved in charity and social enterprises is very energizing. To be personally involved with the disadvantaged and the poor can help you see another side of life, and rekindle your passion for living!

I read the story of a French friar named Abbé Pierre, who was born into a noble family. He had served in the French Parliament until he became disillusioned with the slow pace of political change. After World War II, with Paris still reeling from the effects of Nazi occupation, thousands of homeless beggars lived in the streets. Pierre could not tolerate the endless debates by noblemen and politicians while so many street people starved outside. During an unusually harsh winter, many Parisian beggars froze to death.

He decided to do something. He resigned from his post in the parliament and became a Catholic monk to work among the beggars. Failing to interest politicians or the community in the beggars' plight, he concluded his only recourse was to reorganize the beggars themselves:

- He taught them to do menial tasks better. Instead of sporadically collecting bottles and rags, they divided into teams to scour the city.
- Next, he led them to build a warehouse from discarded bricks and then start a business in which they sorted and processed vast quantities of used bottles from hotels and businesses.
- Finally, Pierre inspired each beggar by giving him responsibility to help another beggar poorer than himself.

- The project caught fire, and in a few years an organization called Emmaus was founded to expand Pierre's work into other countries.

After years of this work, there were no beggars left in Paris. This left him worried as he thought: "I must find somebody for the beggars to help. If I don't find people worse off than my beggars, this movement could turn inward. They'll become a powerful, rich organization, and the whole spiritual impact will be lost. They'll have no one to serve."

So, he scoured the world, and finally found a leprosy colony in India, five thousand miles away. Pierre found at last the solution to the crisis in Paris. He met many hundreds of leprosy patients, many from the low or so-called 'Untouchable' caste, worse off in every way than his former beggars.

Soon, he mobilized the reformed beggars to build a ward at the hospital. The team at the hospital was so deeply moved and thanked Pierre profusely. But Pierre responded: "No, we should thank you. It is you who have saved us. If we don't serve, we die."

Today, Emmaus has 350 organizations in 35 countries.

3. Find Time for Solitude and Reflection

"Far too busy managing our transactive speed, we rarely step back to lead with transformative significance."

Kevin Cashman

The Pause Principle: Step Back to Lean Forward

In our fast-paced world, reflection has become a neglected practice. Taking strategic pauses to reflect on life, your successes and failures, your strengths and your weaknesses must be made a high priority. This can be a life-changing, transformative experience for you.

Reflection has become my regimen, since the day I discovered three blockages in my heart (the main left artery was 99 percent blocked and two others – half- and three-quarters blocked). I have since spent more time taking strategic pauses.

I read Chris Lowney's book *Heroic Leadership*, which recommended the Jesuit practice of *examen*, or 'rumination on the run'. I have since adopted this practice into my lifestyle. Since that near-death experience, I now spend five minutes at the beginning of each day pausing to re-focus on God and on what's important, and re-examine my priorities. During the last five minutes before I sleep, I reflect on what has transpired and thank God for the day's experiences.

In addition, I make time for a 24-hour Sabbath rest every week, from Friday at 6.30 pm to Saturday at 6.30 pm. During this period, I allow myself to do what I enjoy, like watching my favorite soccer team (Manchester United) in action, spending time with family (like watching a movie or going for meals together) and delighting in the beauty of life.

These regimes have made me a more grateful and thoughtful person. I have become emotionally healthier, less reactive and more sensitive, and live a more purposeful life. Indeed, pause powers life!

Daniel Vasella, Chairman and CEO of Novartis for 15 years, has commented: "Pause gives room to oneself and to others. It allows the digestion of things both conceptual, and emotional. Pause can be a way to sense making by bring together a more integrated, complete picture of what is happening in and around us." It's good advice from a man who has spent so long navigating a $58 billion life-science business!

Flow and energy management do not simply happen; they must be actively sought after and worked for in life.

1. How do you find meaning in your work and in your life?

2. How can you encourage others to find meaning in their work and life?

Action Steps

Chapter 5

HOW TO RECOVER
FROM FAILURE
THE POWER OF FORGIVENESS

"Forgiveness is the final and the finest form of love."

Dr. John Ng

"The family and religious community can play an important role here. Their acceptance and support can cushion the fall and make recovery a reality."

Anonymous

Failure is inevitable in life. Whether it is business failure, relational failure, or personal failure, greatness is achieved through recovery. Failure is never final for great people.

A personal failure recovery process is important for you so that you can get back on your feet. Starting over and then ending well should be the focus in the process. In this chapter, I would like to use Father Neil Conway, a Catholic priest, as an example of how failure recovery can take place.

In an article entitled "Confessions of a Fallen Priest", Father Conway shared how he had been luring teenage boys into his sexual trap for over 16 years. He related how he could recover from this sex addiction.

Step One: Admit Failure

This is perhaps the most difficult part of recovery. You often tend to justify, rationalize and deny your mistakes, failures and moral failings. You have to overcome your pride, shame, guilt and self-deception. The higher the status you have and the higher the position you are in, the harder it is to admit failures.

Initially, Father Conway thought his shenanigans with the boys were just intense friendships and it never occurred to him that his actions were inappropriate, much less illegal. He said, "I didn't know how to get the right things in the right way." He never confessed to God or to any living soul.

Finally, he had to come clean with his actions. He admitted, "I violated everything I ever believed in. I caused suffering to the very people I wanted to serve most." That was the beginning of his recovery. For you to recover, there must be an honest admission of mistakes. You must come clean.

Step Two: Be Subject to Discipline

If you have fallen, you must subject yourselves to discipline. This is not an easy process as you are subject to both ridicule and cynicism as well as empathy and support.

Regardless of how others or the media might respond, your true spirit of contrition and courage will be demonstrated by your humility and willingness to be disciplined.

Since going public about his story, Father Conway has received ambivalent responses, ranging from support to outrage. A nun wrote to praise his "courage and honesty." His brothers, however, wrote a letter expressing dismay. He found an unsigned letter informing his neighbors that he was a sexual predator. Father Conway took it in the true spirit of repentance: "I am willing to have my neighbors think I am a pervert. I'm ready for my family to say I betrayed them and dragged the family name into the mud. I'm willing to do that with great sorrow, but I've got to make up for this terrible thing that I did."

Father Conway requested for retirement due to disability. He now regularly attends the 12-step meetings for alcoholism and sexual compulsion. He prays every morning and afternoon and vows never to be alone with a teenager.

For some, this may be in the form of corporate discipline or even doing time in prison. But whatever it takes to recover, so be it. You must do it with moral courage and resolve.

Step Three: Make Restitution

The story of Father Conway models what restitution involves. He confessed, "I committed an abomination. I'm sitting here on the dunghill of my own shame and guilt. I was a predator. I claim full responsibility. Whatever I've done to these men can't be undone by me now, but I am deeply regretful for what I did. How do you make up for something so awful as child abuse?"

Subsequently, the priest went on a journey of intense candor. He tracked down his victims and apologized. Five forgave him, three did not and another two sued. Conway believed there was healing power in confession, not just for himself but also for his victims and the Church. He now hopes to start a movement to allow abusive priests to come out of hiding and to begin the process of healing: "I am challenging these men to come out in the open with me. I want to say, 'Let the discussion begin.'"

Making restitution is part of the healing and recovery.

Step Four: Get Professional Help

Some tendencies like psychological hurt, depression, sexual inadequacies and marital dysfunction need prolonged professional help. It is no shame to seek help. It is not any different from a physical illness.

Father Conway requested professional treatment on his own accord. "I knew I could not stop on my own." He spent a year in a church-sponsored sexual offender program.

For those of us who have failed morally or cheated others in business, this may mean seeking sound financial advice from accounting firms, legal counsel from lawyers, and/or personal counseling from professional therapists.

Step Five: Return to Business and Service

Spouses, family members, and friends must extend support and help to those who have failed. Unfortunately, this is easier said than done. When you have failed, you are often shunned, ostracized and banished. Often, you can become disillusioned, bitter and revengeful. The world is sometimes too unforgiving.

To complete the recovery, the fallen must be embraced and nurtured back into the wounded community. You must not be denied the opportunity to serve and work with appropriate safeguards after the disciplinary period.

The family and religious community can play an important role here. Their acceptance and support can cushion your fall and make recovery a reality.

You must also find mentors who can nurse you back to health. You need to rebuild your credibility. In this entire process of failure recovery, you must continually adopt a spirit of contrition and repentance. The community must take the most redemptive approach to ensure that recovery is complete.

Can This Really Work?

I have personally encountered several people who have been nurtured and mentored back to recovery. I have a business friend, James who had lost millions of dollars through greed, financial mismanagement and failed strategy. He was recently discharged from being a bankrupt after he was willing to make appropriate payment by installments.

He then sought professional financial advice, made restitution, downsized his lifestyle, paid the penalty for his actions, and received support from family and a few close friends. He has since restarted his business. Today, he has been completely rehabilitated and restored. Most of all, he is at peace with himself, family and friends.

I know a pastor and husband, Leo, who committed adultery. Because he could come clean with his wife and his community, he has since recovered through close support and discipline. The couple is now serving in a church, helping couples who have strayed and nursing them back to healthy marriages.

A fairy-tale ending? Absolutely. Can it happen? Yes, if we build the process of failure recovery into the experience of personal failure. You can be transformed again but you must pay the price of moral failures.

So is there hope for Tiger Woods, Peter Lim, Michael Palmer, General Petraeus and others I have mentioned in the previous chapters? Certainly! The road to recovery takes time.

Robert Schuller wrote this poignant poem:

> *Every adversity is an adventure.*
> *Every pain is a pilgrimage.*
> *Every trial is a trail.*
> *Every problem is a path.*
> *Every load is a road.*
> *Every hurt is on the move.*
> *It's leading you somewhere.*
> *Where is it taking you?*

Failure can lead you somewhere. Recovery can lead you to a new adventure, a new experience and a new destiny of greatness again. That is only possible through the power of forgiveness.

Father Conway's recovery was possible only when he learnt to forgive himself. The community that helps him recover has also learnt to forgive. Only then can Father Conway start his new work of helping others to recover through the power of forgiveness. Forgiveness is first and foremost for yourself: It is preventing the pain from hurting you anymore. It releases you from your pain. For truly, forgiveness is the final and the finest form of love.

Final Word on Recovery

Kintsugi, the art of repairing pottery with gold, is based on the understanding that the piece is more beautiful for having been broken. Indeed, Father Conway is the story of a broken life made more beautiful by the *Kintsugi* master.

> All beautiful things carry distinctions of imperfection. Your wounds and imperfections are your beauty. Like the broken pottery mended with gold, we are all Kintsugi. Its philosophy and art state that breakage and mending are honest parts of a past that should be hidden. Your wounds and healing are a part of your history, a part of who you are. Every beautiful thing is damaged. You are that beauty; we are all.
>
> Stuart McGill

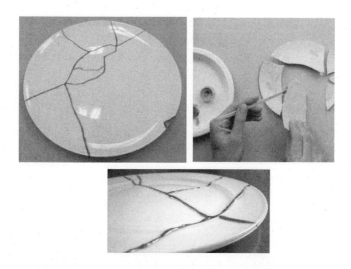

1. What personal, relational, and business failures have you experienced? How did you recover?

2. Which aspect of Father Conway's recovery would you find most difficult to do? Why?

Action Steps

Part 5

LIM HONG JOON AND LEE KUAN YEW
The Power of Two Great Lives
(What you must learn)

Chapter 1

THE GREATNESS OF AN ORDINARY PERSON
LIM HONG JOON

"I chose Lim Hong Joon because he was an ordinary person who rose to greatness and so can you."

Dr. John Ng

*"Keeping promises is very important. I am straightforward
with people. My 'yes' is yes and my 'no' is no.
People generally trust me and I don't overpromise
them anything. If I cannot do it, I will explain to them."*

Lim Hong Joon

You probably have not heard of Lim Hong Joon. He is not on YouTube, Facebook, or LinkedIn.

Lim Hong Joon was the former President-Director of P.T. KL Kepong Agriservindo, taking care of all its plantation operations in Indonesia, until he retired in 2013. I have chosen to highlight him because he is an ordinary man. For me, he exemplifies greatness because he lives out the ten ingredients of greatness.

He served his organization for 53 years. He rose through the ranks to become one of its great leaders. I hope there are more people like Lim Hong Joon and that he will inspire you to become a great person.

In 1958, when he was 16 years old, Hong Joon had to find a job because his father was sick and he could not afford to finish school. Every month, he would send half his salary — about 20 Malaysian ringgits (US$4) — back home to support his three brothers so that they could continue their studies.

After landing the job, he enjoyed it so much that he stayed on with KL Kepong, one of the largest palm oil plantation groups in Malaysia. It is the only company he has ever worked for!

He recently retired. The company honored this longest-serving employee with its 53-year Long Service Award. Here is an account of his life in his words.

1. Greatness is Nurturing Character

"Keeping promises is very important. I am straightforward with people. My 'yes' is yes and my 'no' is no. People generally trust me and I don't overpromise them. If I cannot do it, I will explain to them.

Sometimes, I try to bring their needs to my boss. If he disagrees, I don't badmouth him and position myself as the good guy and the boss as the bad guy, just to win their favor by depreciating him or the company, saying things like 'The company is useless. They don't understand your situation.' Instead, I will explain to my workers why it can't be done now.

At times, I would take their petitions to the boss again and come to him from another angle. Maybe, the first time, it was the wrong occasion. I would always try my best for my workers whenever there was a need. They know they can count on me."

2. Greatness is Enjoying a Healthier Family Life

"I am very happy with my family. I don't have many family problems. I am still happily married with my wife. I don't indulge in extra-marital affairs and don't fool around. My four children have grown up and do respect me. I have imparted my values to them. Now, it's time for them to do their part for the families and impart good values to their children."

3. Greatness is Nurturing Friendships

"I treasure friendship. When you are the top, you must cultivate the habit of helping people so that people can improve their lives and career. When you retire, you are a nobody. You are a blade of grass along the roadside.

One day, people remember you for good or evil. You never know when you need them. Many of my colleagues still remember me for the good that I have done. I don't even remember them.

Friendship is very important. You have to value friendship. You have to make time to cultivate friends in your work place and your community. We meet up for coffee whenever I am in town to catch up. I haven't forgotten them. Friendship doesn't cost us money. You just have to spend time with them. Now, that I am retired, I still enjoy that friendship."

4. Greatness is Becoming Your Best Through Values and Results

"First, I always do my best because I like my work. I like what I am doing. I have had the opportunity to grow with the company.

Second, I always look on the positive side of life even though we have ups and downs. It is so easy to become discouraged by the bad times. There was a time when people thought rubber and oil palm were sunset industries but now they are the golden crops in agriculture.

Third, I keep myself occupied during my time on the estate by being active with my staff and workers in the evening. Sometimes, I would go fishing and hunting around the estate when I have the time during the weekend.

Finally, I have worked with a good company that recognizes my contributions. I moved up the corporate ladder quickly. They promoted me to an executive position within five years even though normally, it would take a long time."

5. Greatness is Developing People

"I see my peers and people as my team and not my competitors. I used to work under a nasty plantation manager. He liked to put down people and create division. I learnt how not to lead. When I was promoted and became a plantation advisor, I was asked to help difficult managers. I knew what their problems were and found ways to improve the processes. We managed to work well and solve problems, and they became better managers.

I lead people by seeing their potential. Whenever I have difficult employees, I always tell them, 'You make me sad and not angry.' I tried to work through the problems with them. My job is to put people in the right positions and get them interested in their work."

6. Greatness is Being Humble

"Generally, I have good PR skills. I work well with people. As a leader, I must learn to interact well with my subordinates. I have been active and participate with my staff and workers in games, even though I am not playing. If not, I would organize sports and football teams to compete with others. I want to be there with them.

I will support them and be with them when we go for matches. And I will buy them jerseys, boots, drinks and food. Our team is always very motivated. We are a winning team and our opponents are afraid of us because of our team spirit.

To be humble means I am willing to be corrected. Once, I had to wait for a truck to pick up the crop from the estate to the mill. It didn't come on time. It was already 8pm and I was late for dinner with my family, so I went home.

In the meantime, the truck came. The manager happened to be there at that time. He stormed into my house and swore at me, in front of my parents: 'You are lazy and irresponsible and not attentive to your job. You are lucky to get a job through the back-door. You are not even fit to be a bus conductor.' I was embarrassed but I didn't retaliate. I knew he could have asked me politely and I could have explained. I apologized for the mistake.

I had another boss who insists on being addressed as 'Sir,' not just 'Mr.' My other colleagues cursed him for demanding respect. But I would just comply. If he wants me to show respect in that way, I will do it because he was my boss. I knew I had nothing to lose.

Second, lead by self-control. On another occasion, a manager tried to insult me, saying 'You are not even fit to be a conductor, how can you become an assistant manager?' I just kept quiet and proved to him that I could do the job. I wouldn't allow my manager to put me down. I only knew that I would not be like him should I become a plantation manager."

7. Greatness is Developing Successors and Successful Systems

"I learnt to be a good role model to others because I have good role-models. I had the unique opportunity to learn from one of our good managers, Nigel Sanderson. He was a firm and straightforward person. He was a retired Gurkha captain. He got along with people very well, had a very good work ethic and was very diligent. Every morning, he would wake up at 6.30am and take me around the plantation, teaching me all the things I needed to learn. He was my mentor; I learnt so much from him.

For the young managers, my advice to them is: Possess strong leadership, integrity, good attitude, good interpersonal skills, communicate well, have sincerity and commitment. It all begins with you. You must be the very best you can be for your own sake. The company will always look for the best employees to do a job and they will settle for second best only when the best is not available.

I have passed this on to others. They are even better than me."

8. Greatness is Recovering from Failures

"First, keep with the times by reinventing yourself. I have been updating myself all these years. When I was 16 years old, I was Chinese-educated and knew that I needed to learn English. I took a correspondence course to learn English for five years in Singapore. I achieved my Diploma in Plantation Management through self-study. In 1984, when I became plantation advisor, I realized that I needed to improve my English further, as it was not sufficient to keep up with the work. And so, I took up English tuition for four years.

Second, be willing to learn from your peers and subordinates. I also learn from the managers during my visits to their operating centers. They have much to teach me. They always inspire me. I also keep up by reading books on relevant subjects and attending seminars. If I stop learning, I am done for.

Third, be resilient in a crisis. Our plantation industry has gone through many crises. There was a time when they said that ours was a sunset industry. But we waded through that. We had to make tough decisions. We even had to take pay cuts, reorganize ourselves and restructure the organization. Now, with the rocketing palm oil prices, people say we are in the golden age of agriculture!"

9. Greatness is Leaving a Legacy of Great Values

Leaving a legacy comes from the people you work with. Their verdict matters more than anything. Hong Joon shared: "The verdict must come from the people who work for me. As a superior, if I wanted to visit their plantations, and they say, 'Oh no, he's coming again!' and show their frustration, then I would have failed. We would have created a culture of fear rather than a culture of trust. But thankfully, the managers welcome me, and say, 'Yes, please come, we have matters to discuss.' That shows that we have achieved as team leaders.

I leave with no regrets. KL Kepong has given me what I want in life."

10. Greatness is Caring for the Community and the Environment

"I also learnt how to be compassionate with people. I remember when my father was very ill and wanted to borrow some money from a close friend to see a doctor. His friend said, 'I can lend you but when will you return it?' I did not feel bad, but thought that he needed to be more compassionate.

"From that experience, I realized that I need to help people in need. When my poor workers came to me because they were short of cash to buy milk for their children or to see a doctor, I would take out my own money to lend them, even though I was not a rich estate manager. In a close community like the estate, these deeds of kindness spread very quickly by word of mouth. My workers knew that I cared for them. When they know that you care, they would be loyal to you.

KL Kepong is very committed to the environment. We must preserve our environment for our children and grandchildren. If I were not a planter, I would be in an NGO. If you don't preserve forests and wild animals, there will be nothing left for the future generations.

The villagers and poorer ones in Indonesia are often neglected and exploited. For example, there is this Plasma scheme in Indonesia where the government gives them two hectares of land. They have to borrow money from the bank to purchase their land. If not, these would be sold. Some do because they don't have enough. So, in KL Kepong, we helped them acquire their land. Instead of borrowing at 15 percent interest from the bank to buy the land, we loan money to them at 8 percent. The savings meant a lot to them."

I chose to share the life of Lim Hong Joon because he was an ordinary person, who rose to greatness by imbibing and living out the ten ingredients of greatness. Perhaps, you may be thinking, 'I am just an ordinary person. Can I be great?' Yes, you can.

If you stay focused and practice these ten ingredients of greatness, you can live a great life.

1. What impresses you most about the greatness in Lim Hong Joon?

2. Which ingredient of greatness do people most admire in you? How can you continue to cultivate this and other ingredients?

Action Steps ▼

Chapter 2

THE GREATNESS
OF A GREAT LEADER
LEE KUAN YEW

"Lee Kuan Yew taught me most deeply that greatness is
measured not just by having great economic successes but
enjoying a great relationship with your wife!"

Dr. John Ng

"Make the people feel that they are wanted. We are one in the Family.
Not step-children or step-brothers. We are part of the family.
And a very important member of the family."

Lee Kuan Yew

Singapore lost a great man on 23 March 2015: Our first and late Prime Minister, Lee Kuan Yew.

Every time I read articles and watched videos about him, I choke and grieve most deeply. When I was at the Parliament House on the first morning of the period of his body lying in State, waiting to pay my last respects, I had the opportunity to speak with many people in the line. Everyone mourned the loss of our Founding Father. Some shed tears and others choked as they recounted personal stories of the way Lee Kuan Yew (fondly called "LKY") led Singapore or shared their own encounters with him.

One 65-year-old man declared unequivocally, "LKY is Singapore and Singapore is LKY. I won't be here if not for him."

I also have my own story about LKY.

My dad was a simple shopkeeper. I remember the times when my dad would take me to the Sepoy Line Branch, which was part of LKY's Tanjong Pagar constituency, where my dad had served as a committee member. LKY would warmly shake hands with every one of his constituents, including me, then a six-year-old boy!

LKY always interacted with and engaged his constituents without airs. He truly lived out one of his speeches: "Make the people feel that they are wanted. We are one in the Family. Not step-children or step-brothers. We are part of the family. And a very important member of the family."

When my dad suffered from dementia, besides recalling my wife's and my name, he remembered LKY fondly. To him, LKY made such an impact in his life that he remembered him as someone who cared for people. He would remind me that if my children needed food, he could get it from LKY because he would always care for the ordinary man. This is certainly an image that many never saw. What a man!

Without his leadership, Singapore would never be what it is today. Lee Kuan Yew truly embodied the essence of greatness.

1. Greatness is Nurturing Character

"I did some sharp and hard things to get things right. Maybe some people disapproved of it. Too harsh, but a lot was at stake and I wanted the place to succeed. That's all."

LKY represented a can-do, work-hard and plough-through spirit, despite the many seemingly impossible odds. He had the conviction to fight for his beliefs, be it meritocracy or multiculturalism. He enacted policies to make sure that no one would be discriminated because of race or religion. He reminded his Cabinet Ministers and, at different opportunities, his people, that no minority was to be mistreated. Challenging conventional wisdom, he ensured that housing estates had minority representation and yet were not just enclaves of any particular race of religion.

Whether it is confronting the racial riots of the 1960s, or starting the mandatory National Service to ensure national security, or cleaning up the Singapore River (which took 10 long years!), he and his team persevered to make things happen.

This spirit can only come from a leader of courage: willing to die in the fight for the nation's survival, making difficult decisions and implementing policies that are good for the country, and standing firm against all odds and not bowing to the pressures of other countries.

He was one leader who led with guts. He was a man of great character.

2. Greatness is Becoming Your Best Through Values and Results

"'This is entrepreneurship on a political stage on a national scale. We change the complexion of Singapore."

LKY gave himself fully, sacrificing his personal interests to pursue the dream of building an economically sustainable nation. His pursuit of nation building was relentless.

He galvanized the people with his lucid oratory and passionate commitment by leading from the front and cheering from the side. He always made clear the purpose of his instructions and explained things in different ways so that the people understood why and what was needed to be done.

As Zuraidah Ibrahim and Andrea Ong wrote, "He pummeled, cajoled and pushed Singaporeans into altering their behavior as he waged war against littering, spitting, men with long hair and singlehood."[xxviii]

He communicated with such passion and persuasion that many mistook him as an authoritarian leader, uncaring and inhuman. Yes, he might have made some mistakes and nailed some of his opponents but his intention was always unalloyed — The Good of the Nation.

The outpouring of emotions and the inundation of eulogies from both the rich and poor, the old and the young, people of all races, global and national leaders, as well as from friend and foe, have demonstrated most clearly that his life, warts and all, has been more than vindicated.

Indeed, he united a nation in life and even in death!

Minister of Education, Heng Swee Keat, who was once his Principal Private Secretary (PPS), recounted with great detail LKY's Red Box. It contained things he had to do and things he wanted his PPS to do from notes on the financial crisis to trees on the expressway which required trimming; from speech drafts to trash floating on the Singapore River.

As Heng Swee Keat wrote poignantly, "Mr. Lee's life revolved around making Singapore better, in ways big and small." The Red Box demonstrated his unwavering dedication to giving his best to Singapore.[xxix]

3. Greatness is Enjoying Healthier Family Life

There is another side of LKY, which has now become one of the more enduring qualities of his life: His undying devotion to his wife and family. His wife, Kwa Geok Choo was his soul mate, intellectual equal and accountability partner.

During her funeral service, LKY gave a eulogy, which aptly described their relationship: "Without her, I would be a different man, with a different life.

[xxviii] Zuraidah Ibrahim and Andrea Ong. "A life devoted entirely to Singapore". The Straits Times. 24 Mar 2015. SPH. Singapore.

[xxix] Heng Swee Keat. "Mr. Lee's red box and his unwavering dedication to Singapore". The Straits Times. 25 Mar 2015. SPH. Singapore.

She devoted herself to our children and me. She was always there when I needed her."

The most touching example of his greatest sacrifice was when LKY made it a point to read Geok Choo's favorite books/poems nightly, a ritual he kept up religiously when she was in a semi-comatose state. At 10 o'clock each night, he would stop, excuse himself and read for her. He extended his passionate commitment from his country to his wife.

For me, in a world of politicians and leaders whose marriages are shams and shenanigans, Mr and Mrs Lee Kuan Yew stood out with their uniquely exemplary marriage. Their love for each other is certainly one of a kind!

LKY taught me most deeply that greatness is measured not just by having great economic successes but enjoying a great relationship with your wife!

4. Greatness is Nurturing Friendships

Another outstanding trait of LKY was his commitment to friendship. To be fair, he only had a few select, close, and trusted friends. Ng Kok Siong, former Chief Investment Officer of The Government of Singapore Investment Corporation (GIC), spoke fondly of LKY's advice to him: "Always honor your friendship with people, never forget your friends, the people who helped you when you were down, when you were never as fortunate. Never forget that."[xxx]

I am a recipient of true friendship and will continue to embrace LKY's legacy by remembering my friends!

5. Greatness is Developing People

LKY described his own generation of leaders as exceptional "dinosaurs, an extinct breed of men who went into politics because of the passion of their convictions."

One of the most enduring legacies was LKY's ability to select, work and nurture a team of equally dedicated men. Men like Dr. Goh Keng Swee, Toh Chin Chye, Hon

---

[xxx] Robin Chan and Sumiko Tan. "Devoted husband and caring father". The Straits Times. 24 Mar 2015. SPH. Singapore.

Sui Sen, Lim Kim San, S. Rajaratnam, and Othman Wok, all shared one common characteristic: they loved Singapore and would sacrifice their lives for their nation. That more than anything drove the team to put aside differences for a common good.

LKY and his team were obsessed with building a nation but they were never possessed by it. They never became personal or arrogant. Their obsession pushed them forward but they were not possessed by their egos.

These leaders were not lackeys. Unlike the public perception of him, many of his closest colleagues have testified that LKY knew the value of diverse views within his cabinet. He expected robust exchanges. He debated with them rigorously over policies and ideas. He selected intellectual equals as well as people with special expertise, whom he could tap on.

People who were smarter or better than him never threatened him. But he would also argue vigorously for his positions, often appearing stern like a combative legal counsel. As Dr. Chan Heng Chee, Former Singapore Ambassador to the United Nations, says, "I think that was his natural outlook. He wanted people to come back to disagree with him, so that he didn't think that everything that were his ideas were all absolutely correct."[xxxi]

6. Greatness is Recovering from Failures

> *"We must never allow ourselves to forget that popular government does not mean that we have to be popular in every act of government. It means that policies in the public interest, however unpopular, must be taken in time for the benefits to be appreciated before the next election."*

LKY was always focused on liberating Singapore from colonial rule and building a vibrant country that all Singaporeans would be proud of. He was a man of the future, never resting on past glories, never feeling contented with mediocrity and never satisfied with his past achievements. He always reminded us that no one owed us a living. We have to constantly create and recreate the future all the time.

[xxxi] Zuraidah Ibrahim and Andrea Ong. "A life devoted entirely to Singapore". The Straits Times. 24 Mar 2015. SPH. Singapore.

But he was realistic about the present. He reminded Singaporeans in one of his public rallies that "We got a little nation 660 square meters. Singapore has only one chance. To go up. Tighter, more discipline, up the ladder. You unwind this and we are finished." Whether battling communists and communalists, or fighting for survival after the abrupt pull out of the British troops or championing the cause of clean government, he never wavered in his resolve.

When Singapore was kicked out of the Malaysian Federation and the situation then exacerbated by the withdrawal of the British troops, which led to severe economic crisis, LKY galvanized his team to rebuild Singapore.

One critical member of his team was Dr. Goh Keng Swee, who was his Deputy Prime Minister. LKY wrote this eulogy of him, "Dr. Goh was both a far-sighted visionary and a pragmatic manager. He was a man of ideas but also excelled at bringing these ideas to fruition. Whatever the challenges, Dr. Goh would stay calm, bring to bear his capacious mind, work out the best course of action and then act decisively to solve the problem."

In many instances, he was far ahead of his time. In his 25 years in office, he created the Economic Development Board (EDB), the Jurong Town Corporation (JTC), the Monetary Authority of Singapore (MAS), and the Government of Singapore Investment Corporation (GIC), which have endured and become distinctive features of Singapore's structure. He always took a long-term perspective, yet recognizing that there was no guarantee of success in all his enterprises.

Failures and crises never frightened LKY and his team. In some sense, they thrived on them and built an even stronger nation.

7. Greatness is Developing Successors and Successful Systems

"I have spent my life, so much of it, building up the country. There's nothing more that I need to do. At the end of the day, what have I got? A better Singapore. What have I given up? My life."

This is the underlying and galvanizing value that made everything he did so stellar. Surrounded by nations where corruption is a way of life, and statesmen who had collapsed under the weight of corruption, he stood as a beacon of light.

He chose and nurtured a team of leaders, ensuring that there was a steady stream of honest, dedicated, and competent leaders to lead Singapore. Were there any fall-outs and failures? Certainly. But by and large, he had developed a succession plan and system, that is second to none in the world. Every leadership transition, from Goh Chok Tong (our second Prime Minister) to Lee Hsien Loong (our third Prime Minister), has been smooth and non-contentious.

He had to persuade many of his older colleagues to step down so that younger leaders could take their place.

He created a system whereby the team selects the most suitable leader. The fact that we are celebrating our 52nd year of independence in 2017, with sustained economic growth and sound infrastructure, is testament to his greatness in developing successors and successive systems.

8. Greatness is Being Humble

Lee Kuan Yew lived a simple life, uncluttered by materialism. He was a simple man who lived in a simple house with simple furniture. He was not one who collected premium or branded watches, shoes, pens, rare books, or art. Material stuff and money never enticed him.

A friend told me this story. LKY was invited to speak in a conference, together with former US President George Bush and Helmut Schmit, the former Prime Minister of Germany. When the invitation came, they asked what his fees were. He said "nothing".

After former President Bush and former Prime Minister Schmitt's speeches, there were thunderous applause. But after Lee Kuan Yew's address, the whole audience gave him a standing ovation.

During the speech, Mrs Lee opined jokingly to my friend, who was with her in the audience: "The two speakers before Kuan Yew were paid a large sum each. He was paid nothing! You better enjoy your lobster and drinks while you can!"

Lee Kuan Yew stated clearly that when he passed away, he did not want monuments to be built or any edifice to be emblazed with his name, unlike many other great leaders.

How he sustained his humble life and lifestyle all these years is truly unmatchable!

9. Greatness is Leaving a Legacy of Great Values

"I would do a lot personally for a friend, providing what we set out together to do is not sacrificed. If you need a hundred thousand dollars, I'll sign it out of my own resources or raise the money... But that personal relationship cannot be transmitted into a concession that will jeopardize state interests."

He chose colleagues who were deeply committed to the same ideal. He could never tolerate any misdemeanor. He showed he was never afraid to prosecute even his friends or colleagues who succumbed to misdeeds.

As S. Dhanabalan, who had held various ministerial portfolios from 1980 to 1992, rightly pointed out, "Many leaders of countries are honest… You must be prepared to demand honesty and be ruthless with your relatives and friends if they are not. Otherwise you can't get the honest culture established."[xxxii] Truly, LKY is a champion of integrity and the rule of law.

He had zero tolerance for corruption. When it came to expose his Cabinet colleague, the late National Development Minister Teh Cheang Wan, for corruption, he did not waver. LKY explained, "The purpose is not just to be righteous. The purpose is to create a system that will carry on because it has not been compromised. I didn't do that just to be righteous. But if I had compromised, that is the end of the system."

He practiced what he preached. He set a rule that any MP who was absent must write in to the Speaker of Parliament. When asked what impressed him most about LKY, Abdullah Tarmugi, a former Speaker of Parliament, shared how when LKY couldn't attend a sitting in the Parliament, he would always write a note to him. He was never above the rules he set up.

His legacy of a good government is:[xxxiii]

> *Give clear signals — don't confuse people.*
>
> *Be consistent — don't chop and change.*

[xxxii] S Dhanabalan. "A leader who's ruthless in demanding honesty". The Straits Times. 24 Mar 2015. SPH. Singapore.

[xxxiii] Zuraidah Ibrahim and Andrea Ong. "A life devoted entirely to Singapore". The Straits Times. 24 Mar 2015. SPH. Singapore.

Stay clean — dismiss the venal.

Win respect not popularity.

Reject soft options.

Spread benefits — don't deprive the people.

Strive to succeed — never give up.

That's the ethos that he has left behind not only in his party and government but to us Singaporeans. This is our legacy.

10. Greatness is Caring for the Community and the Environment

"You can't plant a tree and walk away."

LKY always sought to build the best country for his people. One of the best testaments of this is the amazing greenery of our city. He first conceived the idea of 'The Garden City' and today, it has transformed into 'The City in the Garden'.

He believed in caring for the environment and wanted his people to live in such an environment. His vision of the 'Garden City' was translated into reality. He did something powerfully simple. He set the example by just planting a tree. He meant business and then galvanized all his Members of Parliament to do the same in every constituency every year. He got the schools and students involved. Step by step, he built our 'City in the Garden'.

Conclusion: Our Hero for Life and for Greatness

LKY constantly made my father feel important even though he was only a small businessman. No wonder he was my dad's hero, and my father never stopped admiring him. Before they passed away, my parents kept reminding me that LKY is a '好人' (good person).

When I was in Boston, my son Shun, who had been watching all of Lee Kuan Yew's videos on YouTube, was so excited that he insisted I watch the videos with him throughout the night. He had memorized many of his lines.

It was no surprise that he was the first one to text us about the demise of Lee Kuan Yew. "Today I mourned with all my fellow Singaporeans. I have had one of the best upbringings and environments one could have asked for. I am so proud and honored to have lived in the same time and country as this incredible man. Thank you for your leadership and for dedicating your life to my country at heart."

In a tribute to LKY, my youngest daughter, Meizhi, then a second-year student at NYU Shanghai, posted on Facebook: "Gratitude is all I can express to the founding father of Singapore. A lot of who I am today is because of the environment I grew up in and the community I have in Singapore. Thank you and rest in peace, Mr Lee Kuan Yew."

Subsequently, my eldest child, Meixi, then a Ph.D. student at the University of Washington, followed with this: "Your peace is finally here after giving your life for our little country. We will always be indebted to you. You showed us not just what and how to fight but how to love. You loved our little country and your family. You never stopped being a leader, husband, or father – that for me is a measure of a man. Thank you for giving your life so that we could live ours."

I can say now that Lee Kuan Yew is not only my father's hero, or my hero. He is also my children's hero. They have caught his spirit. That's one of the best gifts my wife and I can give to our children. He is truly a personification of greatness.

Truly, "No Kuan Yew, No Singapore".

1. At the end of your life, what ingredient of greatness would you like people to remember you for?

2. If you had only one more month to live, which ingredient of your life would you cultivate deeper?

Action Steps

ADDENDUM

When I was submitting the manuscript of this book for publication, the Oxley Road episode (a dispute about the house Mr Lee Kuan Yew had lived in) had not happened. I do not wish to rehash the issues, arguments and counter-arguments. This is a piece I wrote soon after it happened.

I needed to put this piece as an addendum to the book so that I could express my feelings and share my concerns about this episode without taking sides.

Having seen me pay tribute to the late Lee Kuan Yew in my last chapter, many had asked if I have lost my faith and want to change my perception of him. Certainly not! This episode has not changed my respect and love for him.

Neither have I lost faith in humanity. Rather, I have only confirmed my belief that greatness is an unending journey. There will be blips and blots but if you do it right, you can get back on track.

So, allow me to include this addendum to my book (written on 23 June 2017).

The Lees' Altercations: A Sad, Sad Day in my Life

June 14, 2017 will be one of the saddest days of my life!

Both the six-page statement by Lee Hsien Yang and Dr. Lee Wei Ling, where they detail losing their trust in their brother (my respected Prime Minister, Lee Hsien Loong) and his leadership, and Lee Hsien Loong's subsequent Facebook reply, have made me very sad.

Why am I so sad?

1. The fight involves the affairs of one of the world's, and my personal hero: the late Prime Minister Lee Kuan Yew. I have always had the highest regard for his children. But their unashamed and unmitigated fight has jolted my senses and numbed my feelings.

2. The fight, at first, seemed to be over a piece of property and concerned the dying wishes of a father. Of course, as more was revealed, it turned out to be a case of much more than what meets the eye. It has become "kitchen-fighting", where everything is thrown into the arena.

3. The fight is between supposedly close-knit siblings, but it played out publicly with no-holds-barred accusations and attacks. Any parent would feel very sad if their children fought so viciously. I would be the saddest parent if my children behaved that way. I am certain that the late Mr and Mrs Lee Kuan Yew would feel the same way too if they were alive.

4. The fight centers around three brilliant leaders and siblings, who should know better. This reminds me that we are all creatures of clay, with instincts of escalating conflicts. What a tragic tale of humanity!

5. The fight has divided the nation and the citizens. The ministers and cabinet have joined in the fray. Opposition parties are up in arms, questioning long-treasured policies and well-guarded traditions. The social media and market talks are all abuzz over this heart-breaking story. This has entrenched People's Action Party (PAP) supporters, while those who oppose them have become more cynical.

6. The fight has negatively affected the reputation of a well-governed Singapore. Our Prime Minister is held as a role model for great governance by many but now his image has been tainted. His apology has appeased some but others are still uncertain. It reminds me that he is human after all.

7. This fight is more terrifying than the external threat of terrorism. Internal divides are even more devastating than external menaces. A house divided can never withstand the onslaught of external onslaught. But a house united can withstand any external enemies.

8. The fight has eroded many people's trust in our government — both Singaporeans and citizens from other countries. Much of the trust that our first-generation and subsequent-generation leaders fought so hard to build over the last 52 years has now has been eroded by this ongoing feud in a matter of days and possibly the coming months.

9. The fight has affected the Lee siblings' spouses and their children, sparking off their accusations of inappropriate behaviour. This has inevitably escalated the conflict.

10. Finally, the fight has escalated from personal differences to sibling conflicts to family disputes to national divide and to international disrepute. My foreign friends are shocked by the news. They have always spoken highly of Singapore. They have always had the highest regard of Singapore. But alas, the last bastion of good governance in our world has suffered a very serious dent! I lament over this.

Truly, I am very, very sad.

I hope and pray that all disputed parties can deal the issues privately, find a third-party to help settle the conflicts amicably (I believe they can never do this on their own), overcome their pain, recover from the rage and learn to forgive. And in so doing, make Singaporeans proud again and make Singapore everyone's home again.

If they do it right, I truly believe that each member of the conflicting parties can be great again!

Dr John Ng is the Chief Passionary Officer of Meta Consulting. He provides transformational leadership development, radical cultural change, and customer-centric consultancy to top international corporations. He serves as Honorary Chair of Eagles Communications, and founded Eagles Mediation and Counseling Centre (EMCC). Well-versed in the art of motivation and leadership, he is a highly sought after speaker and consultant. John has a PhD from Northwestern University, USA. He is the author of seven best-selling books, including *Dim Sum Leadership*, *Smiling Tiger Hidden Dragon*, and *Heart to Heart with Asian Leaders*.

john@meta.com.sg
www.meta.com.sg